W9-ANN-101

FLORIDA STATE
UNIVERSITY LIBRARIES

MAY 26 1995

TALLAHASSEE, FLORIDA

International Comparisons of Household Saving

A National Bureau
of Economic Research
Project Report

International Comparisons of Household Saving

Edited by   James M. Poterba

The University of Chicago

Chicago and London

JAMES M. POTERBA is professor of economics at the Massachusetts Institute of Technology and director of the Research Program in Public Economics at the National Bureau of Economic Research.

HC
79
53
I54
1994

The University of Chicago Press, Chicago 60637
The University of Chicago Press, Ltd., London
© 1994 by the National Bureau of Economic Research
All rights reserved. Published 1994
Printed in the United States of America
03 02 01 00 99 98 97 96 95 94 1 2 3 4 5
ISBN: 0-226-67621-8 (cloth)

Library of Congress Cataloging-in-Publication Data

International comparisons of household saving / edited by James M.
    Poterba.
        p.   cm.—(National Bureau of Economic Research project
    report)
        Companion volume to Public policies and household saving, edited
    by James M. Poterba.
        Includes bibliographical references and index.
        1. Saving and investment—Case studies—Congresses.
        2. Households—Economic aspects—Case studies—Congresses.
    I. Poterba, James M.   II. Public policies and household saving.
    III. Series.
    HC79.S3I54   1994   94-22549
    339.4'3—dc20   CIP

⊗The paper used in this publication meets the minimum requirements of the American National Standard for Information Sciences—Permanence of Paper for Printed Library Materials, ANSI Z39.48–1984.

National Bureau of Economic Research

Officers

Paul W. McCracken, *chairman*
John H. Biggs, *vice chairman*
Martin Feldstein, *president and chief
executive officer*

Geoffrey Carliner, *executive director*
Charles A. Walworth, *treasurer*
Sam Parker, *director of finance and
administration*

Directors at Large

Peter C. Aldrich
Elizabeth E. Bailey
John H. Biggs
Andrew Brimmer
Carl F. Christ
Don R. Conlan
Kathleen B. Cooper
Jean A. Crockett

George C. Eads
Martin Feldstein
George Hatsopoulos
Karen N. Horn
Lawrence R. Klein
Leo Melamed
Merton H. Miller
Michael H. Moskow

Robert T. Parry
Peter G. Peterson
Richard N. Rosett
Bert Seidman
Kathleen P. Utgoff
Donald S. Wasserman
Marina v. N. Whitman
John O. Wilson

Directors by University Appointment

Jagdish Bhagwati, *Columbia*
William C. Brainard, *Yale*
Glen G. Cain, *Wisconsin*
Franklin Fisher, *Massachusetts Institute of
Technology*
Saul H. Hymans, *Michigan*
Marjorie B. McElroy, *Duke*
Joel Mokyr, *Northwestern*

James L. Pierce, *California, Berkeley*
Andrew Postlewaite, *Pennsylvania*
Nathan Rosenberg, *Stanford*
Harold T. Shapiro, *Princeton*
Craig Swan, *Minnesota*
Michael Yoshino, *Harvard*
Arnold Zellner, *Chicago*

Directors by Appointment of Other Organizations

Marcel Boyer, *Canadian Economics
Association*
Mark Drabenstott, *American Agricultural
Economics Association*
Richard A. Easterlin, *Economic History
Association*
Gail D. Fosler, *The Conference Board*
A. Ronald Gallant, *American Statistical
Association*
Robert S. Hamada, *American Finance
Association*

Charles Lave, *American Economic
Association*
Rudolph A. Oswald, *American Federation of
Labor and Congress of Industrial
Organizations*
James F. Smith, *National Association of
Business Economists*
Charles A. Walworth, *American Institute of
Certified Public Accountants*
Josh S. Weston, *Committee for Economic
Development*

Directors Emeriti

Moses Abramovitz
Emilio G. Collado
George T. Conklin, Jr.
Thomas D. Flynn

Gottfried Haberler
Franklin A. Lindsay
Paul W. McCracken
Geoffrey H. Moore

James J. O'Leary
George B. Roberts
Eli Shapiro
William S. Vickrey

Relation of the Directors to the
Work and Publications of the
National Bureau of Economic Research

1. The object of the National Bureau of Economic Research is to ascertain and to present to the public important economic facts and their interpretation in a scientific and impartial manner. The Board of Directors is charged with the responsibility of ensuring that the work of the National Bureau is carried on in strict conformity with this object.

2. The President of the National Bureau shall submit to the Board of Directors, or to its Executive Committee, for their formal adoption all specific proposals for research to be instituted.

3. No research report shall be published by the National Bureau until the President has sent each member of the Board a notice that a manuscript is recommended for publication and that in the President's opinion it is suitable for publication in accordance with the principles of the National Bureau. Such notification will include an abstract or summary of the manuscript's content and a response form for use by those Directors who desire a copy of the manuscript for review. Each manuscript shall contain a summary drawing attention to the nature and treatment of the problem studied, the character of the data and their utilization in the report, and the main conclusions reached.

4. For each manuscript so submitted, a special committee of the Directors (including Directors Emeriti) shall be appointed by majority agreement of the President and Vice Presidents (or by the Executive Committee in case of inability to decide on the part of the President and Vice Presidents), consisting of three Directors selected as nearly as may be one from each general division of the Board. The names of the special manuscript committee shall be stated to each Director when notice of the proposed publication is submitted to him. It shall be the duty of each member of the special manuscript committee to read the manuscript. If each member of the manuscript committee signifies his approval within thirty days of the transmittal of the manuscript, the report may be published. If at the end of that period any member of the manuscript committee withholds his approval, the President shall then notify each member of the Board, requesting approval or disapproval of publication, and thirty days additional shall be granted for this purpose. The manuscript shall then not be published unless at least a majority of the entire Board who shall have voted on the proposal within the time fixed for the receipt of votes shall have approved.

5. No manuscript may be published, though approved by each member of the special manuscript committee, until forty-five days have elapsed from the transmittal of the report in manuscript form. The interval is allowed for the receipt of any memorandum of dissent or reservation, together with a brief statement of his reasons, that any member may wish to express; and such memorandum of dissent or reservation shall be published with the manuscript if he so desires. Publication does not, however, imply that each member of the Board has read the manuscript, or that either members of the Board in general or the special committee have passed on its validity in every detail.

6. Publications of the National Bureau issued for informational purposes concerning the work of the Bureau and its staff, or issued to inform the public of activities of Bureau staff, and volumes issued as a result of various conferences involving the National Bureau shall contain a specific disclaimer noting that such publication has not passed through the normal review procedures required in this resolution. The Executive Committee of the Board is charged with review of all such publications from time to time to ensure that they do not take on the character of formal research reports of the National Bureau, requiring formal Board approval.

7. Unless otherwise determined by the Board or exempted by the terms of paragraph 6, a copy of this resolution shall be printed in each National Bureau publication.

(Resolution adopted October 25, 1926, as revised through September 30, 1974)

Contents

Acknowledgments

This volume is part of a multiyear research program on International Comparisons of Household Saving that is being conducted under the auspices of the National Bureau of Economic Research (NBER). I am grateful to Martin Feldstein, president of the NBER, for his help in formulating the project and his constant interest and advice regarding research strategy. I am also grateful to Lawrence Benenson, the John M. Olin Foundation, and the Dean Witter Foundation for financial support of this research.

The NBER conference department, under the direction of Kirsten Davis, provided its usual outstanding level of logistical support for the meeting at which these papers were presented. I am particularly grateful to Lauren Lariviere, who served as conference coordinator, for assistance with this project.

Deborah Kiernan of the NBER publications department has carefully guided the manuscript through various stages of the editorial process, and I am grateful for her assistance at every stage.

Introduction

James M. Poterba

Household saving rates differ widely across developed nations. Why? Remarkably little economic research has been directed at this question. Although the econometric study of household consumption behavior has been one of the most active topics in applied economics during the last decade, most of this research has been directed at testing, and usually rejecting, standard models of life-cycle consumption and saving behavior. Most of this research has been based on data sets for single nations, most often the United States. The papers in this volume attempt to move beyond this focus by reporting on the patterns of household saving behavior in six OECD nations.

Table 1 presents more precise data on the household saving rates since 1970 for the six countries included in this study. These saving rates are calculated using national income accounts data reported by the OECD and correspond to the net saving of households and unincorporated enterprises divided by their after-tax income. The saving rate is defined as net saving divided by total current receipts less direct taxes and other current transfers to the government. In 1990–91, the most recent year for which data are available, the saving rates in the United States and the United Kingdom were lower than those in the other nations considered in this project. Measured on the OECD basis, the U.S. household sector saved 6.3 percent of its disposable income, less than half the saving rate of households in Italy and Japan. The U.S. saving rate has declined from an average level of 9.3 percent of disposable income in the 1970s.[1] Saving

James M. Poterba is professor of economics at the Massachusetts Institute of Technology and director of the Research Program in Public Economics at the National Bureau of Economic Research.

1. The OECD definition of personal saving differs in several ways from that in the U.S. National Income and Product Accounts (NIPA). The U.S. accounts show an average personal saving rate of 4.4 percent for 1990–91, while the Flow of Funds Accounts show an average of 9.8 percent. The average for a hybrid estimate, the NIPA measure computed using Flow of Funds data, is 6.1 percent. These data are presented in Board of Governors of the Federal Reserve (1993, table F.8).

Table 1   **Personal Saving Rates in OECD Nations (%)**

Country	1970–79	1980–89	1990–91
Canada	10.6	12.8	10.4
Germany	12.4	11.1	12.2
Italy	19.2	17.5	15.7
Japan	18.5	14.2	12.9
United Kingdom	5.7	4.7	3.9
United States	9.3	8.3	6.3

Source: Organisation for Economic Cooperation and Development, *National Income Accounts/ Comptes Nationales: 1960–1991* (Paris: (OECD, 1993).

rates in most of the other nations also declined between the 1970s and the more recent period.

Each of the papers in this volume analyzes a household-level database to develop summary statistics on patterns of saving by age, income, and other demographic characteristics in one of the six nations shown in table 1. Where possible, this information is augmented with data on household asset ownership. The studies concentrate on presenting descriptive information rather than testing particular models of household saving behavior. It is hoped that future researchers will draw upon the data collected in this volume both to develop and to test hypotheses about saving behavior.

Defining Personal Saving

Two basic approaches to defining household saving must be distinguished at the outset of this project. The first, which is the basis for saving in the National Income and Product Accounts (NIPA), equates saving with the flow of income minus the flow of expenditures during a given time period. The second approach defines saving as the change in a household's net worth during a given time period. These two measures can differ substantially whenever there are large capital gains or capital losses on existing assets.

Most discussions of saving, whether focusing on time-series comparisons for a single economy or on international comparisons at a given date, employ the first definition of saving. There are three reasons for this. First, the flow saving measure indicates the amount of resources that an economy has set aside to finance investment. In a closed economy, the flow of saving equals the flow of investment. Investment in turn is of intrinsic interest because it is a direct measure of the new capital being deployed in an economy. In an open economy the equality of saving and investment is broken by international capital flows, but the flow of saving remains of interest because it measures the volume of domestically financed investment and, hence, the asset acquisition that can be expected to contribute to future income.

A second reason for focusing on the NIPA definition of household saving is that it directly reflects individual decisions about how much to consume and how much to save. The alternative definition of saving, the change in net worth, equals the NIPA saving measure plus any capital gains or losses on existing assets. Such gains and losses are often much larger than the NIPA saving flow, which makes it impossible to tell whether households are consuming a higher, or lower, fraction of their flow income at different points in time.

Finally, there are data-based reasons for focusing on the NIPA definition of household saving. Survey data on household income and expenditures are far more common than data on net worth. Most developed nations now collect information on consumption and income with large cross-sectional sample surveys, such as the Consumer Expenditure Survey (CEX) in the United States. Many fewer nations collect information on wealth. Even in those nations that do collect balance sheet data, it is often impossible to construct saving rates, because net worth is sampled once, not twice, for each household. Measuring saving as the *change* in net worth requires at least two observations on the assets and liabilities of sample households.

Defining saving as the difference between income and expenditures does not uniquely identify a measure of personal saving, because there are many plausible definitions of both income and expenditures. In this study, income is measured *after tax;* this corresponds to disposable personal income in the national income accounts. Contributions to mandatory government pension schemes, such as Social Security in the United States, are included in taxes for the purposes of this analysis. Also, following the national accounts, personal income excludes realizations of capital gains and losses.

The one significant way in which the income definition in this study differs from that in the national accounts is in the treatment of imputed income on owner-occupied housing.[2] The national accounts include this as income, while the present analysis excludes it. This is largely because it would be difficult to construct estimates of this imputed income flow in many countries where information on the value of owner-occupied housing is not collected as part of the consumer expenditure survey. Housing tenure usually is recorded, however; so to assess the potential impact of this exclusion on the results, most of the country chapters present disaggregated information on saving rates by owner-occupants and renters.

Expenditures are defined inclusive of spending on consumer durables. One could in principle measure consumption as outlays on nondurables and services plus an accrual-equivalent cost of spending on durables, but this again requires detailed information on the value of the durable stock that is not available in many surveys. While the saving rate for a single household that pur-

---

2. There are other aspects of the income definition used here, such as the absence of any correction for inflation's effects on the household balance sheet, that make the current definition an imperfect proxy for true economic income. Making comparable corrections for inflation, however, would require more detailed information on household asset positions than was available for some nations.

chases a major durable in a given year will be erroneously low, and that of a household that spends very little on durables will be too high, these sources of error should cancel to some degree in the cross section of households.

The unit of observation in the subsequent chapters is the *household*. This avoids the difficult problem of attributing consumption within a household to various family members, but it raises a separate set of concerns. In some of the countries included in this study, notably Japan and Italy, multigenerational households are common. The difficulty of purchasing housing in these two nations, in Italy because of high down-payment requirements and in Japan because of high real estate prices, leads many individuals in their twenties, thirties, and even forties to live with their parents or other older relatives. This raises difficulties for the measurement of age-specific saving rates, because the individuals in a given age group that choose to live in multigenerational households are unlikely to be a random sample of the population. Each of the country chapters discusses the particular problems that household definition raises for analyzing saving behavior.

A final issue of definition and methodology that deserves mention is the choice between *cross-sectional* and *cohort* information on saving behavior. To illustrate the difference between these approaches, consider a snapshot sample survey that collects information on saving rates of a population subsample at a given date. Summary statistics on age-specific saving rates based on such a survey describe cross-sectional saving patterns at a point in time. What inferences about the relationship between age and saving behavior can such data support? The answer depends critically on the degree of heterogeneity in economic circumstances of individuals in different birth cohorts.

Consider the case in which the lifetime incomes of individuals who are currently aged 55 are substantially lower than the lifetime incomes of those who are 45. If saving rates at all ages depend positively on the present value of lifetime resources, then the 45-year-old household might display a higher saving rate than the 55-year-old. We could observe this pattern even if the 55-year-old household's saving rate at age 45 were lower than its current saving rate, and if the saving rate for the currently 45-year-old household were rising and would be higher in 10 years than it is today. If the only available data are from a single cross-sectional survey, it is impossible to identify cohort saving patterns. If saving data are collected as part of a panel-data study, then it is straightforward to disentangle the cohort and cross-sectional effects. Such panel-data sets are rare, however.

A more common situation is one in which *repeated cross sections* of households are surveyed. A random sample of households is drawn in one year, and data on income and expenditures are recorded. The next year, a different random sample is drawn and asked the same battery of questions. If each year's cross section represents a random sample, then following a suggestion developed by Deaton (1985), it is possible to construct "synthetic cohort profiles" by linking together the saving rates of 45-year-olds in the survey at date t, the saving rates of 46-year-olds in the survey at date $t+1$, and so on. In the United Kingdom and the United States, the repeated cross-sectional surveys that constitute the Family Expenditure Survey and the Consumer Expenditure Survey, respectively, can now be linked to create synthetic panel-data sets spanning more than a decade.

Table 2 summarizes the data sources for each of the country studies in this volume. The table illustrates the substantial variation across countries in both the nature of the available data, and the extent to which synthetic panel data can be created. In the United Kingdom, largely comparable cross-sectional data sets are now available for a period of 22 years. In Italy, at the other extreme, there is only a single public-use database, the 1987 Survey of Household Income and Wealth, that provides suitable information for this project. The sample sizes of the underlying surveys vary from slightly more than two thousand in some years of the Canadian Family Expenditure Survey, to fifty thousand in each wave of the Japanese National Survey of Family Income and Expenditure. Such differences in sample sizes imply differences in the precision of the estimates presented in different country chapters.

Hypotheses about Why Saving Rates Differ

The current project was designed to collect information that can inform the question of why saving rates differ across countries. To provide a framework for evaluating the subsequent country chapters, it is useful at the outset to identify several of the leading explanations that have been advanced to account for such international differences.[3]

Demographic Composition

The life-cycle hypothesis of saving, developed by Modigliani and Brumberg (1954), predicts that a given individual will save at different rates at different ages. It is usually applied to a stylized individual whose income rises during the early part of his working life, then stabilizes or declines, and finally falls sharply at retirement. Such an individual will exhibit a rising saving rate as his income rises, and will dissave, consuming more than his current income, after retirement.

The aggregate household saving rate in an economy composed of such life-cycle individuals will depend critically on the relative sizes of different age cohorts in the population. There are substantial differences in the demographic composition of the various developed nations considered in this study. Japan and Germany have the highest average (and median) ages of their populations, while the United States and Canada have the lowest. The potential impact of

---

3. A more detailed discussion of these explanations and several others, along with information on aggregate saving rates in various OECD nations, can be found in Dean et al. (1990).

Table 2   **Data Sources for International Comparisons of Personal Saving**

Country	Data Source	Sample Size	Data Years
Canada	Family Expenditure Survey (FAMEX)	2,100–3,500	1978–90[a]
Germany	German Income and Expenditure Surveys (EVS)	45,000	1978, 1983
Italy	Survey of Household Income and Wealth (SHIW)	8,000	1987
Japan	National Survey of Family Income and Expenditure (NSFIE)	50,000	1979–89[a]
United Kingdom	Family Expenditure Survey (FES)	7,000	1969–90
United States	Consumer Expenditure Survey (CEX)	3,500–7,000	1980–90

Source: Author's tabulations based on individual country chapters.
[a]Data are not available for all years during time span.

demography on aggregate household saving rates suggests a need to compare age-specific saving rates in different nations.

Credit Institutions

The structure of credit institutions is another factor that can affect household saving behavior. If households in one country must accumulate a larger down payment than residents of another nation before they can purchase a home, they may save a higher fraction of their income until they become home owners. They may also respond in other ways, for example, by deferring house purchase and purchasing a smaller house. If the availability of credit for smoothing fluctuations in income, for example due to temporary job loss, is different across nations, this may affect the level of precautionary saving that households undertake. If households can borrow against their illiquid assets to varying degrees using financial instruments such as home equity loans, this may also affect the level and the age profile of household saving rates. Dean et al. (1990) summarize a number of the important changes in the structure of credit markets in OECD nations, and their potential effects on personal saving behavior.

Social Insurance Programs

One of the factors that has received the greatest discussion in international comparisons of saving behavior is the role of social insurance programs, particularly Social Security. Holding fixed the length of retirement, the availability of generous government-provided retirement income programs substantially reduces the incentive for younger households to save. Other social insurance programs can also have important effects on the returns to saving. If a nation offers a comprehensive system of health insurance or health care, for example, the need to set aside resources as a precaution against illness will be reduced. The various country chapters therefore devote some attention to the structure of social insurance programs in each nation, and to the interaction between these programs and household saving behavior.

Lifetime Income Profiles

Another factor that can contribute to international differences in household saving rates, and one that is related to the discussion of demographic differences above, is variation in the profile of income that households expect to receive over their lifetimes. An individual who expects to receive a rapidly rising income stream as he ages will save less than one who expects relatively little income growth. Individual income growth is determined by two factors: the overall rate of income growth in the macroeconomy, and the rate at which an individual's income grows, conditional on the overall level of economic activity. One of the problems in attributing differences in observed saving rates to differences in economic growth is the lack of data on the *prospective* growth rates that individuals currently *expect*. This problem notwithstanding, each of the country studies presents information on the age-income profile of current survey cohorts.

Saving Opportunities

A final significant factor that could account for some international differences is the disparity in the opportunities for saving that individuals face. In some countries, for example, returns on saving are virtually untaxed, while in others, tax rates are high and after-tax rates of return are likely to be lower. In a companion volume, Poterba (1994), teams of authors from each of the countries represented in this volume provide a detailed description of the saving institutions in their countries, and in particular the effects of government policies in affecting the rates of return available to savers.

The foregoing hypotheses do not represent an exhaustive list of the potential explanations for differences in saving behavior. Nevertheless, they provide some guidance for evaluating the empirical findings presented in each of the country chapters.

Principal Findings

The country chapters are not directed at hypothesis testing, but at summarizing the available facts about saving in each nation. Even these summaries, however, provide important information on some of the candidate explanations for international disparities in saving rates. First, the country studies provide very little evidence that supports the life-cycle model, and they consequently raise questions about the power of international differences in demographic composition to explain differential saving rates. Table 3 synthesizes the age-specific saving rates in the six countries. The table shows that, in virtually all nations, the saving rate is *positive* even after retirement. In the nations with the highest

Table 3   Age-Specific Personal Saving Rates, OECD Nations (%)

Age Group	Canada	Germany	Italy	Japan	United Kingdom	United States
<30	0.0	9.8	10.0	17.9[a]	5.0[a]	−2.2
30–34	3.0	9.8	20.0	27.4	8.0	7.1
35–39	3.0	10.6	26.0	31.8	12.0	9.4
40–44	5.0	10.2	22.0	31.8	12.0	9.8
45–49	5.0	10.2	23.0	28.5	11.0	11.2
50–54	8.0	10.4	31.0	31.5	10.0	13.9
55–59	11.0	11.0	32.0	34.5	13.0	16.6
60–64	9.0	12.2	34.0	31.7	6.0	8.6
65–69	6.0	9.2	36.0	32.0	2.0	7.1
70–74	6.0	9.7	31.0	33.8	9.0	1.1
>74	8.0	10.2[a]	n.a.	31.1[a]	n.a.	n.a.

[a]Saving rate for German and Japanese households >75 relates to those 75–79. That for Japanese, U.K., and U.S. households <30 is an arithmetic average of the saving rates for those <24 and 25–29.

overall saving rates, Italy and Japan, the saving rate among elderly households, those aged 65 and greater, actually exceeds 30 percent!

There is some evidence, particularly in low-saving countries, that household saving rates peak in the decade prior to retirement. In the United Kingdom, for example, households aged 55–59 exhibit a saving rate of 13 percent, compared to 2 percent for those aged 65–69 and 7 percent for those aged 70–74. In the United States, the saving rate of 55–59-year-olds is 16.6 percent, compared with 7.1 percent for those aged 65–69. The U.S. data also display the lowest saving rate (1.1 percent) for the oldest age group, in this case the 70–74-year-olds. In Italy and Japan, however, there is very little change in estimated household saving rates once households reach middle age.

A second finding that emerges from the country studies is that most households build up relatively limited financial reserves against financial emergencies, the "precautionary saving" motive. Table 4 shows the age-wealth patterns for the four countries for which it is feasible to make such comparisons. In each case, the estimates are *medians* within each age category. The table shows that in each of the countries except Japan, the median household accumulates very little in financial assets. In Canada, for example, median holdings peak at $17,200 for households between ages 60 and 64. In the United States, the peak is substantially lower, $7,000, for the same age group. Although the mean financial asset holdings for each group are substantially greater than the median, the results do suggest that a very substantial share of households are accumulating relatively little financial wealth.

The contrast between financial asset holdings of Japanese and U.S. households is striking, and it is not confined to any particular age range. At ages 30–34, for example, the median Japanese household has net financial assets 10

Table 4   **Age Profiles of Median Net Financial Assets (thousand 1990 U.S.$)**

Age Group	Canada	Italy	Japan	United States
25–29	0.0	4.1	15.4	0.9
30–34	0.9	4.3	25.1	2.5
35–39	1.3	10.1	33.5	2.0
40–44	2.4	9.3	40.8	2.3
45–49	5.2	10.2	48.5	2.3
50–54	8.2	15.8	51.6	1.6
55–59	11.0	13.6	63.3	2.8
60–64	17.2	8.9	79.5	7.0
65–69	15.4	10.0	76.4	5.8
70–74	11.1	7.4	69.5	6.1

Notes: Entries for Canada are based on the 1984 Survey of Consumer Finances, converted to 1990 Canadian dollars and then converted to U.S. dollars using the 1990 exchange rate. Entries for the United States are from the 1990 Consumer Expenditure Survey. Data for Japan are from the 1989 NSFIE, and for Italy from the 1987 SHIW, converted to U.S. dollars using the average prevailing exchange rate in the year of the survey and then the U.S. inflation rate between the base year and 1990.

times larger than those of the median U.S. household in the same age group ($25,000 vs. $2,500). The disparity widens to more than 20:1 for households nearing retirement age, and is more than 10:1 for elderly households, those in their seventies.

One issue related to the precautionary saving motive is the relationship between income and saving behavior. Lower-income groups in many nations are more likely to experience periods of economic adversity, yet they are also more likely to qualify for social insurance programs in the event of such a change. The various country studies yield consistent evidence that saving rates rise sharply with income. In Canada, Germany, and the United Kingdom, the estimated saving rates are *negative* for households in the bottom quintile of the income distribution. In the top quintile of the income distribution, the saving rate is approximately 17 percent. In the United Kingdom, the comparable saving rate is 24 percent, and in Japan, 42 percent. The United Kingdom and Japan exhibit comparably large changes between the saving rates at the bottom and at the top of the income distribution. In Japan, however, saving rates at all income levels are significantly higher than those in the United Kingdom.

A final finding that emerges from the country studies is a complex linkage between individual saving and the availability of social insurance benefits. In Germany, for example, various social insurance programs provide for most of a household's needs in old age, such as medical care and a substantial level of retirement pension. Yet the saving rate of individuals approaching retirement is substantial. This finding, and related results in other nations, suggests that a bequest motive or similar factors may be a key explanation for some components of saving behavior.

Future Directions

The relatively small sample of countries included in this study makes it impossible to conduct large-scale statistical tests with the resulting data. Yet the high quality and unique character of the data sets should prove a valuable input to further theoretical and empirical work on the determinants of household saving. This conclusion suggests several natural directions for further work.

One potential avenue for future research concerns the relationship between population demography and personal saving behavior. Standard life-cycle analysis suggests that countries in which the elderly account for a relatively high fraction of the population will exhibit lower saving rates than comparable countries with younger populations. Yet such analyses treat the age-specific saving rates of households as independent of the aggregate age structure of the population. Weil (1993) suggests that this may be a strong assumption. He develops an alternative link between age structure and saving, focusing on the effect of anticipated bequests in reducing the saving rate of the currently young cohort in economies with high elderly fractions. His study is the first to use the data in this volume to enlighten further work on saving decisions.

A second important issue is the link between social insurance systems, particularly those directed at retirement saving, and personal saving rates. In keeping with this project's focus on presenting facts rather than testing hypotheses, none of the studies explicitly analyze the link between social insurance programs and age-specific household saving rates. Such a study requires a detailed codification of the social insurance system in each nation to compute measures of social security wealth and other similar summary statistics that might affect household saving patterns. This is left for future investigation. Yet in light of the patterns of saving behavior presented in this volume, future researchers should be able to provide new insights on the effects of social insurance and other government policies on individual saving decisions.

References

Board of Governors of the Federal Reserve System. 1993. *Flow of funds accounts: Flows and outstandings.* Publication Z.1. Washington: Board of Governors, September 17.

Dean, Andrew, Martine Durand, John Fallon, and Peter Hoeller. 1990. Saving trends and behavior in OECD countries. *OECD Economic Studies* 14 (Spring): 7–58.

Deaton, Angus. 1985. Panel data from a time series of cross sections. *Journal of Econometrics* 30:109–26.

Modigliani, Franco, and Richard Brumberg. 1954. Utility analysis and the consumption function: An interpretation of cross-section data. In *Post-Keynesian economics,* ed. Kenneth K. Kurihara, 388–436. New Brunswick, N.J.: Rutgers University Press.

Poterba, James M., ed. 1994. *Public policies and household saving.* Chicago: University of Chicago Press.

Weil, David N. 1993. Comparing personal saving in six countries. Brown University. Mimeograph.

1

Household Data on Saving Behavior in Canada

John B. Burbidge and James B. Davies

1.1 Introduction

This paper uses Canadian microdata to examine age profiles of income, consumption, saving, and wealth holding. It looks not only at the most recent cross-sectional evidence, but, except for wealth holding where data limitations do not permit, constructs synthetic longitudinal data over the period 1978–90. This is a shorter time span than used for some of the other G7 countries in this volume, which are favored with longer-running consistent sample survey data.

In earlier work with Lonnie Magee and Les Robb, one of us has developed a set of statistical techniques for studying age profiles and has employed them on Canadian microdata sets to examine how earnings, consumption, and wealth holding vary over the life cycle.[1] This paper synthesizes and extends this research to consider saving. We begin by describing the data.

Statistics Canada releases public-use microdata tapes which record responses to questionnaires based on subsamples of the Labour Force Survey sampling frame. Family Expenditure Surveys ((FAMEX) are conducted in February and March and collect information on each household's income, expenditures, and changes in assets and liabilities during the previous calendar

John B. Burbidge is professor of economics at McMaster University, Hamilton, Canada, and holds the Faculty of Social Science Chair in Public Policy at the University of Western Ontario, 1993–94. James B. Davies is professor of economics and chairman of the Department of Economics at the University of Western Ontario, London, Canada.

The authors thank conference participants, seminar participants at Tilburg University, the University of Toronto, and Rob Alessie, Annamaria Lusardi, Lonnie Magee, and Les Robb for helpful comments. In addition, we thank Ulysse Nevraumont, Family Expenditure Surveys Section, Statistics Canada, for providing an unpublished document outlining the relationship between FAMEX estimates of income and expenditure and the corresponding estimates in the National Accounts. All calculations were performed with GAUSS 2.2 and the figures were drawn with STATA 3.0.

1. See Burbidge and Robb (1985), Burbidge, Magee, and Robb (1988), Robb and Burbidge (1989), Magee, Burbidge, and Robb (1991), Robb, Magee, and Burbidge (1992), Bar-Or et al. (1992), and Burbidge and Davies (1994).

year; FAMEX is publicly available for the 1978, 1982, 1984, 1986, and 1990 calendar years.[2] The Survey of Consumer Finances (SCF) is conducted in April and May every year. About every seven years, prior to 1984, the SCF measured family assets and debts as of the date of the survey and, as it always does, income for the previous calendar year. We have SCF assets and debts data for April/May 1977 and 1984. Public-use tapes for surveys of income exist for 1971–81 (biennial) and 1982–90 (annual).

The definition of saving used here is after-tax income minus current consumption. It is important to keep in mind that, as is common in such sample surveys, income excludes capital gains and capital income is not adjusted for inflation. In line with the practice throughout this volume, contributions to state-mandated and employer pension schemes are excluded from after-tax income. Current consumption includes expenditures on durables, which, of course, in truth embody a significant saving component. The upshot is that "saving" here means saving solely in financial form plus net payments made when purchasing housing, business equity, or producer durables.

What is known about the reliability of these data? First, response rates are quite high—78.4% in the 1984 SCF and 72.0% in the 1990 FAMEX.[3] But differential response and misreporting are always potential problems with survey data, so it is important to consider validation studies as well.

Statistics Canada has conducted validation studies that examine the coherence between expenditure estimates from FAMEX and the corresponding estimates from the National Income and Expenditure Accounts. Category by category, FAMEX numbers are quite close to those obtained in the National Income and Expenditure Accounts with the exception of expenditures on tobacco and alcoholic beverages, which are about half of the National Accounts estimates. If we adjust for conceptual differences between FAMEX and the National Accounts, total consumption expenditure in the 1986 FAMEX is about 8 percent lower than in the 1986 National Accounts (see Statistics Canada 1993). This is a concern for the present study, since we measure saving as the difference between after-tax income and consumption in the FAMEX surveys. An error of 8 percent in consumption could, in principle, translate into a much larger error in the saving residual.

In fact we believe that, within the limitations of the FAMEX saving definition, the saving numbers provided by this survey are reasonably reliable. First, it is not just consumption which is low relative to the National Accounts. The same is true for income, and the percentage shortfall is of similar magnitude.[4] Second, there is an internal check in the FAMEX questionnaire. Direct ques-

2. Microdata tapes may be purchased from Statistics Canada, Tunney's Pasture, Ottawa, Ontario, Canada. A sixth FAMEX tape for the 1969 calendar year will be publicly available shortly.

3. Response rates for earlier surveys were higher, ranging from 76.6% for the 1986 survey to over 80% for the 1978 and 1982 surveys.

4. Comparisons are regularly reported between SCF income aggregates and National Accounts data. These have been quite consistent over time. Wages and salaries, in aggregate, are quite accu-

tions are asked to establish the net change in assets minus liabilities for each household. If this is dissimilar to the gap between income and expenditure which one may deduce from answers to other questions, the discrepancy is brought to the interviewer's attention and the household is reinterviewed to see if "income − expenditure" can be reconciled with net change in assets and liabilities. Also, overall income minus consumption can be compared with the overall net change in assets minus liabilities. The sample means are within 10 percent of each other in all five surveys.

Studies have also been done on the relationship between SCF estimates of assets and debts and the National Balance Sheet (NBS) totals (Oja 1986; Davies, forthcoming). These comparisons are less illuminating than those for FAMEX because of the differences in scope and definition between the SCF and the NBS, and the fact that the NBS numbers themselves have many limitations. Overall, the SCF aggregates are much more reasonable for nonfinancial than for financial assets. Some financial assets are vastly underestimated; corporate shares, for example, are underrepresented by 80 percent.[5] Equally important for the purposes of this paper is the issue of whether one can assemble a picture of income, consumption, and saving from FAMEX data that is consistent with the income, assets, and debts picture from SCF data, at least for certain types of households. To the best of our knowledge this is an open question; this paper will begin to address this issue, but it cannot provide a complete answer.

While both FAMEX and SCF are multistage, stratified, clustered samples drawn from the Labour Force Survey sampling frame, Statistics Canada publications note some important differences which are relevant here:

(1) the unit surveyed differs;
(2) FAMEX reconstructs the household as it existed during the previous calendar year, while SCF describes the household as it existed at the time of the survey;
(3) there are differences in the population covered (see Statistics Canada 1992, 107).

With reference to the third point, prior to 1990, FAMEX focused on a "spending unit"—"a group of people living in the same dwelling who depend on a common or pooled income for major expenses or one financially indepen-

---

rately reported. Transfer income is underestimated by about 20%, and investment income by about 50%. The overall underestimation is about 8% in the SCF. Statistics Canada (1993) reports that FAMEX income estimates are about 97% of the SCF estimates.

5. The severe underestimation of corporate shares likely reflects the twin facts that (1) share ownership in Canada is highly concentrated, and (2) in part due to differential response by income and wealth level the SCF does not include any extremely wealthy families. On the latter point, the wealthiest family in the 1984 survey had a net worth of $6 million (1984 dollars). We work with quantiles below the affected region, and we use the SCF weights. If these weights accurately reflect the number of households in the extreme upper tail of the wealth distribution, the results reported below will also be accurate.

dent individual living alone." The unit surveyed in the 1990 FAMEX was "a person or group of persons occupying one dwelling unit." The SCF examines "economic families"—"a group of individuals sharing a common dwelling unit and related by blood, marriage or adoption." This difference in unit should be borne in mind when comparing FAMEX and SCF variables. A strict and accurate cumulation of FAMEX saving per unit up to age 45, say, would not produce observed SCF wealth per family at age 45, for example, even in the absence of measurement error. There are about 10 percent more family units than spending units, which tends to make per unit SCF numbers correspondingly lower.

Some important themes emerge from this paper. For example, it becomes clear that it is not safe to assess age patterns of consumption, saving, or wealth holding using isolated cross-sectional data. Second, apparent saving rates vary much more by income level than they do by age. Another finding is that Canadians save in essentially two phases. When young they do so by building up home equity. It is only in middle age that most make the transition to saving in the form of pension rights and financial assets. Finally, in common with several recent studies we find that continued saving after retirement is more the rule than the exception.

The remainder of the paper is organized as follows. Section 1.2 sets out the recent cross-sectional age profiles of household saving rates. Sections 1.3–1.5 explore how these cross-sectional profiles are determined by age profiles of income and consumption using FAMEX data. Section 1.6 then employs the 1977 and 1984 SCFs to examine how components of assets and debts vary with age. Section 1.7 presents a summary and conclusions.

1.2   Saving and Wealth: Recent Cross-Sectional Evidence

Tables 1.1–1.3 present a summary picture of household saving in Canada, as estimated by the 1990 FAMEX. Tables 1.4 and 1.5 provide comparable information on wealth holding from the 1984 SCF. The population of families and unattached individuals is grouped into five-year age groups, and within each age range into five after-tax income quintiles. For each variable we show overall medians by age group, and also medians for each quintile.[6]

Table 1.1 shows traditional saving rates: household saving divided by disposable money income. The overall median saving rate is .05. The age profile is humped, except for an interesting upturn for the 74+ age group (which is largely the result of an interesting jump for the top quintile). The saving rate peaks at ages 55–59. Note that the age pattern of these saving rates is quite different from what would be predicted by the life-cycle model (LCM), how-

---

6. The number of observations in each age-income cell is given for the two surveys in tables 1A.1 and 1A.2 in the appendix.

Table 1.1   **Median Saving Rates by (After-Tax) Income Quintile and Age Group**

Income Quintile	All	<29	30–34	35–39	40–44	45–49	50–54	55–59	60–64	65–69	70–74	>74
						Age Group						
1	−0.05	−0.15	−0.06	−0.07	−0.04	−0.11	−0.03	−0.11	−0.02	−0.06	−0.05	0.02
2	−0.00	−0.04	−0.03	−0.01	0.02	0.07	0.05	0.04	0.06	−0.04	0.05	0.08
3	0.06	0.01	0.06	0.04	0.02	0.09	0.08	0.12	0.11	0.09	0.02	0.02
4	0.09	0.03	0.09	0.09	0.08	0.07	0.18	0.18	0.14	0.06	0.13	0.08
5	0.17	0.11	0.13	0.19	0.17	0.10	0.19	0.27	0.19	0.21	0.09	0.33
All	0.05	−0.00	0.03	0.03	0.05	0.05	0.08	0.11	0.09	0.06	0.06	0.08

Source: FAMEX for 1990 (all observations).

ever. While the median saving rate drops after ages 55–59, it remains at .06 or above.

Looking across quintiles, there is a monotonic increase of the saving rate with income up to, and including, ages 65–69. Thereafter there are some wobbles, but still a positive correlation. (The breakdown of the monotonic relationship after ages 65–69 may be due to declining sample size at these ages. See table 1A.1 in the appendix.) Median saving rates range from −.15 for bottom quintile households aged less than 29 to .33 for top quintile units aged 74+.

Table 1.2 looks at saving rates defined relative to total expenditure, rather than income. Under the permanent-income hypothesis (PIH) total expenditure serves as a proxy for permanent income. Compared with Table 1.1, the overall age profile is little affected, but differences in saving rates across income groups are increased.[7] The saving rates for bottom quintiles, whose total expenditure and income are very similar, are little affected, but saving rates for the top quintiles (whose expenditures falls short of income by a considerable margin) are increased. Actual median amounts saved are shown in Table 1.3, which shows that the variation in saving rates with age found in the first two tables can be traced very much to differences in amounts saved. To put these figures in perspective, it helps to keep in mind that median after-tax income overall was $44,610.

Tables 1.4 and 1.5 present some key information from the 1984 SCF wealth survey. Note that the influence of the nonsampling errors which especially affect surveys of assets and debts is considerably reduced here by the use of medians and other quantiles rather than means (which are so sensitive to extreme values). Even so, the numbers do need to be viewed with caution. In addition, it should be noted that SCF assets exclude equity in employer-based

7. Saving is not necessarily more stable relative to permanent income (PI) than relative to current income, even if this is true for consumption. In fact, it is precisely by having the saving rate jump around that smoothness in consumption can be maintained.

Table 1.2 The Ratio of Median Saving to Total Expenditure by (After-Tax) Income Quintile and Age Group

Income Quintile	All	Age Group <29	30–34	35–39	40–44	45–49	50–54	55–59	60–64	65–69	70–74	>74
1	−0.05	−0.13	−0.06	−0.07	−0.04	−0.10	−0.03	−0.10	−0.03	−0.05	−0.05	0.00
2	−0.00	−0.04	−0.03	−0.01	0.02	0.07	0.05	0.04	0.06	−0.04	0.05	0.08
3	0.06	0.01	0.07	0.04	0.02	0.10	0.08	0.14	0.12	0.10	0.02	0.02
4	0.10	0.03	0.10	0.10	0.08	0.07	0.22	0.22	0.16	0.07	0.15	0.09
5	0.21	0.12	0.15	0.23	0.21	0.11	0.23	0.37	0.23	0.27	0.09	0.49
All	0.05	−0.00	0.03	0.04	0.05	0.05	0.08	0.12	0.09	0.06	0.06	0.09

Source: FAMEX for 1990 (all observations).

private pension plans and life insurance, as well as durables other than homes and cars. All consumer debt, however, is included. These limitations in coverage lower estimated financial assets and net worth significantly.

Table 1.4 shows that net financial assets for Canadian households are very low up to about age 45, when the overall median is still just $2,845. At that point financial assets are built up very rapidly in the run-up to retirement, peaking at $20,046 at ages 60–64, and then declining in retirement. Table 1.5 also shows a hump shape, and a peak for ages 60–64, but the shape of the profile is very different. Net worth increases quite rapidly in the early years, when financial assets are creeping upward very slowly. The reason is that most of the accumulation taking place is in nonfinancial form, principally in housing equity. As we shall see later, the representative form of wealth accumulation for young Canadians is home purchase followed by fairly rapid paying off of mortgage debt.

Like the saving tables, tables 1.4 and 1.5 show sharp differences in wealth holding across income quintiles. It is instructive to note, however, that inequality in the holding of financial assets and net worth declines with age. The net worth of the top income quintile as a ratio to that of the bottom quintile declines from 65.7 at ages 30–34 to 8.0 at ages 60–64, for example.[8]

Finally, although all the data shown in these tables are from cross sections, they already point out pitfalls of relying too much on isolated pieces of cross-sectional evidence. Looking at the wealth-holding tables alone one would think that the Canadian data provide strong confirmation of the LCM: median wealth holding declines by 46 percent from ages 60–64 to 74+. But the saving tables suggest that this picture may be highly misleading. Apparent saving rates remain positive and large throughout all the retirement years that we can observe

8. The top/bottom quintile net worth ratio rises after ages 60–64, ending up at 27.6 for those aged 74+. This rise is not found, however, if households are ranked according to wealth rather than income. Unlike the United States, standard measures of inequality indicate that wealth inequality continues to rise in retirement in Canada. See, e.g., Davies (1979) or Siddiq and Beach (1993).

Table 1.3   Median Saving by (After-Tax) Income Quintile and Age Group (1990 Canadian $)

	All	<29	30-34	35-39	40-44	45-49	50-54	55-59	60-64	65-69	70-74	>74
							Age Group					
1	-622	-1,653	-796	-1,089	-758	-1,164	-567	-1,103	-468	-799	-443	111
2	-24	-799	-844	-394	606	2,109	1,534	973	1,448	-598	605	854
3	1,800	342	2,003	1,448	825	3,977	3,295	4,461	3,435	2,289	367	305
4	4,125	1,056	4,009	4,379	4,270	3,636	10,358	9,705	4,275	2,585	3,254	1,749
5	11,611	5,459	7,132	12,712	14,095	9,354	15,444	20,054	10,535	11,083	4,167	12,462
All	1,228	-189	829	1,008	1,708	1,886	3,140	3,020	2,070	1,295	856	1,257

Source: FAMEX for 1990 (all observations).

Table 1.4 **Median Net Financial Assets by (After-Tax) Income Quintile and Age Group (1990 Canadian $)**

Income		Age Group											
Quintile	All	<25	25–29	30–34	35–39	40–44	45–49	50–54	55–59	60–64	65–69	70–74	>74
1	300	1	8	26	3	32	304	259	647	1,565	1,659	1,681	2,612
2	1,940	6	22	1,035	647	1,373	2,889	5,220	5,314	13,104	8,154	6,848	5,186
3	2,716	−39	−59	1,132	1,849	3,765	5,348	10,424	15,720	19,399	17,947	11,407	12,092
4	5,381	0	0	2,085	4,475	6,034	11,180	15,720	26,900	27,413	32,853	27,071	25,135
5	19,923	252	3,207	10,088	11,624	15,138	27,146	39,264	37,001	66,126	66,504	74,818	65,161
All	3,350	3	26	1,044	1,526	2,845	6,080	9,577	12,867	20,046	17,938	12,998	10,772

Source: SCF for 1984 (all observations).

Table 1.5   Median Net Worth by (After-Tax) Income Quintile and Age Group (1990 Canadian $)

Income Quintile	All	<25	25–29	30–34	35–39	40–44	45–49	50–54	55–59	60–64	65–69	70–74	>74
1	2,438	12	136	1,377	3,829	5,348	11,041	2,615	25,736	32,850	14,226	5,561	5,734
2	26,404	243	2,781	16,211	33,419	40,472	64,787	66,394	66,204	81,775	53,246	28,996	35,177
3	42,627	936	10,890	32,319	55,829	60,125	107,990	98,395	112,536	104,943	85,124	78,628	47,612
4	70,549	5,458	19,077	43,649	68,174	91,556	122,958	135,278	146,097	131,269	124,492	127,163	86,105
5	139,494	14,453	44,948	90,433	119,720	142,909	197,880	194,045	200,990	263,967	178,567	171,917	158,001
All	50,980	1,429	10,090	33,902	55,459	67,439	95,162	99,855	106,627	109,380	84,485	74,212	59,582

Source: SCF for 1984 (all observations).

in the FAMEX data. The apparent hump shape of the age-wealth profile may therefore very well simply be a cross-sectional artifact. If Canadian cohorts were observed longitudinally, no evidence of a decline of wealth in retirement might be found.

It is also instructive to think about the implications of the positive relationship between saving rates and current income found in the saving tables. With zero mobility in the income distribution, this pattern would suggest wealth inequality rising with age. In fact we find declining wealth inequality in the SCF data, as noted above. In addition to appealing to possible data problems, one way to reconcile these observations is to note that there is considerable income mobility over the life cycle. Thus, the representative spending unit in the bottom quintile has not spent its entire existence in that quintile, and its accumulated wealth is much larger than one would expect if it had been in the same quintile all along.

1.3   Data and Methods

The 1978, 1982, and 1986 FAMEX cover both urban and rural areas, but those for 1984 and 1990 cover only major urban centers with populations in excess of 100,000. To achieve comparability with all five surveys we restrict our attention to major urban centers. All spending units, that is, nonfamily households, families, and unattached individuals, are included in the following analysis. We exclude units whose heads were less than 25 or more than 75 years of age, however.[9]

Family expenditure surveys in most countries use a diary method, whereby the household records every expenditure over, say, a two-week period. The Canadian FAMEX is different; households are asked to recall their financial transactions during the previous calendar year using whatever records they happen to have at hand.[10] The surveyor tries to obtain a complete list of expenditures, total income before taxes, and net change in assets and liabilities. A basic test of data accuracy is that income minus expenditure minus net change in assets and liabilities (call this difference "TEST") be zero. Statistics for these and other variables are shown in table 1.6 for the 1990 FAMEX. The mean of TEST is small relative to pretax income or total consumption.

After the head's age, we list pretax income and its major components— earnings, capital income, government transfer income (which includes unemployment insurance receipts, welfare receipts, Canada and Quebec Pension Plan [C/QPP] benefits, Old Age Security [OAS] and Guaranteed Income Sup-

9. There are very few spending units with heads aged less than 25 years, so we have begun our age profiles at age 25 for the sake of reliability. At the other end of the age scale, all units with heads aged 76 or more were coded "76" in the survey. In the absence of some correction, including these units would distort the age profiles toward the end of the life cycle.

10. The surveyor interviews one or more members of the household in the household over a three to four hour period. Second visits are made occasionally.

Table 1.6   **Selected Statistics for Extracts Drawn from FAMEX Data Sets (1990 Canadian $)**

Variable	Mean	Standard Deviation	Minimum	Maximum
	1978 Data Set ($N = 4{,}671$)			
Age	45.6	13.8	25.0	75.0
Pretax income	49,086.9	28,231.5	320.7	238,014.5
Earnings	0.0	0.0	0.0	0.0
Capital income	0.0	0.0	0.0	0.0
Government transfer income	0.0	0.0	0.0	0.0
Other income	0.0	0.0	0.0	0.0
After-tax income	39,090.4	20,870.3	320.7	210,937.8
C/QPP contributions	424.5	288.9	0.0	2,802.6
Other pension contributions	756.7	1,565.1	0.0	20,949.9
Total consumption	35,190.7	17,274.1	2,501.2	148,586.2
Nondurbles	27,683.5	12,473.1	2,393.2	137,472.0
Durables	7,507.2	7,571.0	0.0	77,795.8
Health expenditures	548.4	781.6	0.0	20,501.0
Saving	3,899.7	12,419.2	−74,761.3	153,776.6
Change in RRSPs	713.7	2,235.9	−14,964.2	29,928.4
Home value	78,210.5	77,876.8	0.0	641,323.8
Number of adults	2.1	0.9	1.0	8.0
Number of children under 18	0.9	1.2	0.0	9.0
Total expenditure	45,666.5	24,462.5	3,223.7	172,383.6
Net change in assets/liabilities	3,334.7	11,822.0	−61,793.7	153,526.5
Test	85.8	3,854.0	−23,587.9	19,152.1
	1982 Data Set ($N = 6{,}100$)			
Age	45.6	14.2	25.0	75.0
Pretax income	47,020.1	29,447.5	1,285.0	276,551.8
Earnings	37,836.4	29,121.7	0.0	229,434.3
Capital income	2,904.7	7,882.8	0.0	147,768.8
Government transfer income	3,939.9	5,008.9	0.0	42,831.5
Other income	1,412.7	5,001.9	0.0	103,758.0
After-tax income	36,838.2	21,589.2	−33,368.6	266,300.8
C/QPP contributions	417.8	296.8	0.0	2,370.0
Other pension contributions	750.1	1,426.2	0.0	15,967.6
Total consumption	32,613.3	17,300.7	3,171.0	220,094.2
Nondurables	25,696.9	12,562.0	3,171.0	172,415.5
Durables	6,916.5	7,567.7	−20,463.5	118,210.8
Health expenditures	831.9	988.2	0.0	29,900.7
Saving	4,224.9	12,915.2	−107,891.2	208,909.4
Change in RRSPs	598.1	3,268.4	−127,066.9	51,397.8
Home value	69,109.7	78,819.0	0.0	1,427,716.6
Number of Adults	2.0	0.8	1.0	8.0
Number of children under 18	0.8	1.1	0.0	7.0
Total expenditure	42,795.1	24,905.0	3,171.0	279,365.9
Net change in assets/liabilities	3,991.9	12,662.3	−105,773.9	208,027.1
Test	233.1	5,263.9	−61,517.5	120,419.4

(*continued*)

Table 1.6 (continued)

Variable	Mean	Standard Deviation	Minimum	Maximum
	1984 Data Set (N = 4,232)			
Age	45.5	14.1	25.0	75.0
Pretax income	46,978.1	30,736.1	0.0	240,552.0
Earnings	37,676.6	30,905.7	−142.3	222,963.2
Capital income	2,579.9	9,044.0	−64,664.5	215,176.3
Government transfer income	4,132.2	5,248.3	0.0	49,817.5
Other income	1,567.4	5,318.8	0.0	90,530.3
After-tax income	36,457.4	22,040.9	0.0	240,552.0
C/QPP contributions	446.7	334.5	0.0	2,247.7
Other pension contributions	734.2	1,420.1	0.0	11,827.1
Total consumption	33,284.6	17,773.6	1,579.1	156,618.7
Nondurables	25,834.9	12,783.0	2,452.1	143,877.2
Durables	7,449.7	7,767.5	−18,325.9	68,713.8
Health expenditures	817.5	840.0	0.0	9,964.8
Saving	3,172.8	13,314.7	−60,339.7	187,894.3
Change in RRSPs	761.9	2,751.9	−42,678.6	49,145.0
Home value	65,706.8	73,262.4	0.0	646,645.0
Number of adults	2.0	0.9	1.0	7.0
Number of children under 18	0.8	1.0	0.0	6.0
Total expenditure	43,805.3	26,311.5	1,777.0	219,329.1
Net change in assets/liabilities	3,025.7	12,689.8	−63,604.0	192,312.2
Test	147.1	3,779.2	−20,245.2	21,704.0
	1986 Data Set (N = 5,851)			
Age	45.4	13.9	25.0	75.0
Pretax income	49,647.0	37,266.8	−3,907.7	1,553,461.8
Earnings	39,976.0	33,947.1	−11,950.0	1,552,783.0
Capital income	2,402.9	13,073.3	−14,340.0	659,042.5
Government transfer income	4,073.6	5,369.7	0.0	74,217.9
Other income	2,097.2	10,373.8	0.0	394,583.0
After-tax income	37,837.1	26,662.0	−25,446.3	947,202.4
C/QPP contributions	507.4	377.9	0.0	2,048.2
Other pension contributions	613.1	1,293.5	0.0	14,777.4
Total consumption	35,932.3	20,570.1	−15,354.5	352,213.1
Nondurables	27,400.2	14,505.4	2,608.7	254,940.1
Durables	8,532.2	9,521.8	−61,438.5	102,398.4
Health Expenditures	827.1	980.9	0.0	20,452.4
Saving	1,904.8	17,146.3	−103,898.1	594,989.3
Change in RRSPs	932.9	4,062.7	−108,169.0	110,637.9
Home value	81,877.8	98,391.8	0.0	1,193,805.0
Number of adults	2.0	0.9	1.0	8.0
Number of children under 18	0.8	1.1	0.0	8.0
Total expenditure	47,742.2	30,858.0	2,762.8	958,472.4
Net change in assets/liabilities	2,107.7	16,971.7	−119,393.6	651,275.0
Test	−202.9	4,273.5	−56,285.7	46,818.9
	1990 Data Set (N = 4,089)			
Age	45.3	13.8	25.0	75.0
Pretax income	52,892.4	38,787.2	695.0	948,000.0
Earnings	42,638.1	34,840.4	−7,468.0	339,500.0

Table 1.6   (continued)

Variable	Mean	Standard Deviation	Minimum	Maximum
	1990 Data Set ($N = 4,089$)			
Capital income	2,188.8	7,273.1	−22,500.0	112,402.0
Government transfer income	4,125.0	5,738.2	0.0	42,448.0
Other income	2,273.7	7,093.4	0.0	99,000.0
After-tax income	39,385.0	29,742.2	−16,695.0	929,000.0
C/QPP contributions	587.9	417.0	0.0	3,055.0
Other pension contributions	738.9	1,513.6	0.0	17,500.0
Total consumption	36,082.2	20,602.6	1,549.0	266,711.0
Nondurables	27,180.8	14,901.7	3,607.0	257,242.0
Durables	8,901.4	9,536.6	−17,385.0	87,018.0
Health expenditures	688.2	1,025.8	0.0	15,500.0
Saving	3,302.8	22,737.2	−204,188.0	786,720.0
Change in RRSPs	1,076.1	3,984.0	−50,000.0	68,000.0
Home value	97,610.1	113,400.4	0.0	999,999.0
Number of adults	1.9	0.8	0.0	7.0
Number of children under 18	0.7	1.0	0.0	6.0
Total expenditure	49,589.6	30,358.9	3,607.0	311,200.0
Net change in assets/liabilities	3,326.4	22,807.8	−220,000.0	821,000.0
Test	−23.6	5,041.6	−66,642.0	45,247.0

plement [GIS] payments), and other income (which are primarily payments from private pension plans).[11] Note that the components are unavailable for the 1978 FAMEX and that all relevant variables are measured in 1990 dollars. The definitions change somewhat across the surveys; for example, earnings excluded self-employment income in the 1982 and 1984 surveys, but then included this item after 1984. One consequence is that "earnings" could be negative in the 1986 and 1990 surveys.

Our measure of after-tax income is pretax income from all sources (excluding capital gains, which FAMEX does not measure) less mandatory deductions for income and payroll taxes, and government and employer-sponsored pension plans. Since saving is after-tax income less consumption this means that our measure of saving excludes contributions to employer-sponsored pension plans but does include tax-sheltered savings instruments like Registered Retirement Savings Plans (RRSPs). This definition of saving is somewhat more consistent with our assets and debts data, which provide no estimate of assets in employer-sponsored pension plans but which do include an estimate of RRSP wealth.[12]

11. Note that, contrary to what might be expected, mean age of head declines slightly over the five FAMEX surveys, from 45.6 in 1978 to 45.3 in 1990. This trend is opposite to the aging trend of the Canadian population as a whole. It must reflect compositional changes among spending units, for example a tendency for the number of units with younger heads to increase as the rate of divorce and marital separation increases over time and the population of single-headed families increases.

12. Similarly, life insurance contributions are excluded from after-tax income (and thus saving), and our SCF assets data provide no estimate of the value of assets held in life insurance policies.

Table 1.6 indicates that over the five FAMEX surveys from 1978 to 1990 both pretax and after-tax income exhibit a U-shaped time series. Pretax income fell from about $49,000 in 1978 to around $47,000 in each of 1982 and 1984. It then moved slightly higher than the 1978 level in 1986, reaching $49,647; in 1990 it peaked at $52,892. Due to increasing tax rates, after-tax income in 1990 was, in contrast, only slightly above its 1978 level, standing at $39,385 versus a 1978 figure of $39,090. Neglecting 1978, where information on income components is unavailable, earnings follows a time path qualitatively similar to that of pretax income. In contrast, capital income was at its peak, $2,905, in 1982, and declined in each subsequent year. As discussed below, saving was also at its peak in 1982, and declined in 1984 and 1986. This crude association raises the question of whether there are differential saving rates out of earnings versus capital income. Addressing this question is unfortunately beyond the scope of this paper.

Table 1.6 indicates that total consumption (which includes expenditures on durables but not down payments on housing or payments of principal on mortgages) declined sharply between 1978 and 1982, and surged upward from 1984 to 1986. Given the, somewhat larger, decline in after-tax income from 1978 to 1982, saving rose in this time period. Consumption moved up faster than income, however, from 1982 to 1986, producing a halving of personal saving between these years. The decline was far from permanent, however, with a jump from $1,905 to $3,303 occurring between 1986 and 1990. Thus, aggregate personal saving is quite volatile in the FAMEX data. This volatility is the result of variations over time in after-tax income and in consumption, and of the fact that changes in these variables over time are typically far from being equal in size.

Health expenditure in table 1.6 includes direct expenditures on items like drugs, dental care, and health care services, as well as public and private health insurance premiums. Over the entire period 1978–90 the compulsory and universal public health insurance scheme, known as Medicare, was in force. This scheme covers most physician services. In our survey years of 1978–86, three of Canada's ten provinces, with about half the country's population, levied health insurance premiums, which ranged up to $30 per month for a single individual and $60 per month for a family. In the 1990 survey year, the most populous province (Ontario) had discontinued its health insurance premiums, so that only a small minority of Canadian families paid such premiums.

One can deduce from table 1.6 that health expenditures are under 3 percent of total expenditure but they did rise significantly in 1990 despite the discontinuation of health insurance premiums in Ontario. And health expenditures are not small relative to personal saving, ranging from 25 percent to 45 percent. Thus, the numbers in table 1.6 are not inconsistent with precautionary saving motivated by the threat of future health expenditures. It remains to be seen at what ages, if any, this saving motive might be especially important. This issue is examined in the next section.

The market value of the household's dwelling, "Home value," is one variable that is common to both FAMEX and SCF data sets, but there are some important differences. FAMEX asks the household to estimate the value as of December 31st (a month or two before the survey is conducted). SCF asks the household to estimate market value at the time of the survey but then, if some part of the dwelling is used for business purposes (e.g., renting a room to a boarder), only the value of that part of the house used for nonbusiness purposes is recorded as "Home value" and the rest is included in another category. Thus the SCF numbers tend to be lower than those for FAMEX. Given the presence of zeros and outliers in this variable, the mean of this variable probably conveys very little information. FAMEX also monitors the net change in holdings of RRSPs, which are an important form of tax-sheltered savings; once again, means and standard deviations are not very informative, but as we shall see the distribution of this variable conditional on age is.

Table 1.6 also indicates that the representative spending unit is quite small. Rounding off the means, the typical spending unit has two adults and one child. Of course, there is considerable variation in these numbers, especially in the number of children.

Table 1.7 provides selected summary data for the 1977 and 1984 SCF wealth surveys. It indicates mean net worth per family of $103,857 in 1984, in 1990 dollars. For the reasons discussed in the introduction it is clear that this is an underestimate, reflecting in large part the absence of the extreme upper tail of the wealth distribution from the SCF samples. This error in means provides further justification for our concentration on medians and quantiles elsewhere in the paper. The surveys also suggest that nonfinancial assets almost eclipse financial assets in aggregate. The NBS figures make clear that this is misleading in terms of the aggregate picture. However, it is not necessarily misleading for the bottom 95 percent of the population, for which these surveys may be "reasonably" accurate. Note finally that the figures for home value, which U.S. validation studies indicate is quite reliably estimated on average in sample surveys, are about 10 percent lower than the FAMEX estimates shown in table 1.6, for the reasons discussed earlier.

The minimum and maximum columns of table 1.6 and table 1.7 show that some variables assume extremely high or low values. Predicted values obtained from standard regression techniques of, say, net worth on age are known to be sensitive to the presence of outliers and to functional form. This is why we have chosen to estimate age profiles with "kernel-smoothed quantiles," which are relatively insensitive to the presence of outliers in the data and place weaker restrictions on the shape of the age profiles. A "quantile" is a generalization of the concept of a median. For example, the .8 quantile of family income at age 40 is the income level such that 80 percent of those aged 40 have lower incomes; the median is the .5 quantile. We obtain a "kernel-smoothed quantile," say at age 40, as follows. Let $F(\text{age} - 40)$ be the "kernel" function which determines the weight to place on incomes at ages in a neighborhood of

Table 1.7   **Selected Statistics for Extracts Drawn from the Assets and Debts SCFs (1990 Canadian $)**

Variable	Mean	Standard Deviation	Minimum	Maximum
		1977 Data Set ($N = 5,037$)		
Age	45.1	14.4	25.0	75.0
Net worth	104,664.4	176,665.3	−515,795.1	16,337,206.0
Total assets	127,751.4	183,491.3	0.0	16,479,558.0
Total debt	23,087.1	35,888.7	0.0	931,773.9
Net financial assets	19,238.5	57,887.7	−852,291.3	1,411,835.4
Home equity	55,351.9	69,363.5	−487,084.8	815,302.1
Home value	73,856.7	79,842.9	0.0	815,302.1
Home-owner dummy	0.6	0.5	0.0	1.0
		1984 Data Set ($N = 6,819$)		
Age	45.5	14.1	25.0	75.0
Net worth	103,857.6	157,271.6	−179,250.0	1,764,500.3
Total assets	122,087.3	163,137.9	0.0	1,783,678.5
Total debt	18,229.8	31,684.3	0.0	461,991.7
Net financial assets	25,097.2	65,540.4	−321,650.3	1,284,330.1
Home equity	48,179.7	68,417.3	−43,971.9	1,166,677.0
Home value	61,749.9	76,268.1	0.0	1,216,856.6
Home-owner dummy	0.6	0.5	0.0	1.0

40. We assume F is a parabola with a peak at age 40.[13] The "bandwidth" is the distance between the two age values where the parabola cuts the age axis. The "weight" on age levels outside this range is zero, and relative weights on age levels within this range are determined by the height of the parabola and are then scaled so that they sum to unity.[14] The .8 kernel-smoothed quantile at age 40 is then the weighted average of the .8 quantiles of the income distributions at and around age 40. Since age is recorded as an integer in our data, bandwidths of 2 or smaller imply the "raw" or unsmoothed quantile is being used. An infinite bandwidth places equal weights on all ages.

Since the shape of the kernel-smoothed quantiles of some dependent variable conditional on age depends on the bandwidth chosen, it is useful to specify some criterion for choice of bandwidth. We employ the "L1 loss function with cross-validation."[15] The median income at age 40, M40, minimizes the

13. Our earlier work suggests that results are insensitive to the kernel function assumed so long as one uses "cross-validated bandwidths" (see below).

14. This is slightly oversimplified. As noted above the Labour Force Survey is not a random sample. On each public-use microdata tape Statistics Canada releases its estimate of the inverse of the probability that the household is included in the sample ("universal weights"). The kernel-smoothed estimates reported below use these weights in conjunction with the kernel weights.

15. The following is an "intuitive" explanation; technical details are in Magee, Burbidge, and Robb (1991), which also discusses limitations of the approach, such as edge effects.

sum of absolute deviations of all incomes at age 40 from M40; the .8 quantile, .8Q40, minimizes a weighted sum of absolute deviations of incomes above and below .8Q40 (.8 on incomes above, .2 on incomes below). A sensible loss function in this context (the L1 loss function) is a weighted sum of absolute prediction errors from "out of sample" (or "leave one out") prediction. For each bandwidth one can calculate the value for the L1 loss function, and the "cross-validated" (CV) bandwidth is the one that minimizes this loss function.

CV bandwidths tend to vary with the size of the data set (larger data sets have lower CV bandwidths) and the quantile being estimated (quantiles away from the median where the data are thinner tend to have larger CV bandwidths). Nevertheless, in our experience, pictures drawn with different bandwidths for different quantiles in the same diagram focus attention on unimportant details, and we shall use a single "typical" bandwidth for each variable in this paper.

We have used the kernel-smoothing technique to isolate year and cohort effects, and to remove them from the estimated "pure" age profiles, which are shown below. In doing so, we have first removed the year effects, on the argument that inspection of the raw year-to-year changes for particular age groups suggests that year effects are likely quite important. This involves iterating to find the assignment of year effects which will minimize the L1 loss function. Cohort effects are then removed, conditional on the initial identification of year effects.[16]

For each variable in the FAMEX data, we present a two-part figure. The first part (A) shows the pure age effect—a kernel-smoothed median with cohort and year effects removed (denoted by a solid line). It also traces the raw medians for six different cohorts across the 1978, 1982, 1984, 1986, and 1990 surveys. The cohorts consist of spending units with heads whose ages in 1978 were less than 25, 25–34, 35–44, 45–54, 55–63, and 64+.[17] The second part of the figure (B) graphs the estimated pure age effects (most often) for the .25, .5, and .75 quantiles.

1.4 Age Profiles

We now turn to a step-by-step examination of the age profiles of income, consumption, saving, and wealth in Canada. Except for wealth, all the data come from the FAMEX surveys. In the case of wealth, the data sources are the 1977 and 1984 SCFs.

16. The order in which cohort and year effects are removed is arbitrary. We have experimented with removing them in the opposite order. Results are little affected.

17. There are no observations on the first group (aged less than 25) in 1978. The cutoff for the last group (64+) was set at age 64 so that this group is just eliminated in the 1990 survey year. At that point, the group who were aged 55–63 in 1978 are 67–75, i.e., just covering the top available ages. (Recall that observations on those coded with age "76" are not used here.)

1.4.1   Income

Pretax Income

This variable includes all forms of income measured by FAMEX, but there are no imputations, e.g., for imputed rent on owner-occupied housing. Figure 1.1 shows quantiles peaking later for higher income groups, but with the overall median peaking between ages 45 and 50; the quantiles tend to fan out from age 25 to age 50 and then compact somewhat from age 50 to age 75. The .25 quantile appears to be forced closer to the median late in the life cycle, probably as a consequence of public pension programs. From a preretirement peak of over \$55,000, median pretax income declines to a postretirement level of about \$18,000. Note from Figure 1.1A that 1982 and 1984 were low-income years, as we observed in our discussion of table 1.6; this pattern is reflected in many of the subsequent figures.

Earnings

Figure 1.2 indicates, not surprisingly, that age profiles for earned income are similar to those for total income.[18] There is, however, a more pronounced hump and a clear retirement effect. In addition, there is no noticeable convergence of the .25, .5, and .75 quantiles in the higher age ranges.

Capital Income

Figure 1.3A shows that median capital income rises with age up to about age 70, peaking at about \$1,500. The increase is slow, however, prior to about age 50. The raw medians show strong year effects, but, in contrast to the income pictures, 1982 is here the best year. Year effects decline and become negative over 1984–90. In interpreting these year effects it is important to keep in mind that inflation rates were also declining over this period, so that part of the fall in capital income is due simply to the drop in its purely inflationary component. Ideally, it can be argued, capital income should be measured gross of capital gains (here omitted) and net of the inflationary component. Dagenais (1992) implements this approach for Canada over the period 1962–85. The result is that measured capital income becomes highly volatile. The same also becomes true of measured saving, as will be noted later.

Figure 1.3B shows that one-quarter of all households have negligible capital income in retirement, and even the median household has under \$1,200. The quantiles do fan out, however, and the top quarter of spending units receive over \$5,500 of capital income in retirement.

Government Transfer Income

Figure 1.4 reveals a huge change at retirement as median government transfers switch from about \$1,000 to about \$10,000. Figure 1.4A shows that gov-

---

18. Note that, in contrast to figure 1.1A, we have only four observations for each cohort. This is because, as mentioned earlier, the 1978 FAMEX does not break income into its components.

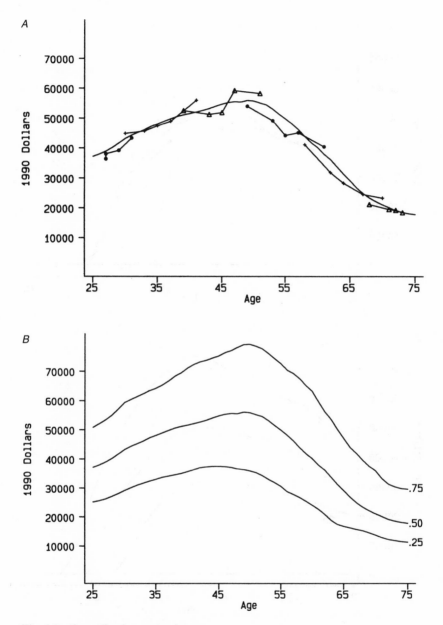

Fig. 1.1   Quantiles for pretax income
Note: The bandwidth is 8. (*A*) Cohort and smoothed medians. (*B*) Kernel-smoothed quantiles.

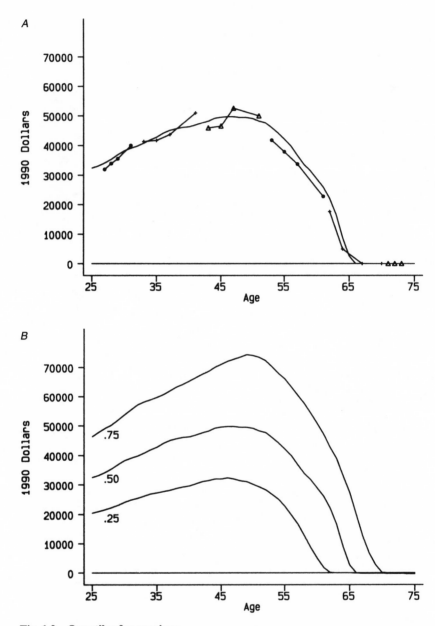

Fig. 1.2   Quantiles for earnings

Note: The bandwidth is 8. (*A*) Cohort and smoothed medians. (*B*) Kernel-smoothed quantiles.

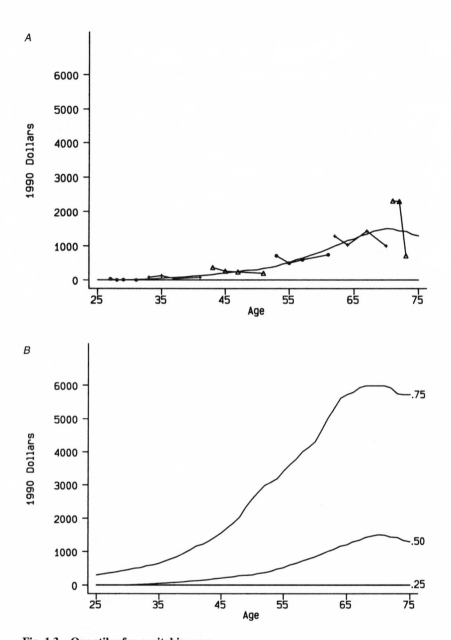

Fig. 1.3   Quantiles for capital income

Note: The bandwidth is 12. (*A*) Cohort and smoothed medians. (*B*) Kernel-smoothed quantiles.

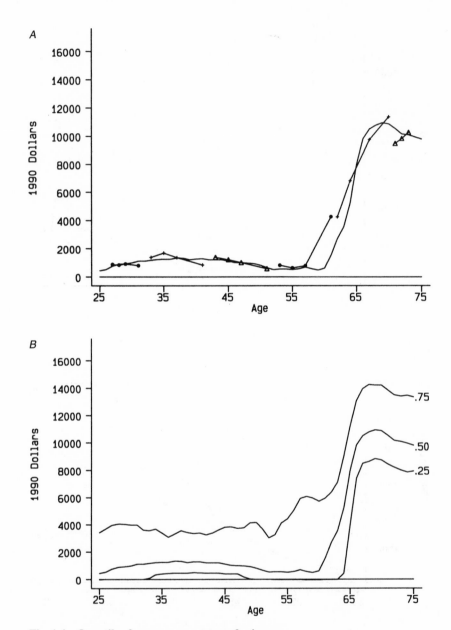

Fig. 1.4   Quantiles for government transfer income
Note: The bandwidth is 3. (*A*) Cohort and smoothed medians. (*B*) Kernel-smoothed quantiles.

ernment transfers prior to retirement have fallen over this period while median transfers postretirement have risen sharply. Year effects are therefore highly nonlinear here. Figure 1.4B shows that even the .25 quantile receives about $8,000 in government transfers in retirement. The decline during retirement is related to an increasing incidence of unattached individuals. Much of the spread in transfers between the quantiles in retirement is likely due to differences in size of spending units (i.e., in number of pensioners).

Other Income

This source of income is primarily income from private pension plan receipts. Like the previous category, figure 1.5A indicates an upward trend in retirement income. About one-half of all retirees are covered by a private pension plan but median payments are small relative to their receipts from public sources (see above). Over 90 percent of members of private pension plans are in defined-benefit pension plans.

After-Tax Income

This and pretax income are the comprehensive measures of income available in FAMEX data sets. Comparing figure 1.6A with 1.1A we see that after-tax income is flatter than pretax income; the hump shape is muted. Also, 1990 is still a relatively good year, but does not stand out as much as for pretax income. This reflects the fact that average tax rates rose significantly in the late 1980s (see Burbidge and Davies 1994). Figure 1.6B shows that quantiles for after-tax income, like those for pretax income, fan out until income of the higher quantiles peaks around age 50. Thereafter, the .5 and .75 quantiles are roughly parallel, but the .25 quantile comes closer to the median.

It is useful at this point to summarize some of the numbers underlying these figures by calculating replacement rates. The figures show that ages 45–54 are peak years for income, ages 55–65 are years when almost all individuals exit the labor force, and ages 66–75 are spent in retirement. Table 1.8 calculates replacement rates as the ratio of quantile income in retirement to quantile income in peak-income years. Using either pretax or after-tax income, except for 1986, replacement rates have been trending upward over the data period, and as one would expect they are higher for after-tax than for pretax income. Government transfers replace just under one-quarter of peak earnings. The replacement rate built into the C/QPP is 25 percent on earnings up to the average industrial wage, which was about $30,000 in 1990. OAS (payable at age 65 and taxable) and the GIS (age and income conditioned) provide a safety net for low-income elderly. This is one reason why the numbers in the Government Transfer Income/Earnings column fall sharply as one moves from lower to higher quantiles. The opposite occurs for pretax and after-tax income. Here median "other income," for those with private pensions, is over $10,000 per annum and replacement rates rise with the quantiles.

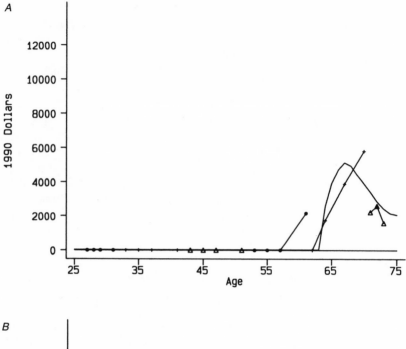

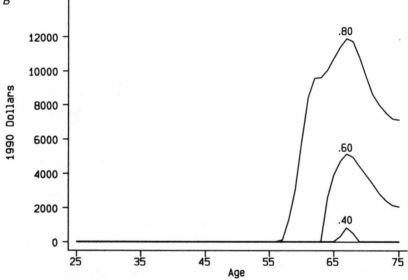

Fig. 1.5 Quantiles for other income

Note: The bandwidth is 5. (*A*) Cohort and smoothed .6 quantiles. (*B*) Kernel-smoothed quantiles.

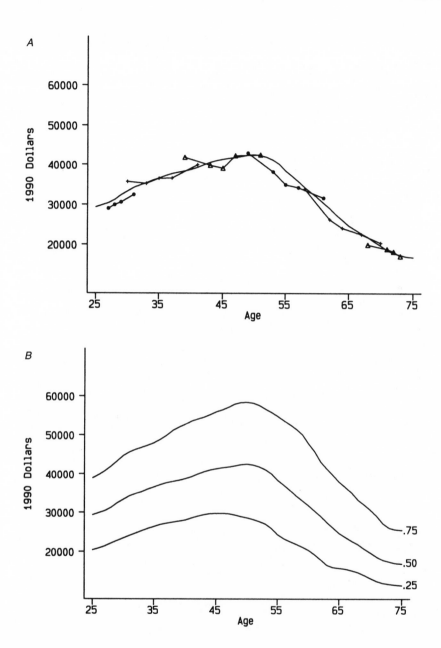

Fig. 1.6   Quantiles for after-tax income
Note: The bandwidth is 7. (*A*) Cohort and smoothed medians. (*B*) Kernel-smoothed quantiles.

Table 1.8   Replacement Rates for Various Income Measures, Years and Quantiles

	Pretax Income	After-Tax Income	Government Transfer Income/Earnings
Year			
1978	0.36	0.43	n.a.
1982	0.39	0.47	0.21
1984	0.39	0.48	0.22
1986	0.35	0.45	0.20
1990	0.41	0.49	0.22
Quantile			
.25	0.38	0.45	2.52
.5	0.38	0.47	0.24
.75	0.46	0.53	0.20

C/QPP Contributions

Having looked at what retirement income spending units receive from public and private sources it is of some interest to know what contributions they make prior to retirement. Since major components of the public system (e.g., OAS and GIS) are financed out of general revenue we can trace only contributions to C/QPP. Over our data period, employee contribution rates have been about 2 percent of earnings up to a three-year moving average of the average industrial wage, roughly $550 per annum. The raw cohort median trajectories in figure 1.7A show that rates have been rising over time.

Contributions to Other Pension Plans (not RRSPs)[19]

About one-half of all employees are members of private pension plans. In the FAMEX data median contributions are zero, or very close to zero, for all years 1978–90. Therefore we graph the .75 quantile in figure 1.8A. This figure shows that, broadly speaking, contributions have risen over the data period, although not smoothly. However, relative contributions fell in 1986 and 1990 early in the life cycle and before retirement. The latter presumably reflects the trend towards earlier retirement. The former suggests that younger households may be increasingly likely to hold jobs in companies that do not have pension plans and are using RRSPs to save for retirement (see fig. 1.15A).

19. We should emphasize that this item, like C/QPP taxes and life insurance premiums, is excluded from our measure of saving.

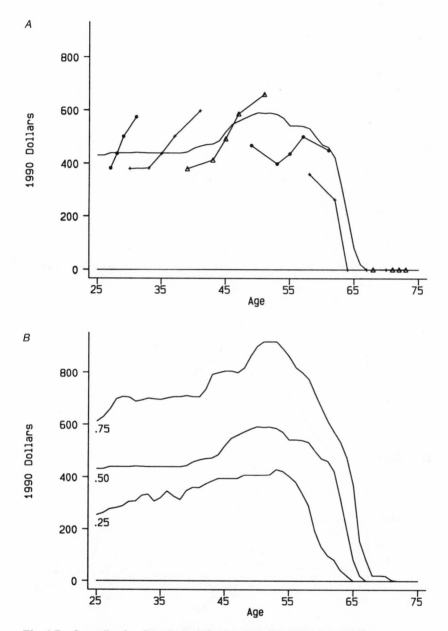

Fig. 1.7 Quantiles for Canada and Quebec Pension Plan contributions

Note: The bandwidth is 3. (*A*) Cohort and smoothed medians. (*B*) Kernel-smoothed quantiles.

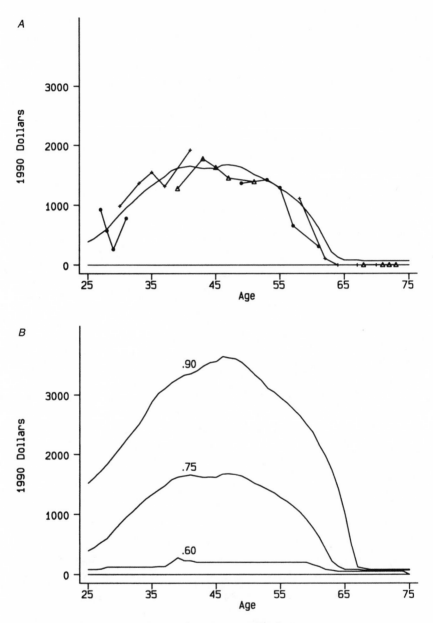

Fig. 1.8   Quantiles for other pension plan contributions
Note: The bandwidth is 8. (*A*) Cohort and smoothed .75 quantiles. (*B*) Kernel-smoothed
quantiles.

1.4.2   Consumption

Total Consumption

Figure 1.9*A* shows that the median total consumption profile is similar to that of after-tax income. An interesting aspect of the year effects is the sharp upturn in the raw cohort medians from 1984 to 1986. That this did not occur for after-tax income means that saving dropped sharply in 1986. Like income, however, figure 1.9*B* shows that consumption quantiles tend to fan out until they peak and then the .25 quantile moves closer to the median later in the life cycle. Also note that all the consumption quantiles peak at about the same age, around 45. This is about the same age as the income peak for the .25 quantile, but is earlier than the income peak for the higher quantiles, suggesting that we should see an increase in their relative saving past about age 45 in later figures.

Martin Browning (1992) has documented how important familial interactions are to an understanding of consumption patterns. Figures 1.9*A* and 1.9*B* are drawn without controlling for family size. Figure 1.9*C* uses adult-equivalence scales to illustrate the idea that much of the hump-shaped pattern in consumption vanishes when one controls for family size but that there is still a significant decline (about 25 percent) in consumption during retirement (see Robb, Magee, and Burbidge 1992). Browning (1992, 1444, table 2) shows that existing empirical studies place only weak restrictions on what scale one employs. Figure 1.9*C* uses the weighting in Robb, Magee, and Burbidge—head 1.0, spouse 0.5, other adult 0.5, first child 0.3, and other children 0.15.

Nondurables

Consumption of nondurables comprises about three-quarters of total consumption. Figure 1.10*A* shows that nondurable consumption peaks later than total consumption and that the profile is flatter. Year effects and quantile differences are similar to those for total consumption.

Durables

The differences between total and nondurable consumption profiles are explained by the durables consumption profile shown in figure 1.11. As one might expect, expenditures on durables are skewed toward the first half of the life cycle. We have an early peak, and a decline to a low level of expenditure above about age 60. When young, median households are spending between $6,000 and $8,000 on durables. This expenditure in fact reflects capital accumulation more than consumption and is impressive relative to the "regular" median saving of between $1,000 and $2,000 per year reported in table 1.3.

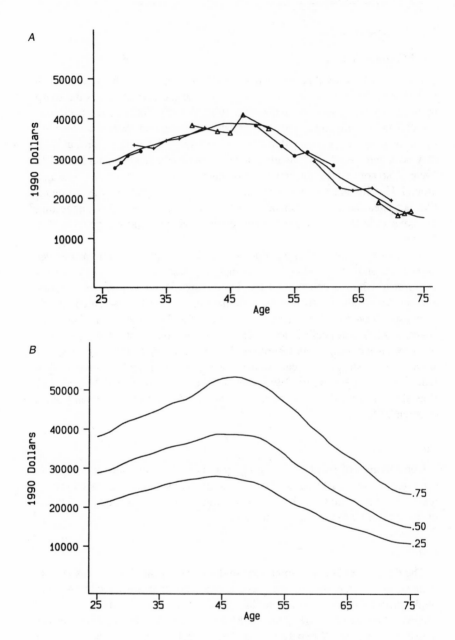

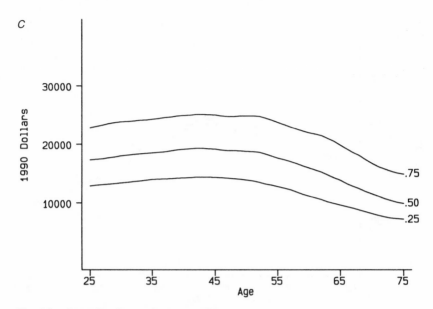

Fig. 1.9   Quantiles for total consumption

Note: The bandwidth is 7 for panels (*A*) and (*B*), and 9 for (*C*). (*A*) cohort and smoothed medians. (*B*) Kernel-smoothed quantiles. (*C*) Kernel-smoothed quantiles using an adult-equivalent scale.

Health Expenditures[20]

Figure 1.12*A* shows that median health expenditures have a hump-shaped age profile, peaking at about age 45. The hump is very similar to, and is essentially explained by, that in family size. This suggests that while there may well be some precautionary saving motivated by concerns about health expenditures, this phenomenon exists at all ages and is not especially related to saving for retirement. Also note that for the older groups there is a distinct cohort effect, with younger cohorts having higher expenditures at a given age. Figure 1.12*B* shows that quantiles fan out to a peak near age 50 and then move closer together. In addition, it would appear that at any age, the gap between the .75 quantile and the median is larger than the gap between the median and the .25 quantile. A comparison with figure 1.9*B* shows that health expenditures are more unequal and more skewed at all ages than is total consumption. There may be households in the top quartile who spend very large amounts on health care.

1.4.3   Saving

This subsection combines the numbers generated in the previous two sections to study saving, which is defined to be after-tax income less consumption.

---

20. At all ages, health expenditures for 1978 are about one-third of those for 1982. Statistics Canada's public-use microdata tape documentation does not admit the possibility of obtaining a consistent definition of health expenditures for these two years. Here we focus on 1982–90.

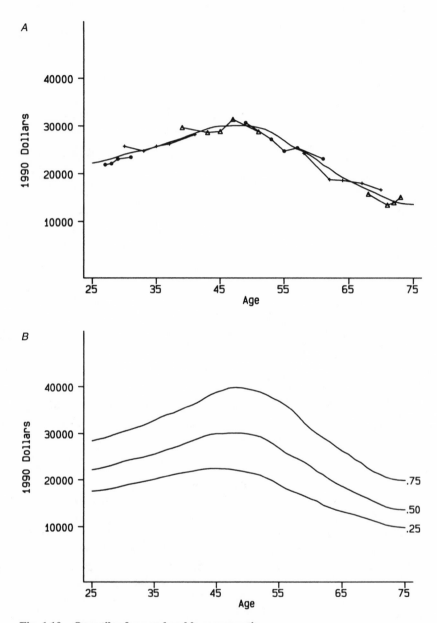

Fig. 1.10   Quantiles for nondurable consumption
Note: The bandwidth is 8. (*A*) Cohort and smoothed medians. (*B*) Kernel-smoothed quantiles.

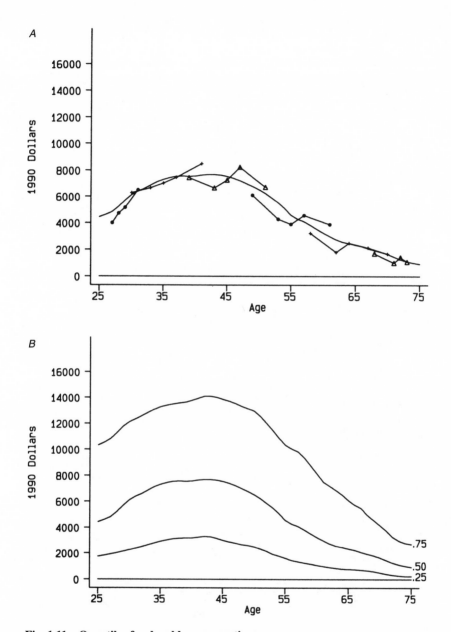

Fig. 1.11   Quantiles for durable consumption
Note: The bandwidth is 7. (*A*) Cohort and smoothed medians. (*B*) Kernel-smoothed quantiles.

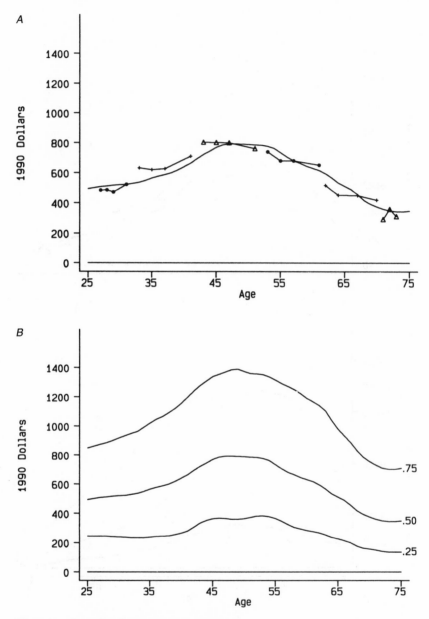

Fig. 1.12   Quantiles for health expenditures
Note: The bandwidth is 9. (*A*) Cohort and smoothed medians. (*B*) Kernel-smoothed quantiles.

One might be tempted simply to overlay the after-tax income and total consumption quantiles to get a picture of saving. Unlike averages, however, the difference of the medians is not the median of the difference. As with other variables studied in this paper we must first construct saving for each household and then examine its distribution conditional on age.

Saving

Like after-tax income and consumption, saving is hump shaped. It peaks near age 55, which is later than income or consumption. It then declines between ages 55 and 65 and is quite flat after age 65. Figure 1.13A shows strong year effects, as one would anticipate from our discussion of table 1.6. There is a marked trough for most age groups in 1986, and peaks in 1982 and 1990. As in our discussion of capital income above, it is important to note that including capital gains in income and removing the purely inflationary component from capital income would have a marked effect on the apparent year effects. As noted above, Dagenais (1992) performs such an exercise at the aggregate level for Canada up to 1985. He finds that, in contrast to the picture shown here, 1982 was a low-saving year. Measured saving is highly volatile in his time series, so that year effects would be much larger in our exercise if we performed similar adjustments for capital gains and inflation.

Figure 1.13B shows that, at any age, more than one-fourth of all households dissave and that the hump shape is more pronounced the higher the quantile.

Saving Rates

Among other things, changes in tax structure redistribute income across private households. If all households had the same marginal propensity to save then aggregate private saving would be unaffected, on this account, by a (balanced-budget) change in tax policy. Therefore, it is important to know how marginal propensities to save vary across households. We do not have panel data, and thus we cannot observe the change in saving in response to a change in income for any household. In the next few paragraphs we present some information on saving rates out of after-tax income, defined to be saving/after-tax income,[21] in the hope that such information may suggest important determinants of *marginal* propensities to save. The household saving rates so generated may be very large positive or negative numbers. Our data contain some huge outliers, to such an extent that the average saving rate is meaningless. We think this is a setting where quantile estimation is extremely helpful.

From figure 1.14A one can see that saving rates rise gently to about age 60 and then fall slightly to age 75. Year effects similar to those for total saving (fig. 1.13A) are found. Figure 1.14B shows that saving rates at many quantiles rise to age 60 and then fall a little. Once again, at any age, more than one-

---

21. For the purposes of this section, any household with zero income is assigned an income of $1.

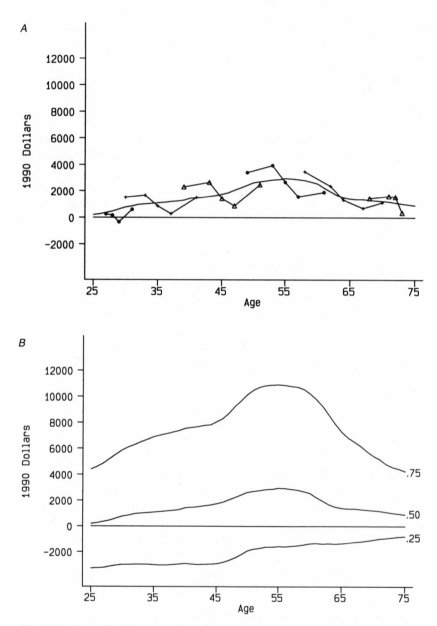

Fig. 1.13   Quantiles for personal saving
Note: The bandwidth is 10. (*A*) Cohort and smoothed medians. (*B*) Kernel-smoothed quantiles.

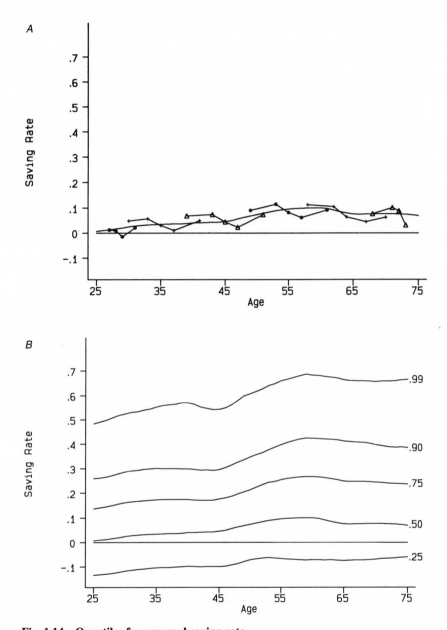

Fig. 1.14 Quantiles for personal saving rate

Note: The bandwidth is 10. (*A*) Cohort and smoothed medians. (*B*) Kernel-smoothed quantiles.

fourth of families have negative saving rates. It is also interesting to observe how the quantiles spread out at higher values.

An important question concerns the extent to which the pattern of saving rates shown here depends on our inclusion of families of all types, and the varying importance of different kinds of families with age. In an earlier version of this paper we standardized for family type by confining our attention to married-couple families. When that is done, saving rates at the various quantiles are somewhat higher, except for the .99 quantile. The saving rate for the .99 quantile is lower for married couples than for all families taken together. This indicates that, while most unattached individuals have lower saving rates than married couples, there is a small group of such individuals with extremely high saving rates. Importantly, there is little change in the age pattern of saving rates when married couples, rather than all types of family units, are examined. This suggests that lack of standardization for family type is not biasing our assessment of the age pattern of saving.

It should be emphasized again, as in our earlier discussion of table 1.1, that according to these FAMEX data, personal saving rates in Canada vary much more across income quantiles than they do with age. Figure 1.14B makes this very clear.

Change in RRSP Holdings

As noted above, the FAMEX structure requires an estimate of each household's net change in assets and liabilities, and the one category reported on the public use tapes is net change in RRSP holdings. Figure 1.15A shows that prior to retirement about one-quarter of families make significant additions to their RRSPs each year (the median is zero for all years). It also shows a very strong cohort effect: contributions at any given age have been trending upward over the data period. The absence of a similar cohort effect for total saving indicates that there is a compositional switch in saving vehicles toward greater use of RRSPs. Burbidge and Davies (1994) argue that this is due to a closing down of many alternative tax shelters for saving in the 1980s.

Figure 1.15B shows a wide range of quantiles. Note first, that all quantiles between .10 and .60, inclusive, are very close to zero. That is, there is a very large group, at any age, making no RRSP contributions or withdrawals. (It would be quite consistent with this for the majority of spending units to make contributions and withdrawals at some point in their lives. There may be many spending units for which such transactions occur in only a few years.) Second, note that it is only a very small minority who are making RRSP withdrawals at any age. It is not until past age 65, for example, that the .05 quantile dips below the zero axis. In part this may reflect the general lack of dissaving in retirement, and in part it may simply point to a data problem. Finally, on average it is only about 25 percent of spending units who are contributing to RRSPs at any particular age.

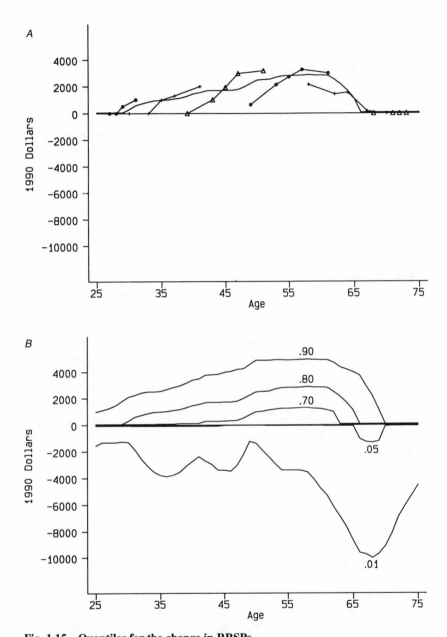

Fig. 1.15 Quantiles for the change in RRSPs

Notes: The bandwidth is 8. All quantiles between .10 and .60 are virtually zero. (*A*) Cohort and smoothed .8 quantiles. (*B*) Kernel-smoothed quantiles.

1.4.4   Wealth

We now turn to the SCF data for 1977 and 1984 to study the age dependence of net worth and its components. It is impossible to identify year, cohort, and "pure" age effects with just two cross sections, so the previous format cannot be adopted here. In the first draft of this paper we graphed age profiles for each cross section separately and found the shapes of the profiles to be quite similar. Accordingly, we now pool the two SCF data sets. The *A* graphs for each variable depict raw and smoothed medians; the *B* graphs show the median and other quantiles.

Net Worth

Figure 1.16*A* shows that net worth, i.e., total assets minus total debts, rises with age to 48, flattens out until age 63, and declines thereafter. As mentioned earlier, this hump shape cannot be taken as confirmation of the naive LCM, although such an interpretation is tempting. The danger of such an interpretation is suggested by the positive median saving rates we have found at all ages up until age 75.[22] Figure 1.16*B* shows that the net worth quantiles fan out with age, and that the higher quantiles have a more strongly peaked age profile.

It is interesting to note in figure 1.16*A* that the data are quite noisy after age 48. Given that we are looking at quantiles and that the sample sizes are quite large, this is striking. The noisiness of the data is behind the bumpiness of the age profile which comes through despite the use of a bandwidth of seven years. A smoother profile would be obtained if the kernel-smoothing procedure allowed longer bandwidths to be selected in particular age ranges where the data are noisier. Also note that higher-quantile age profiles are less smooth. Again, if our smoothing procedure allowed different bandwidths for different quantiles this differential bumpiness would likely be reduced.

Net Financial Assets

Median net financial assets rise with age until 65 and then fall slightly. Note, however, that these assets are not large relative to median net worth at any age, and that they are particularly small up to age 45. Thus, for the *typical* Canadian household most saving takes place in nonfinancial form, and this is especially true for young households. Figure 1.17*B* shows that financial assets are relatively much more important for higher quantiles. The .75 quantile, for example, has peak net financial assets over $60,000, which is more than a quarter of the peak for the .75 net worth quantile. If we penetrated further into the upper tail of the distribution we would find net financial assets becoming even more important. Given the skewness of the wealth distribution, if we therefore

---

22. Recall that net worth has a downward bias for at least two reasons. First, "total assets" ignores any equity the family may have in private pension plans or life insurance. Second, consumer durables other than housing and automobiles are excluded from "total assets," but money borrowed to purchase any consumer durable is counted as part of "total debt."

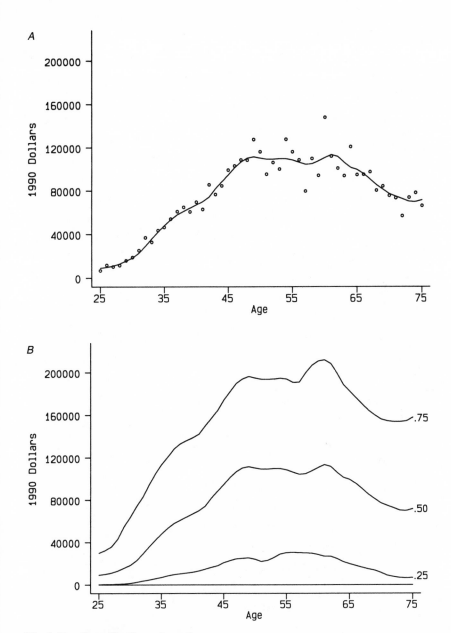

Fig. 1.16 Quantiles for net worth
Note: The bandwidth is 7. (A) Raw and smoothed medians. (B) Kernel-smoothed quantiles.

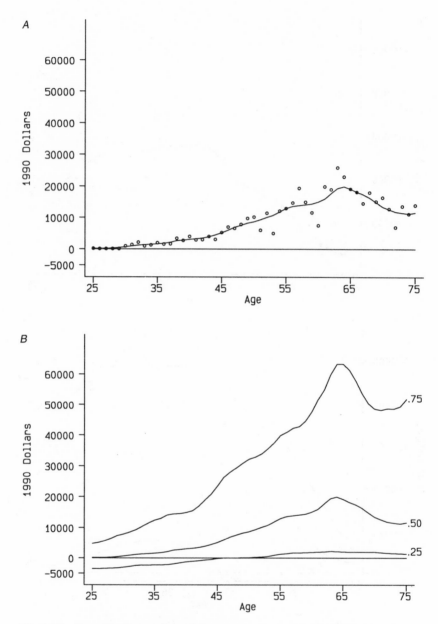

Fig. 1.17 Quantiles for net financial assets
Note: The bandwidth is 8. (*A*) Raw and smoothed medians. (*B*) Kernel-smoothed quantiles.

looked at means, rather than medians, net financial assets would appear to be considerably more important "on average" than figure 1.17A suggests.

It is also interesting to compare the age profiles of owners of net financial assets with those of the corresponding flow, capital income (see fig. 1.3). The capital income profiles show less of a hump shape. This suggests some caution in accepting that median net financial assets decline significantly in retirement.

Home Equity

Figure 1.18A shows median home equity for home owners. This rises to about age 45 and then is remarkably flat with age. The quantiles shown in figure 1.18B are very similar. Note that the quantiles fan out slightly at early ages, but in contrast to net financial assets are, overall, very similar in shape.

Finally, figure 1.19 indicates a rapid rise in the proportion of home owners up to about .75 at age 45, and only a small decline in this fraction at advanced ages. This confirms the great importance of investment in owner-occupied accommodation as a form of saving for young Canadians.

1.6 Summary and Conclusions

We have presented a summary of what Canadian microdata sets have to say about the variation of income, consumption, saving, and wealth both across quantiles and over the life cycle. All of these variables and their components exhibit age dependence. Of all the variables studied, saving rates out of disposable income were least dependent on age; here intracohort variation appears to dominate. Tax policies that redistribute income across low- and high-income households within age groups, rather than policies that redistribute across households with similar incomes but different ages, are more likely to affect aggregate saving.

Other important themes have emerged. For example, there is a general message that it is not safe to assess age patterns of consumption, saving, or wealth holding using isolated cross-sectional data. While this is not the case for *all* variables, cohort and year effects are often quite strong. Another finding is that Canadians save in essentially two phases. When young they do so by building up home equity. It is only in middle age that most make the transition to saving in the form of pension rights and financial assets. This suggests, as we believe is echoed in the studies for other countries, that the institutional structure and tax provisions affecting home ownership, mortgage lending, and speed of buildup of home equity are a very important determinant of the overall personal saving rate in Canada. Finally, in common with several recent studies, we find that continued saving after retirement is more the rule than the exception. This paper thus repeats the challenge to the naive life-cycle model as an organizing tool for thinking about personal saving.

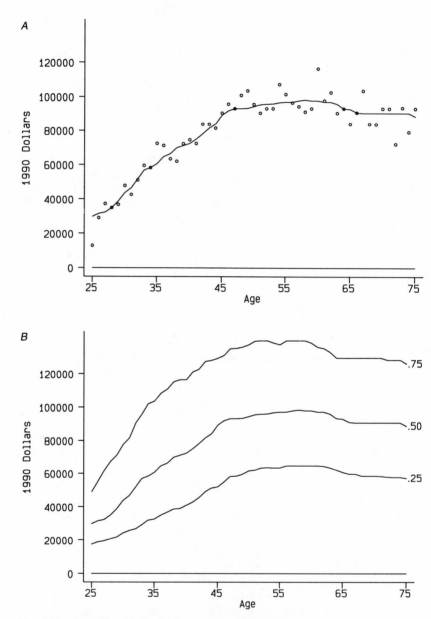

Fig. 1.18 Quantiles for equity in owner-occupied homes
Note: The bandwidth is 10. (*A*) Raw and smoothed medians. (*B*) Kernel-smoothed quantiles.

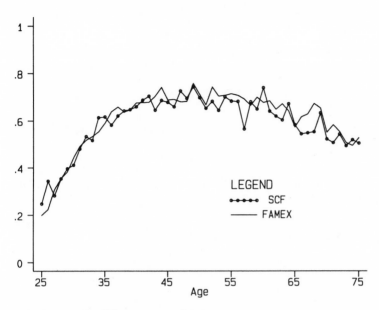

Fig. 1.19 Proportion of home owners by age

Table 1A.1   Numbers of Observations by (After-Tax) Income Quintile and Age Group

Income quintile	All	<29	30–34	35–39	40–44	45–49	50–54	55–59	60–64	65–69	70–74	>74
						Age Group						
1	994	154	139	124	112	76	82	69	57	57	43	70
2	953	145	129	129	101	85	67	64	59	54	39	71
3	942	144	131	112	103	75	61	68	56	58	51	61
4	916	136	139	121	105	72	67	57	47	52	59	63
5	764	126	112	94	83	74	59	45	42	57	46	67
All	4,569	705	650	580	504	382	336	303	261	278	238	332

Source: FAMEX for 1990 (all observations).

Table 1A.2   Numbers of Observations by (After-Tax) Income Quintile and Age Group

	All	<25	25–29	30–34	35–39	40–44	45–49	50–54	55–59	60–64	65–69	70–74	>74
							Age Group						
1	2,755	216	315	336	311	276	219	219	220	200	171	138	184
2	2,919	208	330	339	294	254	217	235	233	213	177	141	179
3	2,842	212	322	313	303	232	218	238	218	212	191	166	195
4	2,779	217	316	331	294	255	213	214	206	217	185	158	190
5	2,734	222	326	310	297	244	213	231	215	203	172	147	208
All	14,029	1,075	1,609	1,629	1,499	1,261	1,080	1,137	1,092	1,045	896	750	956

Source: SCF for 1984 (all observations).

References

Bar-Or, Yuval, John B. Burbidge, Lonnie Magee, and A. Leslie Robb. 1992. Canadian experience-earnings profiles and the return to education in Canada: 1971–1990. McMaster University. Mimeograph.

Browning, Martin J. 1992. Children and household economic behavior. *Journal of Economic Literature* 30:1434–75.

Burbidge, John B., and James B. Davies. 1994. Government incentives and household saving in Canada. In Public policies and household saving, ed. James M. Poterba, 19–56. Chicago: University of Chicago Press.

Burbidge, John B., and A. Leslie Robb. 1985. Evidence on wealth-age profiles in Canadian cross-section data. *Canadian Journal of Economics* 18:854–75.

Burbidge, John B., Lonnie Magee, and A. Leslie Robb. 1988. Alternative transformations to handle extreme values of the dependent variable. *Journal of the American Statistical Association* 83:123–27.

Dagenais, Marcel G. 1992. Measuring personal savings, consumption, and disposable income in Canada. *Canadian Journal of Economics* 92:681–707.

Davies, James B. 1979. Life cycle saving, inheritance and the distribution of income and wealth in Canada. Ph.D. Thesis. University of London.

———. Forthcoming. The distribution of wealth in Canada. In *Research in Economic Inequality,* ed. E. Wolff, vol. 4. New York: Academic.

Magee, Lonnie, John B. Burbidge, and A. Leslie Robb. 1991. Computing kernel-smoothed quantiles from many observations. *Journal of the American Statistical Association* 86:673–77.

Oja, Gail. 1986. The wealth of Canadians: A comparison survey of consumer finances with national balance sheet estimates. Labour and Household Surveys Analysis Division Staff Reports. Ottawa: Statistics Canada.

Robb, A. Leslie, and John B. Burbidge. 1989. Consumption, income and retirement. *Canadian Journal of Economics* 22:522–44.

Robb, A. Leslie, Lonnie Magee, and John B. Burbidge. 1992. Kernel smoothed consumption-age quantiles. *Canadian Journal of Economics* 25: 669–80.

Siddiq, Fazley K., and Charles M. Beach. 1993. Characterizing life-cycle wealth distributions in Canada using dominance criteria. Discussion Paper no. 886. Institute for Economic Research. Queen's University.

Statistics Canada. 1992. Documentation for the public use microdata tape for the 1990 Family Expenditure Survey. Ottawa: Statistics Canada.

———. 1993. The relationship between estimates from the 1986 FAMEX and data in the National Accounts. Ottawa: Statistics Canada. Unpublished.

2 Personal Saving in the United States

Orazio P. Attanasio

2.1 Introduction

Saving is an intrinsically dynamic phenomenon: what is saved is to be consumed later, either by oneself or others. As such it is hard to formalize; it is difficult to assess the importance of uncertainty, expectations, changes in income and demographic variables, and so on. The most elegant theory of saving behavior is the life-cycle model of Modigliani and Brumberg (1954). According to this theory, people save to smooth consumption in the face of an uneven income profile. Its simplest version, which assumes a constant utility function, no uncertainty, no changes in the interest rate, and perfect capital markets, has very sharp implications for the life-cycle pattern of consumption, saving, and wealth. The theory can then be extended to allow for uncertainty about income and/or life length, changing discount rates, family composition, income endogeneity, and so on. In general, saving will depend on the duration of total and working life, the nature of pension arrangements, and the shape of the age profile of earnings.

While the life-cycle model can be considered a benchmark, alternative models and modifications of the original model have been proposed. In a recent paper, Deaton (1991) analyzes the implications of liquidity constraints for optimal saving under different assumptions about the dynamics of lifetime income. Kotlikoff and Summers (1981, 1988), in a lively exchange with Modig-

Orazio P. Attanasio is professor of economics at Stanford University and at the University of Bologna, a faculty research fellow of the National Bureau of Economic Research, and a research fellow of the Centre for Economic Policy Research (London) and of the Institute for Fiscal Studies (London).

The participants at the conference and the discussant, David Wise, provided helpful comments. This project was financially supported in part by NSF grant SES-9057511. The author is very grateful to Catherine C. de Fontenay for able and dedicated research and editorial assistance. Dean Maki helped in the construction of the data set on real estate wealth.

liani (1988), have argued that most wealth is not accumulated to smooth consumption over the life cycle but rather to provide bequests. The precautionary motive for saving has also received a considerable amount of attention (see, e.g., Kimball 1990; Skinner 1988).

No matter what the main motive for saving is (life-cycle, precautionary, or bequest) it is clear that aggregate savings will depend crucially on the composition of the population. In the life-cycle case, for instance, aggregate savings will depend on the relative number of young and old consumers and on the total amount of resources available to them. It is therefore essential, in order to understand aggregate savings, to analyze and model individual behavior and consider aggregation and composition effects carefully.

Unfortunately, studies of individual saving behavior are not numerous, especially for the United States, the main reason being the lack of microdata sets containing individual data on income and consumption.[1] This paper uses data from the Consumer Expenditure Survey (CEX) from the 1980s to describe and characterize individual saving behavior. The CEX is the only U.S. microdata set that contains exhaustive information on consumption, and it has been available, on a continuous basis, since 1980.[2]

The rest of the paper is organized as follows. In section 2.2 we discuss the data sources and the statistical techniques we use in what follows. The CEX contains detailed data on income, consumption, and wealth. These data are described in detail in the first part of section 2.2; in the second part, we illustrate the statistical techniques employed in the analysis. In section 2.3 we analyze the last available cross section: that for the year 1990. We estimate and tabulate the cross-sectional age profiles of some key variables: income, consumption, saving, saving rates, and wealth. In addition to age, we also control for the level of income, the years of schooling of the household head, and the number of children. The measure of location used for all the variables considered in this section is the median. This avoids the problem of dealing with top-coded observations and makes the analysis robust to the presence of outliers.

The cross-sectional analysis in section 2.3 supplies a snapshot which is easily summarized and is useful for comparison with data from other countries. However, the interpretation of the cross-sectional profiles estimated on a single year of data as age profiles can be misleading in the presence of strong cohort effects. The availability of a time series of cross sections and the use of average

1. Early evidence on individual consumption and saving behavior is contained in Friend (1954), Goldsmith (1956), Friedman (1957), Juster (1966), and in the volume edited by Friend and Jones (1960).

2. Before then various surveys were available: the first CEX was run in 1917–18. Various students have analyzed the 1960–61 and the 1972–73 surveys. In this paper we will not use them for two reasons. First, we will stress the dynamic aspects of saving behavior and use cohort techniques: surveys that are 10 years apart are therefore of limited use. Second, and more important, many important methodological aspects of the surveys are substantially different, making a comparison extremely difficult, if not impossible. Bosworth, Burtless, and Sabelhaus (1991) compare the 1972–73 CEX to those from the 1980s.

cohort techniques helps in circumventing this problem. In sections 2.4 to 2.7 we characterize the age profiles of several variables of interest using data from the 11 available CEX surveys (1980–90) and average cohort techniques.

In section 2.4 we analyze data on disposable income and pension contributions. We estimate age profiles for both total family income and its various components. In particular, income is divided into four components: labor income, capital income, transfers, and pensions. In section 2.5 we estimate age profiles for total consumption expenditure and its components. We analyze one by one those forms of expenditure that could be considered saving: durables, education, and health. In section 2.6 we construct several definitions of saving and analyze their age profiles. The relationship between the cross-sectional distribution of saving and various controls is analyzed. In section 2.7 we estimate financial wealth–age profiles, while section 2.8 concludes the paper.

2.2 Data and Methods

2.2.1 Data

The data used in this paper are primarily from the CEX 1980–90. Since 1980 the CEX has been a rotating panel of approximately 7,000 households interviewed four times over a period of one year;[3] each quarter one-fourth of the sample is replaced by new households. The sample is representative of the population of the United States:[4] each household is assigned a weight proportional to the reciprocal of the probability of its being included. For the purpose of our analysis, the information collected in the interview can be divided into three groups: expenditure information, data on income and transfers, and other variables.

The sample unit is the so-called consumer unit. The consumer unit does not necessarily coincide with a household: it may include individuals not related to the households provided they "share responsibility for at least two out of three major types of expenses—food, housing and other expenses." In this respect, the definition is similar (but not identical) to the definition of household used in the Current Population Survey (CPS).

Expenditure Information

In each interview the household's reference person is asked to report expenditure during each of the three months preceding the interview on each of about 500 different commodity categories. This level of detail is never used in the analysis that follows. As a first step, we aggregate these 500 categories into 28 expenditure categories. This level of aggregation was chosen on the basis

---

3. Each household is actually interviewed five times. The first interview, however, is a contact interview from which no public data are available.

4. In 1982 and 1983, nonurban households were excluded from the population of reference. For consistency, we exclude nonurban households from our sample.

of the availability of monthly price indexes at the regional level.[5] These 28 categories are then used to create monthly household-specific price indexes for the consumption aggregate we analyze (durables, nondurables, education, etc.). This is done by taking the geometric weighted average of the relevant price indexes at the regional level, with weights given by household expenditure shares.

Annual expenditure is constructed by summing over the monthly figures. Annual price indexes are given by geometric averages of monthly price indexes, with weights given by monthly expenditures. Expenditure on items for which no price index is available is deflated by the household-specific CPI.[6] In the analysis that follows we consider six categories: durables, health, education, housing (inclusive of mortgage payments), finance charges other than mortgages, and other nondurables and services. Nominal figures are converted into real figures, when necessary, using the household-specific price indexes.[7] If one attempts to estimate aggregate Personal Consumption Expenditure (PCE) by aggregating individual figures with the appropriate weights, one typically underestimates the aggregate figures. These differences exist for three reasons, the first and foremost being the fact that the CEX data come from a recall interview: it is well known that substantial omissions arise from these interviews, especially for frequently purchased items.[8]

The second reason is the presence of definitional differences between the CEX and PCE. The most important of these are in the definition of health and housing expenditures. The CEX counts as health expenditures only out-of-pocket expenditures, while the PCE includes all expenditures on health, regardless of who ultimately pays the bill. Indeed, because health insurance refunds can be given out for expenditures incurred in months previous to those covered by the interviews, in the CEX net health expenditure can be (and for some households is) negative. The PCE includes in housing expenditures the imputed rent of owner-occupied housing; no such attribution is made for the CEX. Finally, the third reason is that the universe of reference, because of the exclusion of nonurban households, is different for the CEX and the PCE.

Given these problems, it is important to assess the importance of the difference between CEX and PCE aggregates. A detailed study of this issue has been made by Gieseman (1987) and Paulin et al. (1991), who report that for

5. Our categorization of household expenditure matches closely the Bureau of Labor Statistics (BLS) classification used in the construction of the CPI. There are few exceptions: the most noticeable is the inclusion of personal computers into "entertainment goods" along with hi-fi equipment, televisions, and so on; the BLS includes them in home furniture.

6. An example is expenditure on finance charges. The household-specific CPI is constructed by excluding this expenditure from the weights.

7. Most expenditure items are not top-coded in the CEX (exceptions include boats, airplanes, etc.): we therefore decide to ignore this problem at this point.

8. The BLS runs another survey on food and other frequently purchased items based on diaries. Large differences emerged between aggregate food expenditure between the diary and the interview surveys in the early years of the survey. These differences became negligible in 1983. In what follows we do not use diary survey data.

most components of personal expenditure the differences between CEX and PCE are roughly stable.[9] A further indication of the quality of the CEX data is the evidence in Attanasio (1993b), who reports that the correlation between the rate of growth of aggregate CEX consumption and PCE is as high as .71 over the period analyzed.[10]

Income and Wealth Data

The CEX contains detailed information on total household income and various of its components. In particular, it is possible to construct four variables: labor income, capital income, transfers (including social security, food stamps, unemployment insurance, etc.), and pension income. Extensive information is also available on tax payments and refunds. Unfortunately, the tax information is not in general matched to the income source to which it refers. It is possible to construct total household after-tax income as the sum of the various income components minus tax payments net of refunds; the components, however, are before taxes.

The income questions are always asked in the first and fourth interviews. In the second and third, these questions are asked only if the employment status of some household member has changed; otherwise the figure from the first interview is repeated. The questions on income typically refer to the 12 months before the interview, and so it is not possible to construct changes in income over quarters. The timing of the income questions has implications for the construction of saving that are discussed later.[11]

Income figures are top-coded in the CEX. Until 1982 the top-coding level was $75,000; it was raised to $100,000 in 1983. In addition, in 1980 and 1981, if any of the components of income was above the top-coding level, all income variables would be top-coded. After 1981, only the components above the top-coding level are top-coded: total income for top-coded observations can therefore exceed the top-coding level. We discuss how top-coded observations are dealt with in section 2.2.2.

In addition to top-coding, income variables are plagued by another problem: that of incomplete income responses. Incomplete responses for household income are those observations that do not report all income sources. The large majority of these observations do not report any income. We decided to exclude these observations, which account for about 12 percent of the total, from the sample we analyze.[12]

9. A similar analysis has been implemented recently by Slesnick (1992), who stresses that the amount by which the CEX underestimates PCE aggregates was very different in the 1980s relative to the 1960–61 and 1972–73 surveys.

10. A further difference between CEX and PCE aggregates is the definition of a "year" used in this paper and in Attanasio (1993b).

11. The CEX contains separate files on individual household members which include information on individual members' income. We do not use this information in this paper.

12. Surprisingly enough, the average level of total consumption for these observations is not statistically different from that of the households with complete income responses. The BLS routinely publishes averages for the subsample with complete income responses.

A sizeable number of households report negative values for before- and after-tax income. After consultation with the BLS statisticians, we decided to keep these observations in the sample (most of them are self-employed individuals).

If we aggregate CEX income data and compare them to the National Income and Product Accounts (NIPA) statistics, the result is much less satisfactory than for consumption. Attanasio (1993b) reports that the correlation coefficient between the aggregated CEX disposable income growth computed using the figures published by the BLS and the NIPA equivalent series is only .21. Interestingly enough, the correlation of NIPA disposable income and the CEX aggregate obtained from the sample used in this paper and in Attanasio (1993b) is much higher (around .71).[13]

Admittedly, the income data in the CEX are not of the highest quality. Other data sets, such as the CPS or the Survey of Income and Program Participation (SIPP) are much more reliable. The CEX, however, has the unique advantage of having income and consumption data simultaneously, thereby making it possible to study *saving* at the individual level. In addition, the main features of the CEX income data are not dissimilar from those of other data sets. When we estimate income-age profiles similar to those presented in section 2.4 using CPS data, we obtain very similar results, the main difference being that the CPS profile looked much smoother than the CEX. This is probably due partly to the much larger size of the CPS sample and partly to greater measurement error in the CEX.

The CEX also contains information on financial assets held by the household as of the last day of the month preceding the fourth interview. Total assets are divided into four categories: checking accounts, saving accounts, U.S. saving bonds, and other bonds and equities. In section 2.3 we describe the 1990 cross-sectional profile for total financial assets, while in section 2.4 we aggregate these four components into *liquid assets,* which include savings and checking accounts, and into *nonliquid assets,* which include the last two categories.[14] As far as top-coding is concerned, financial asset variables are treated in the same way as income variables; the top-coding level is also the same.

The quality of the CEX data on financial assets is equivalent to that of the data on income. The survey is not designed to investigate asset holding in detail. Nor can it be used to estimate aggregate household wealth: the relatively large number of nonresponses for these variables, the low level of top-coding, and the lack of oversampling among wealthy households prevent it. On the

13. The BLS published figures and the aggregates from our sample are different for three reasons. First, we exclude several groups of households from our sample (see the selection rules used). Second, the way in which we assign observations to time periods is different. Third, the BLS has access to the original data; therefore, there are no top-coded observations.

14. In addition to stock variables in the CEX, there is also a question on the change in the stock over the last year. Unfortunately, the quality of the answers to these questions is dubious: there are many missing values and a large number of zeros. We therefore decided not to use this information.

other hand, the main features of the financial asset data are similar to those found in other surveys. Attanasio (1993a) reports that the financial wealth–age profiles estimated using the CEX are similar to those typically estimated in the literature. Furthermore, while it is true that the proportion of households reporting zero assets is higher than in other surveys (about 18 percent overall, 15 percent in our sample), if one looks at the proportion of households with, say, less than $5,000, one gets figures similar to those of other data sources.[15]

The information on real estate wealth was very limited in the early years of the survey.[16] However, since 1988, the BLS has started releasing detailed information on the value of household estate property, as well as details on outstanding mortgages. In section 2.3, we use the 1990 data to estimate the cross-sectional profile of the net and gross value of real estate wealth. The gross value is the defined as the total market value of all real estate owned by the household (even if it does not live in it) and should therefore reflect capital gains and losses. The net value is obtained from the gross by subtracting total outstanding debt on real estate.

Other Variables

The "income and characteristics" file of the CEX contains information on about 500 different socioeconomic variables that range from pension contributions to family composition, region of residence, education, and so on. Detailed information on the variables available is in the CEX manual. In this section we will discuss briefly the variables that are used in the analysis below.

The information on the region of residence is not very detailed. The United States is divided into the four standard census regions: Northeast, Midwest, South, and West. In addition to the region of residence, some information is provided on the size of the city of residence.[17]

Information on pension contributions is extremely valuable to the analysis of savings. The CEX contains information on employees' contributions to both private and government pension schemes in the form of deductions from their pay. In addition, we have information on contributions to individual retirement accounts (IRAs). No information on employers' contributions to pension schemes is provided.

---

15. For a comparison of wealth data from the Survey of Consumer Finances, PSID, and SIPP, see Curtin, Juster, and Morgan (1987).

16. We know whether the household rents or owns (possibly with a mortgage) the house it lives in. We also know whether the consumer units live in student housing. We exclude these observations from our sample. The few observations of units that live in a nonowned house without paying rent are aggregated with the renters. Finally, a question is asked on the market value of owned homes. Unfortunately, the answers to this question are very few and extremely unreliable.

17. This information is absent for the West. Most restrictions on data availability in the CEX are motivated by confidentiality. The reason for the exclusion of city size information for the West is that there is only one city with more than 4 million people in the West.

Attrition, Sample Size, and Construction of Saving

The response rate in the CEX is reasonably good. The BLS reports that about 15 percent of the households contacted do not participate in the survey. Of the remaining 85 percent, we exclude an additional 12 percent because of incomplete income responses (see above). Various additional selection criteria were used to eliminate observations that presented apparent inconsistencies. In particular, we eliminated all observations with missing consumption or income data, those for which the age of the reference person increases by more than one during the period of interview, and those living in student housing.

In section 2.3, we focus on the 1990 sample and on 11 age groups, while in the following sections we use data from 1980–90 to analyze the behavior of 10 cohorts, defined on the basis of their year of birth. We eliminate from the sample used for the cross-sectional analysis of section 2.3 all households headed by individuals younger than age 21 or older than age 75. The sample used in the cohort analysis of sections 2.4 to 2.7 excludes all the households headed by individuals born before 1910 or after 1959. We refer to the former as the *cross-sectional* sample and to the latter as the *cohort* sample.

After all selection criteria are used, we are left with 4,623 households in the cross-sectional sample and 47,647 households in the cohort sample. The definition and size of the age groups of the cross-sectional sample are reported in table 2.1. In table 2.2 we report, for each year from 1980 to 1990, the size of the cohort sample.[18]

While, in theory, each household is interviewed four times, not all households complete the four interviews. It is common for a household to drop out of the sample and/or to miss an interview (not necessarily the last). In table 2.3, we report the number and percentage of households completing any set of interviews. As can be seen, only half the households complete four interviews. We did not eliminate households with fewer than four interviews, deciding rather to make some adjustment in the computation of saving.

Saving is defined as disposable income minus consumption. Disposable income is defined as total family income net of taxes *and* social security contributions. Deductions for and contributions to private and government retirement schemes are included in income but not in consumption. Therefore they are considered as saving. Employers' contributions to pensions are not considered as saving because of the lack of data on this item. Several definitions of saving can be constructed by using different definitions of consumption.

---

18. As explained below, we aggregate all the interviews of a given household: therefore we have only one observation per consumer unit. In 1986 the CEX sample was discontinued, so that it is not possible to follow into 1986 households that had their first or second interview in 1985. This explains the larger sample sizes of 1985 and 1990 (which is the last year in the sample): households that normally would have completed their cycle of interviews in 1986 and 1991 are not observed so that their "last" recorded interview is in 1985 and 1990. The size of the cohort sample in 1990 differs from the cross-sectional sample because the definition of the age groups in the latter does not coincide with the definition of the cohorts in the former.

Table 2.1   **1990 CEX: Sample Size by Age Group**

Age Group	Observations
21–25	497
26–30	639
31–35	640
36–40	572
41–45	523
46–60	375
51–55	335
56–60	251
61–65	259
66–70	303
71–75	229

Table 2.2   **CEX: Sample Size by Year**

Year	Observations
1980	4,027
1981	3,920
1982	3,954
1983	4,140
1984	4,105
1985	7,200
1986	4,315
1987	4,221
1988	3,507
1989	3,655
1990	4,603

Table 2.3   **Interviews Completed**

Interviews	Frequency	Percentage
2	4,406	9.25
3	658	1.38
3,2	3,316	6.96
4	607	1.27
4,2	88	0.18
4,3	556	1.17
4,3,2	2,923	6.13
5	3,203	6.72
5,2	71	0.15
5,3	109	0.23
5,3,2	308	0.65
5,4	2,993	6.28
5,4,2	330	0.69
5,4,3	3,558	7.47
5,4,3,2	24,521	51.46

The time span used to define the flow of consumption is the year. This is done so as to match the time spans to which consumption and income refer. Therefore, while income is taken from the last completed interview, annual consumption is defined as the sum of the monthly figures from all the interviews. For households that do not complete the four interviews, the total figure for consumption is adjusted to take into account the fact that it refers to less than 12 months. Of course this introduces some measurement error that can be particularly severe in the case of durables.

Households are interviewed every month, and, as discussed, consumption and income refer to the 12 months preceding the interviews. To construct annual aggregates, it is therefore necessary to assign households to a specific year. We chose to assign to year $n - 1$ all the households interviewed between July of year $n - 1$ and June of year n.[19]

2.2.2 Statistical Methods

All the cell statistics in sections 2.3 to 2.7 are obtained by weighting each household by the corresponding weight from the Bureau of the Census, which is proportional to the inverse of the probability of the household's being included in the sample. This procedure is used to compute percentiles (in sections 2.3 to 2.7) as well as means (estimated either by sample mean or by maximum likelihood in sections 2.4 to 2.7). The results were not dramatically affected by the weighting scheme.

The analysis of section 2.3 is based on group medians and/or other percentiles and does not present any difficulty. All the figures in that section are in current dollars.

To analyze an intrinsically dynamic phenomenon such as saving, one would like to follow the same individuals over time. If long panel data are not available, one can circumvent this difficulty by using average cohort techniques. This has the advantage, relative to the cross-sectional analysis used in section 2.3, that it controls for cohort effects. In the presence of cohort effects, the cross-sectional profile of a variable such as consumption, income, or saving, observed in a given year, might not correspond to the age profile of any individual in the population. Shorrocks (1975) constructs an example in which every individual in the population has a strictly increasing wealth-age profile and yet, because of strong cohort effects, the cross-sectional profile at a given point in time will be "hump-shaped."

---

19. The BLS follows a different procedure. First it constructs monthly income figures. Then it aggregates the consumption and income figures for all households in a given year. As a consequence, observations on a given household are going to be divided between different periods, except for those households interviewed in January. Given that I am interested in matching exactly income and consumption for a given household in order to construct savings, I preferred to use the alternative procedure described in the text, even though the assignment to a given year might sound arbitrary.

The use of average cohort techniques amounts to following as they age individuals born in the same time interval.[20]

Consider a variable of interest X_t^{ch} observed for household h, belonging to cohort c at time t. It is always possible to define ε_t^{ch} by the following equation:

$$(1) \qquad X_t^{ch} = \delta_t^c + \varepsilon_t^{ch},$$

where δ_t^c is a measure of location for the cell defined by households belonging to cohort c and observed at time t. The age corresponding to cell (c,t) is given, if we identify c by the year of birth, by $t - c$.

In this paper, cohorts are defined by five-year bands. We analyze a total of 10 cohorts; data for each cohort are averaged in every year: this gives us a total of 110 cells. The cohort definition, the median age in 1980 and in 1990, and the average cell size in our sample are reported in table 2.4. The relative sizes of different cohort cells reflect approximately the composition by age of the U.S. population.[21] Changes in size across years reflect changes in the dimension of the total sample.

If δ_t^c in equation (1) is the cell mean and the data present no particular problems, a sensible and robust estimator is given by the sample mean. If, however, some observations are top-coded, as is the case both for income and financial wealth, estimation of the mean is substantially more complicated. In general, it will not be possible to use nonparametric methods. If we are willing to parametrize a density function for the cross-sectional distribution and believe that such a density fits the (unobserved) tail of the distribution, it will be possible to estimate the mean by maximum likelihood. The reliability of such an estimate hinges in a crucial way on the parametric specification used: in this respect it is important to use a flexible functional form, capable of allowing for the substantial amount of skewness and kurtosis which characterizes both income and wealth distribution.

Consistent estimates of the population quantiles can be easily obtained using the sample quantiles, as long as the top-coding level is above the quantile we are interested in estimating.[22] The sample quantiles can be compared to the quantiles of the estimated density as a specification test. When we perform this exercise in our applications, we obtain satisfactory results.

To parametrize the cross-sectional distribution of income we choose a mix-

---

20. Cohort techniques have been used by Browning, Deaton, and Irish (1985) and are discussed by Deaton (1985) and more recently by Moffitt (1991) and Attanasio (1993b). Particular emphasis is usually given to means; other measures of locations can however be used.

21. Of course there are sampling errors and possible biases caused by differing attrition and nonresponse rates.

22. This is true for income and wealth, where we can safely assume that the top-coded observations are on the right tail of the distribution. The same is not necessarily true for savings. The bias introduced is however much less than for the estimation of the mean.

Table 2.4   Cohort Definition and Cell Size

Cohort	Year of Birth	Age in 1980	Age in 1990	Average Cell Size
1	1955–59	23	33	759
2	1950–54	28	38	672
3	1945–49	33	43	580
4	1940–44	38	48	432
5	1935–39	43	53	350
6	1930–34	48	58	325
7	1925–29	53	63	334
8	1920–24	58	68	340
9	1915–19	63	73	295
10	1910–14	68	78	243

ture of two normal densities with different means and variances. Therefore we fit five parameters for each cell.

The unconditional distribution of financial asset holdings is parametrized as a distribution with mass p at zero (where p is the proportion of observations with zero assets) and the remaining mass distributed on the positive axis as a mixture of two log-normal distributions, which results in six parameters to be fitted for each cell.

Finally, these techniques can also be modified to control for within-cell heterogeneity. One can either define new cells, interacting year cohort dummies with other dummies (education, race, and sex of the household head), or allow these variables to affect the within-cell conditional mean, possibly imposing across-cell restrictions.

To analyze data from several years it is necessary to transform current into constant dollars. Given that we construct household-specific price indexes (see section 2.2.1), we have a choice between estimating cell means in nominal terms and deflating them by cell-specific price indexes[23] and estimating cell means of quantities deflated at the individual level. We chose the former alternative to avoid the possibility that measurement error in consumption would affect income indirectly through the individual price level, while preserving the heterogeneity in price indexes determined by the different expenditure patterns of different cohorts. In practice, the two procedures give extremely similar results.

2.3   Cross-Sectional Analysis

In this section we use the 1990 CEX survey, which includes all households interviewed during 1990. In what follows, we tabulate and plot the cross-sectional profiles for income, consumption, saving, and wealth. Because in-

23. The cell-specific price indexes are constructed by averaging individual price indexes in each cell.

come and consumption refer to the 12 months preceding the interview, for most households the period of reference includes some months of 1989. All figures are obtained using current dollars: no attempt was made to correct for inflation. Given the short length of the period considered, we do not think this is a serious issue. The sample is divided into the 11 age groups described in section 2.2.1.

2.3.1 Income

In the first column of table 2.5 we tabulate median disposable income[24] by age group for the total sample. In the other four columns we divide each age group on the basis of income quartiles and compute the median within each group.[25] The numbers in parentheses are cell sizes.[26] The figures in table 2.5 are plotted against age in figure 2.1. The evidence is not particularly surprising: the cross-sectional profile for income presents the usual hump shape. Family income peaks between ages 41 and 55 (it is reasonably flat over that interval) and declines afterward. The difference among the percentiles plotted in figure 2.1 evidentiates the degree of inequality of the cross-sectional distribution of income at various ages. Inequality is more pronounced for the central age groups as the cross-sectional profile is steeper for higher percentiles than for lower percentiles.

For reasons discussed below, we divide the sample not only by income quartiles but also on the basis of the educational attainment of the household head. The three groups we consider are high school dropouts, high school graduates, and college graduates. The cross-sectional profile of median household after-tax income of these three groups is reported in table 2.6 and plotted in figure 2.2. Household income peaks slightly earlier for high school dropouts than for high school and college graduates. In addition, the hump is much more pronounced for more highly educated households: this indicates that the returns to education,[27] and especially college education, increase strongly with age, at least until age 50. Median income for college graduates in the 51–55 age group is 1.67 times that of high school graduates in the same age group and 2.84 times that of high school dropouts. The same figures in the 26–30 age group are 1.38 and 1.88, respectively. The median income of high school graduates is (not surprisingly) just around the overall median.

Some of the cells (especially for college graduates) are very small: for instance we have only 19 households whose head is in the 71–75 age group and

24. As stressed in section 2.2, we subtract Social Security contributions from the BLS definition of "after-tax family income."
25. This is done only for comparability with the subsequent tables that report median consumption and saving by income quartiles. The second to fifth columns table 2.5 are the 12.5, 37.5, 62.5, and 77.5 percentiles of each age group.
26. These are not the same in the second to fifth columns because income quartiles (and medians) are computed on the basis of the Bureau of Census weights.
27. The figures reported in table 2.6 refer to total household income, not wages. As a consequence they can vary because of variations both in wages and in household labor supply.

Table 2.5   **Median Disposable Income by Age Group and Income Quartile**

Age Group	Total Sample	Below First Quartile	Between First and Second Quartiles	Between Second and Third Quartiles	Above Third Quartile
21–25	12,855	4,486	10,375	15,699	29,890
	(497)	(120)	(120)	(124)	(133)
26–30	20,663	8,428	15,689	25,738	41,557
	(639)	(152)	(157)	(160)	(170)
31–35	24,137	8,609	18,847	30,377	49,909
	(640)	(151)	(148)	(163)	(178)
36–40	28,057	8,726	21,920	33,482	56,099
	(572)	(141)	(138)	(146)	(147)
41–45	31,573	11,040	24,980	39,836	64,280
	(523)	(120)	(132)	(135)	(136)
46–50	29,719	8,920	24,728	40,626	65,886
	(375)	(83)	(96)	(92)	(104)
51–55	30,127	9,251	22,003	37,852	62,435
	(335)	(79)	(85)	(85)	(86)
56–60	25,511	8,409	19,521	29,452	55,252
	(251)	(63)	(56)	(60)	(72)
61–65	20,617	6,300	16,923	28,871	56,112
	(259)	(64)	(62)	(68)	(65)
66–70	17,718	6,608	12,759	22,178	45,137
	(303)	(75)	(78)	(78)	(72)
71–75	13,996	6,535	11,331	17,879	31,666
	(229)	(52)	(65)	(53)	(59)

Note: Numbers in parentheses are cell sizes.

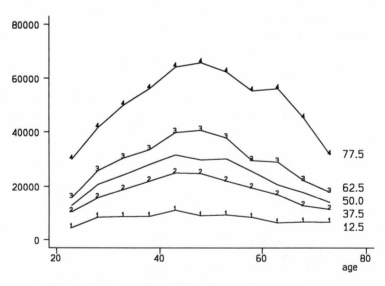

Fig. 2.1   Median and various percentiles of disposable income

Table 2.6   **Median Disposable Income by Age and Education Groups**

Age Group	Total Sample	High School Dropouts	High School Graduates	College Graduates
21–25	12,855	12,649	12,235	16,566
	(497)	(64)	(342)	(91)
26–30	20,663	13,911	18,937	26,108
	(639)	(63)	(388)	(188)
31–35	24,137	12,688	22,138	36,083
	(640)	(65)	(399)	(176)
36–40	28,057	18,050	25,660	38,111
	(572)	(59)	(316)	(197)
41–45	31,573	19,000	26,464	46,772
	(523)	(60)	(288)	(175)
46–50	29,719	13,341	28,307	47,900
	(375)	(69)	(200)	(106)
51–55	30,127	16,748	28,520	47,572
	(335)	(74)	(193)	(68)
56–60	25,511	16,095	25,894	39,653
	(251)	(84)	(105)	(62)
61–65	20,617	16,176	18,184	37,686
	(259)	(79)	(120)	(60)
66–70	17,718	13,618	16,610	30,993
	(303)	(101)	(154)	(48)
71–75	13,996	11,648	15,244	28,597
	(229)	(113)	(97)	(19)

Note: Numbers in parentheses are cell sizes.

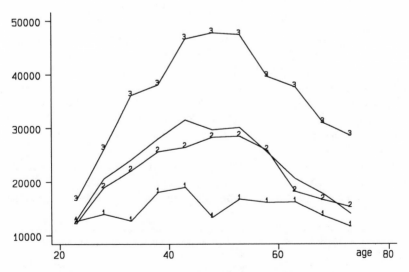

Fig. 2.2   Median income cross-sectional profile by education group

is a college graduate. Therefore we need to use some caution in interpreting these and other statistics computed on such small cells.

2.3.2 Consumption

The consumption definition we use in this section is the closest we can get to the NIPA. Therefore it includes all consumption expenditures reported in the CEX. As discussed in section 2.2, the main differences are in that it includes only out-of-pocket health expenditure and that it excludes imputed rents on owner-occupied housing. Pension contributions are not included in consumption.

Median consumption cross-sectional profiles for the total sample and by income quartile are reported in table 2.7 and plotted in figure 2.3. Median consumption by age-education group is tabulated in table 2.8 and plotted against age in figure 2.4. The cross-sectional profile of consumption is similar to that of income in that it presents a pronounced hump. However, the consumption profile peaks slightly earlier and is flatter than the income profile.

The differences in consumption cross-sectional profiles across education groups mirror those observed in income profiles. This evidence is consistent with that reported, for instance, by Carroll and Summers (1991), who show that differences in cross-sectional age profiles for consumption across different occupational groups parallel corresponding differences in income profiles.[28] Median consumption of college graduates in the 51–55 age group is 1.5 times that of the high school graduates and 2.23 times that of the high school dropouts in the same age group. The same figures are 1.27 and 1.83 respectively for the 26–30 age group.

2.3.3 Saving

In table 2.9 we report median saving by age group and by age-income quartile group and plot them in figure 2.5. Saving is always negative for the lowest income group. Median saving is also negative for the two youngest and the oldest groups of households whose disposable income is between the first and second income quartiles (for their age group). In general, saving increases with income and, with the exception of households with income below the first quartile, increases until ages 51–55 and declines afterward. This hump shape is more pronounced for the households with income in the highest income quartile.

Median saving rates for the whole sample and by disposable income quartile are tabulated and plotted in table 2.10 and figure 2.6, respectively.[29] Saving rates are very flat for the two groups above the median, exhibit a substantial

---

28. Attanasio and Browning (1992) argue that this is not necessarily inconsistent with the life-cycle model. It should be remembered, for instance, that the profiles considered here do not control for either cohort effects or changes in family composition.

29. We do not plot the saving rates for the first income group because their variability would swamp that of the other groups.

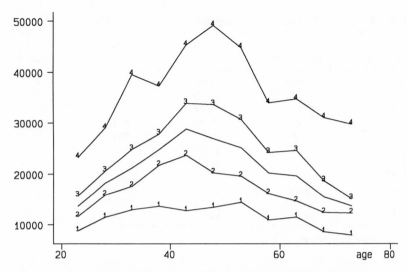

Fig. 2.3 Median consumption cross-sectional profile by income quartile

Table 2.7   Median Total Consumption by Age Group and Income Quartile

Age Group	Total Sample	Below First Quartile	Between First and Second Quartiles	Between Second and Third Quartiles	Above Third Quartile
21–25	14,359	8,771	11,644	15,728	23,279
26–30	18,902	11,503	15,927	20,618	29,005
31–35	21,987	12,992	17,651	24,845	39,564
36–40	24,820	13,693	21,758	27,839	37,299
41–45	28,041	12,785	23,713	33,868	45,294
46–50	24,467	13,489	20,245	33,624	49,109
51–55	25,704	14,455	19,581	30,670	44,776
56–60	19,653	10,934	16,199	24,217	33,934
61–65	21,042	11,513	14,705	24,608	34,696
66–70	16,823	8,563	12,423	18,672	31,018
71–75	14,362	7,899	12,323	15,177	29,705

Note: Cell sizes are the same as in table 2.5.

hump for the households with disposable income between the first and second quartiles, and are negative and extremely variable for households with income below the first quartile.

The fact that, beside their life-cycle dynamics, both saving and saving rates are an increasing function of disposable income is not inconsistent with the life-cycle permanent-income theory. Households in the lowest income quartiles are affected, on average, by lower transitory income shocks than households in higher income quartiles. According to the theory, transitory

Table 2.8   **Median Total Consumption by Age and Education Groups**

Age Group	Total Sample	High School Dropouts	High School Graduates	College Graduates
21–25	14,359	13,343	13,453	16,543
26–30	18,902	12,372	17,896	22,699
31–35	21,987	15,246	20,112	29,732
36–40	24,820	19,260	23,160	32,681
41–45	28,041	16,790	25,170	37,925
46–50	24,467	15,907	24,285	41,645
51–55	25,704	17,276	25,704	38,952
56–60	19,653	13,484	19,653	32,669
61–65	21,043	15,267	19,972	32,115
66–70	16,823	12,301	16,273	24,929
71–75	16,362	11,686	15,245	35,280

Note: Cell sizes are the same as in table 2.6.

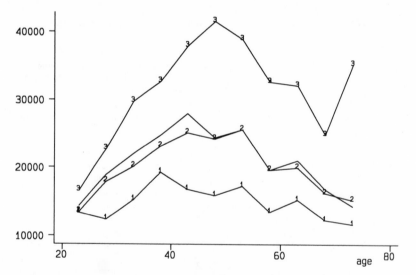

Fig. 2.4   Median consumption cross-sectional profile by education group

shocks to income should be smoothed by saving. Households receiving large negative shocks should dissave to smooth consumption.[30]

To characterize the relationship between saving and income we should therefore divide the households in the sample according to their permanent rather than disposable current income. An instrumental variable approach is to divide the sample on the basis of a variable which is correlated with permanent

30. If measurement error in income is uncorrelated with that in consumption, it introduces a similar bias: measurement error in income is fully reflected in saving.

Table 2.9   **Median Saving by Age Group and Income Quartile**

Age Group	Total Sample	Below First Quartile	Between First and Second Quartile	Between Second and Third Quartile	Above Third Quartile
21–25	−1,431	−4,620	−1,857	723	5,673
26–30	1,414	−2,951	−58	4,905	13,910
31–35	1,570	−3,925	1,065	4,648	11,299
36–40	2,341	−4,329	1,395	5,657	18,922
41–45	2,895	−3,732	1,359	6,249	15,635
46–50	2,461	−4,060	2,681	7,278	19,789
51–55	3,411	−5,111	2,805	8,293	22,331
56–60	2,574	−2,862	4,523	6,525	21,606
61–65	1,059	−7,148	1,766	4,531	18,124
66–70	914	−2,017	465	3,383	11,930
71–75	139	−600	−1,535	2,840	6,413

Note: Cell sizes are the same as in table 2.5.

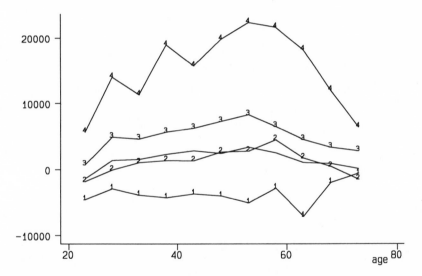

Fig. 2.5   Median saving cross-sectional profile by income quartile

income and uncorrelated with transitory shocks. For such a purpose we use the educational attainment of the household head.[31]

In tables 2.11 and 2.12 we report median saving and saving rates by age-education group. The same figures (with the exception of saving rates for the lowest education group) are plotted in figures 2.7 and 2.8.

For high school dropouts, median saving and saving rates are negative for 4

31. Of course this approach would not solve the problem if different education groups have been affected by different transitory shocks in the year considered.

Table 2.10   Median Saving Rates by Age Group and Income Quartile

Age Group	Total Sample	Below First Quartile	Between First and Second Quartiles	Between Second and Third Quartiles	Above Third Quartile
21–25	−11.8	−111.8	−16.7	4.3	20.0
26–30	7.4	−28.8	−0.4	19.2	33.8
31–35	7.1	−44.0	5.4	17.2	24.2
36–40	9.4	−55.3	5.4	17.1	35.6
41–45	9.8	−35.3	5.1	13.8	28.2
46–50	11.2	−33.5	12.4	20.3	32.1
51–55	13.9	−65.4	12.4	22.7	33.9
56–60	16.6	−34.0	26.6	23.8	41.4
61–65	8.6	−148.3	11.0	14.4	34.7
66–70	7.1	−28.4	4.2	16.9	24.4
71–75	1.1	−8.1	−15.8	14.5	21.0

Note: Cell sizes are slightly different from those in table 2.5 because of zero-income observations.

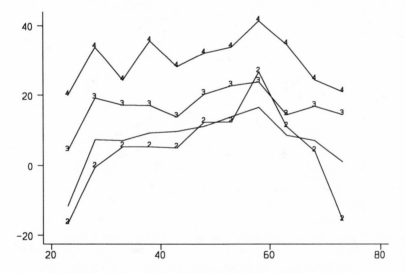

Fig. 2.6 Median saving rates cross-sectional profile by income quartile

of the 11 age groups, and not as variable as for the households in the lowest income quartile. For this group, both saving levels and saving rates do not have a distinctive pattern over age. For the other two groups, the level of saving exhibits a distinctive hump which is more pronounced for college graduates. Saving rates are substantially flat for college graduates, while for high school graduates they are highest before retirement.

Saving rates are not defined for households with zero or negative income. It is therefore useful to consider the ratio of saving to consumption rather than

Table 2.11   **Median Saving by Age and Education Groups**

Age Group	Total Sample	High School Dropouts	High School Graduates	College Graduates
21–25	−1,431	60	−2,245	298
26–30	1,414	112	1,013	2,960
31–35	1,570	−651	1,157	4,074
36–40	2,341	−426	1,843	4,879
41–45	2,895	−50	1,378	7,695
46–50	2,461	−1,338	3,374	5,209
51–55	3,411	1,537	3,488	5,762
56–60	2,574	1,725	4,904	2,174
61–65	1,059	909	−198	5,294
66–70	914	900	1,236	1,524
71–75	139	139	584	−3,287

Note: Cell sizes are the same as in table 2.6.

Table 2.12   **Median Saving Rates by Age and Education Groups**

Age Group	Total Sample	High School Dropouts	High School Graduates	College Graduates
21–25	−11.8	0.7	−18.8	2.2
26–30	7.4	1.6	6.9	14.8
31–35	7.1	−7.2	6.0	11.5
36–40	9.4	−2.0	7.7	16.1
41–45	9.8	−0.2	7.0	19.0
46–50	11.2	−13.4	13.6	14.0
51–55	13.9	8.8	14.4	17.7
56–60	16.6	16.6	21.5	10.6
61–65	8.6	10.1	−2.0	15.2
66–70	7.1	4.2	6.0	7.7
71–75	1.1	1.7	5.3	−10.0

Note: Cell sizes are slightly different from those in table 2.6 because of zero-income observations.

to income. This variable, besides being defined at zero income, has several advantages. First, it is a monotonic transformation of saving rates (for those values of income when they are defined). Second, consumption might be a more appropriate denominator because, in theory, it reflects variations to permanent income and is therefore less affected by transitory shocks. Third, the monotonic transformation that maps saving rates into the variable we consider has the effect of damping extreme observations, just as a log transform or a Box-Cox transform would do.[32] This can be useful given the enormous variability of individual saving rates.

32. Think, for instance, what happens when income goes to zero. Saving rates diverge to minus infinity, whereas our measure goes to minus one.

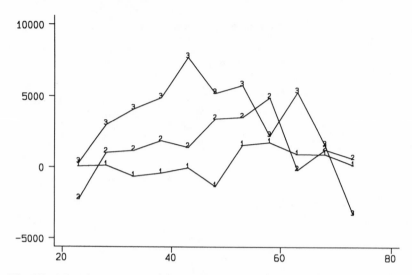

Fig. 2.7   Median saving cross-sectional profile by education group

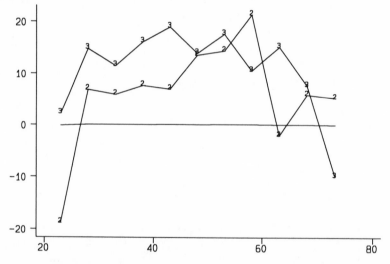

Fig. 2.8   Median saving rates cross-sectional profile by education group

Ratios of median saving to consumption by age group for the whole sample and by income quartile and education group are reported in tables 2.13 and 2.14 and the latter are plotted against age in figure 2.9.

The picture that emerges is substantially similar to that in tables 2.10 and 2.12, and it does not deserve further comment except to note that the corresponding figure 2.9 is, as expected, substantially smoother than figures 2.6 and 2.8 for saving rates.

Table 2.13   **Median Saving to Consumption Ratio by Age Group and Income Quartile**

Age Group	Total Sample	Below First Quartile	Between First and Second Quartile	Between Second and Third Quartile	Above Third Quartile
21–25	−10.8	−53.2	−14.3	4.5	24.9
36–30	7.5	−26.8	−0.4	23.7	51.0
31–35	7.5	−31.2	5.8	20.8	32.0
36–40	9.8	−38.9	5.7	20.7	55.3
41–45	10.8	−26.1	5.4	16.1	39.2
46–50	11.1	−31.0	14.1	25.5	47.2
51–55	16.0	−39.8	14.2	29.3	51.2
56–60	18.6	−40.2	36.3	31.2	70.6
61–65	9.5	−59.7	12.4	16.9	53.0
66–70	6.3	−25.7	4.3	20.3	32.2
71–75	1.1	−7.5	−13.6	17.0	26.5

Note: Cell sizes are the same as in table 2.5.

Table 2.14   **Median Saving to Consumption Ratio by Age and Education Groups**

Age Group	Total Sample	High School Dropouts	High School Graduates	College Graduates
21–25	−10.8	0.7	−16.3	2.3
26–30	7.5	1.7	6.2	17.3
31–35	7.5	−6.7	6.1	12.9
36–40	9.8	−2.2	8.0	19.2
41–45	10.8	−0.2	7.6	23.5
46–50	11.1	−11.8	14.9	16.2
51–55	16.0	6.8	16.9	21.5
56–60	18.6	19.9	27.3	9.6
61–65	9.5	11.2	−2.0	17.9
66–70	6.3	4.3	6.3	7.7
71–75	1.1	1.8	5.6	−9.1

Note: Cell sizes are the same as in table 2.6.

Controlling for demographic changes in saving behavior is not an easy task. In table 2.15, however, we report a very simple attempt to control for the number of children in households. We will not give any interpretation to these results. In particular, we tabulate ratios of median saving to consumption by age and number of children. With the exclusion of some cells which are extremely small (and should be ignored), these results do not show strong effects of children on saving behavior. The only possible exception is that of households with no children (*at that point in time*), which exhibit consistently higher saving than the households with children. This probably reflects the greater consumption needs of larger households.

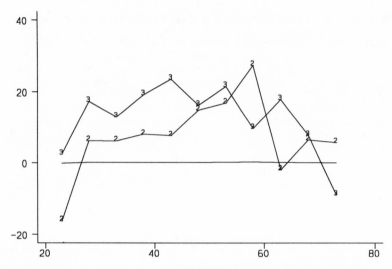

Fig. 2.9 **Ratio of median saving to consumption cross-sectional profile by education group**

Table 2.15 **Median Saving to Consumption Ratio by Age Group and Number of Children**

Age Group	No Children	One Child	Two Children	Three or More Children
21–25	−16.3	−1.0	−3.1	6.7
	(351)	(77)	(46)	(23)
26–30	16.8	5.6	3.2	−7.3
	(344)	(135)	(96)	(64)
31–35	12.2	9.6	−5.6	−0.7
	(227)	(135)	(165)	(113)
36–40	19.3	2.9	7.5	7.8
	(183)	(130)	(156)	(103)
41–45	12.1	20.6	9.4	6.3
	(196)	(132)	(114)	(81)
46–50	10.3	14.4	13.1	8.1
	(221)	(86)	(37)	(31)
51–55	17.8	−0.3	0.8	60.9
	(255)	(43)	(24)	(13)
56–60	19.9	2.8	21.2	−4.6
	(219)	(20)	(8)	(4)
61–65	11.2	−11.2	10.2	38.2
	(238)	(16)	(4)	(1)
66–70	7.7	5.0	14.6	2.3
	(289)	(7)	(3)	(4)
71–75	1.1	23.6	−49.5	62.4
	(217)	(8)	(2)	(2)

Note: Numbers in parentheses are cell sizes.

2.3.4 Wealth

Because the life-cycle model (at least in some simple versions) has strong implications for the pattern of wealth accumulation (and decumulation) the latter has been studied extensively.[33] In spite of the large volume of the literature on this issue, no firm answer on the shape of a typical age profile for wealth (and in particular on the issue of asset decumulation by the elderly) or on the main motivation for savings has emerged. This is both because of the scarcity and poor quality of data sets and because of difficult conceptual issues.[34]

We conclude this section describing the cross-sectional age profile of real and financial wealth (see section 2.2 for definitions). These two components do not exhaust household net wealth. The main exclusions are, on the asset side, pension wealth and durable commodities and, on the liability side, loans and debts other than mortgages.

In table 2.16 we report mean, median, and standard deviation for financial wealth (in the first two columns) and for gross and net real estate wealth (in the fourth to sixth columns). In the last column we report the percentage of home owners (with or without mortgages).

Mean and median financial wealth are plotted by age group in figure 2.10. Two considerations are in order as far as financial wealth is concerned. First, the median level of financial wealth is very low: for all age groups it is below $7,000. For most groups it is around one-tenth and for all groups is well below one-half of median annual disposable income. Second, there is no tendency for either the mean or the median to decline in the last part of the life cycle. This could be due, of course, to a variety of reasons and does not necessarily contradict the life-cycle model.[35]

Real wealth is substantially higher than financial wealth, confirming that real estate constitutes a very important part of households' portfolios. Both the mean and the median (plotted in fig. 2.11) increase very rapidly in the first part of the life cycle and show a slight tendency to decline in the last part. The difference between net and gross wealth (which roughly corresponds to mortgage debt) tends to decline in the last part of the life cycle as households repay their mortgage debts.[36]

A pattern similar to that of the stock of real estate wealth is followed by the percentage of home owners by age. The percentage of home owners is as low

33. The papers on this topic are too numerous to be cited here. Some interesting studies are those by Shorrocks (1975), King and Dicks-Mireau (1982), Hurd (1989), and Jianakoplos, Menchik, and Irvine (1987).

34. Wealth information (especially for rich households) is very difficult to obtain and no long panels exist. For a comparison of different data sets containing wealth information see Juster et al. (1987).

35. See Attanasio (1993b) for a discussion of these issues and Attanasio and Hoynes (1993) for a discussion of differential mortality by wealth class.

36. The difference between median gross and net real estate wealth is obviously *not equal* to median mortgage debt.

Table 2.16   **Real and Financial Wealth Holdings by Age Group**

	Financial Assets		Gross Real Estate		Net Real Estate		Percentage of Home Owners
Age Group	Mean	Median	Mean	Median	Mean	Median	
21–25	1,801 (6,466)	500	7,020 (26,898)	0	3,844 (20,126)	0	0.105
26–30	4,233 (9,583)	850	36,913 (61,175)	0	25,163 (48,876)	0	0.397
31–35	7,763 (16,928)	2,527	59,732 (81,523)	35,000	38,079 (63,630)	5,000	0.570
36–40	10,579 (24,198)	2,000	66,380 (103,064)	33,000	43,842 (87,517)	6,803	0.556
41–45	14,060 (28,860)	2,286	83,515 (97,421)	45,000	59,488 (80,193)	37,660	0.725
46–50	14,151 (27,928)	2,275	97,657 (104,619)	70,000	71,224 (89,113)	45,000	0.729
51–55	14,177 (31,313)	1,575	98,098 (131,458)	60,000	79,136 (116,350)	45,000	0.831
56–60	21,795 (41,267)	2,819	91,620 (102,945)	62,500	80,133 (94,759)	57,500	0.773
61–65	34,777 (50,136)	6,950	107,269 (106,318)	79,000	95,391 (98,490)	65,000	0.816
66–70	27,107 (45,744)	5,750	105,707 (107,420)	75,000	100,984 (104,955)	67,350	0.811
71–75	33,663 (56,815)	6,093	81,539 (98,192)	55,000	77,042 (95,949)	52,500	0.775

Note: Numbers in parentheses are standard deviations.

as 10 percent for the first age group, and it is already equal to 57 percent for the third group. It peaks at 83 percent for the 51–55 age group. This indicates that most of the sharp increase in average real estate wealth in the first part of the life cycle is explained by an increase in home ownership rather than by an increase in the stock owned.[37]

The same words of caution used for the interpretation of the financial asset age profile are in order here. The fact that the cross-sectional profile for total assets declines in the last part of the life cycle it is not necessarily an indication of asset decumulation: it could be due to cohort effects or to biases introduced by differential mortality. For instance, the decline in mean and median real estate wealth, as well as in the percentage of home owners in the last age group could be explained either by some of the elderly liquidating their real estate wealth or by the fact that the percentage of home owners (and their average real estate wealth) for that particular cohort had always been lower.

37. The variable reported in the survey should, at least in theory, be equal to the market value of the house and therefore reflect capital gains and losses as well as "active" additions to the household's estate wealth.

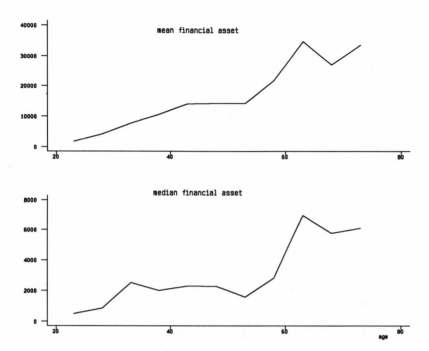

Fig. 2.10　Mean and median financial assets cross-sectional profile

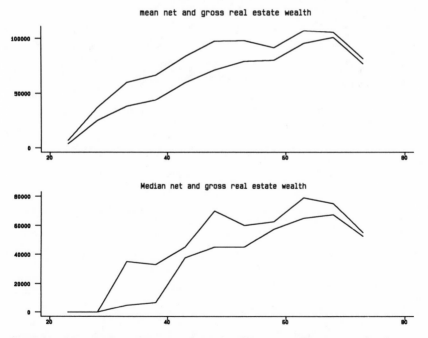

Fig. 2.11　Mean and median net and gross real estate wealth cross-sectional profile

2.4   Income and Pension Contribution Age Profiles

As stressed in the introduction, the analysis of a single cross section can provide only a useful snapshot of a given phenomenon, but it is of very limited use in describing the behavior of a dynamic variable such as saving. In the presence of strong cohort effects, the interpretation of the cross-sectional profile as the life-cycle profile of a given variable can introduce serious biases. In the absence of panel data and repeated cross sections there is not much one can do to control for cohort effects. In this and in the following sections we use the 11 CEX surveys available since 1980 to construct synthetic cohort averages in the attempt to measure life-cycle and cohort effects on the variables of interest.

Before proceeding with the analysis, however, it might be of some interest to assess the importance and the magnitude of the potential bias introduced by interpreting cross-sectional profiles as life-cycle profiles. One can use the techniques discussed below to identify a (smoothed) age profile and compare it to a cross-sectional profile. As a representative variable we chose total household consumption expenditure.

In figure 2.12 the line labeled "cross-section profile" is constructed using the 1984 survey to compute consumption averages for different age groups. The line labeled "age profile" is the same as that in figure 2.26 (in section 2.5 below) with cohort effects removed. It is constructed by regressing average cohort data on a fifth-order polynomial in age and cohort-specific intercepts. What we plot is the age polynomial with the intercept of the first cohort. As can be seen, because of the presence of sizeable and positive cohort effects, the cross-sectional profile exaggerates the hump in consumption. A similar picture can be obtained choosing different cross sections and different variables (provided that there are sizeable cohort effects). The method used to remove cohort effects from the consumption profile is crude and based on some strong identification assumptions. The picture makes clear, however, the potential importance of these effects.

2.4.1   Total After-Tax Household Income

In this subsection we use the cohort techniques outlined above to estimate total household age-income profiles. We correct the CEX definition of total after-tax income by subtracting from it Social Security contributions which will be considered (here and in the section on saving) as a tax rather than as a form of saving.

As discussed in section 2.2.2, we parametrize the cross-sectional distribution of disposable household income within each cell as a mixture of two normal densities.[38] The estimated means are, as expected, higher than the simple

---

38. It is not possible to fit a log-normal distribution (or the mixture of two log-normals) because of the presence of negative and zero income. These densities are fitted to the CES definition of disposable income. The corrected means are obtained by subtracting from the maximum likelihood means the sample means of Social Security contributions.

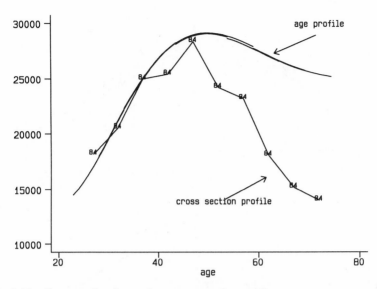

Fig. 2.12 Cross-sectional vs. cohort consumption profile

averages one obtains setting the top-coded observations at the top-coding value. The magnitude of the difference between these two estimates obviously depends on the number of top-coded observations.[39] Because the proportion of top-coded observations varies systematically with age and cohort, the distortion introduced by ignoring top-coded observations will also have a systematic pattern.

In the top panel of figure 2.13 we plot the estimated means for year-cohort cells against age. Because this kind of graph will be used extensively throughout the rest of the paper, it is worthwhile spending a few moments explaining it in detail. Each connected segment represents the behavior of a cohort over the 11 years of our sample. For instance, the first segment on the left is average household income for the first cohort—i.e., for households headed by a person born between 1955 and 1959—in each year from 1980 to 1990. These individuals were, on average, 23 years old in 1980, 24 in 1981, and so on until 1990 when they were 33. Because a cohort is defined by a five-year interval and we have 11 years of data, each cohort overlaps at six ages with the following cohort: for instance, cohort 2 is observed between ages 28 and 38, while cohort 3 is observed between ages 33 and 43.

In the bottom panel, the same data points are smoothed by regressing them on a fifth-order polynomial in age, cohort-specific intercepts, and year dummies whose coefficients are constrained to sum to zero and to be orthogonal to a linear trend.[40] The smooth profiles in the graph are given by the polynomial

---

39. Without top-coded observations the maximum likelihood estimator is the sample mean.

40. Deaton and Paxson (1992) use a similar procedure. Estimates of the coefficients can be obtained either by OLS or by weighted least squares, using as weights the standard errors of the cell means. The results are almost identical.

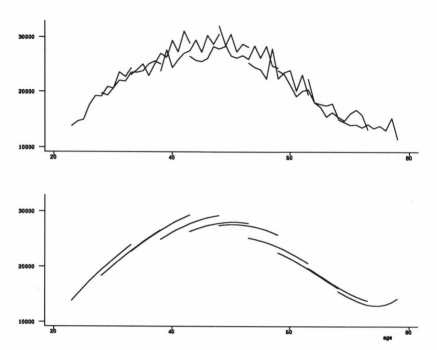

Fig. 2.13   Mean disposable income

in age with the cohort-specific intercepts. One should not give any structural interpretation to this graph: without a structural model or additional information it is not possible to identify cohort, age, and time effects separately because of the linear relationship that links them.[41] The only aim of the bottom panel is to smooth the estimated means; to interpret them as pure age profiles we would have to assume that time effects are common for all cohorts, sum to zero, and are orthogonal to a linear trend.

Figure 2.14 is similar to 2.13 except that we plot cohort medians instead of means against age.[42] Because of the skewness of income distribution, medians are lower than means; otherwise the picture that emerges from this figure is similar to that from figure 2.13.

Several elements of interest emerge from figures 2.13 and 2.14. First, household disposable income has the typical hump-shaped profile that is often found in the literature: a similar profile emerges from CPS data. The smoothed age profile peaks at age 51 for the means and at age 48 for the medians.

Cohort effects are also quite evident: for all cohorts but one, the smoothed profiles lie above that of the next older cohorts. In table 2.17 we report the

41. For a discussion of identification issues in this framework see Heckman and Robb (1987), MaCurdy and Mroz (1990), and Attanasio (1993b).
42. In this figure and in figure 2.15 I use sample quantiles. The figures obtained using the quantiles of the density estimated by maximum likelihood are very similar.

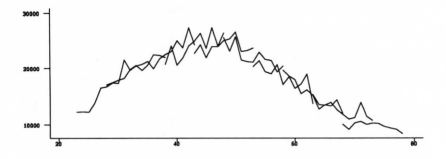

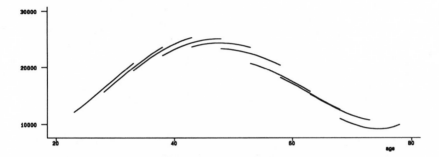

Fig. 2.14   Median disposable income

Table 2.17   **Cohort Intercepts and Their Changes for Income Profiles**

Cohort	Intercept for Medians	Percentage Increase	Intercept for Means	Percentage Increase
1	25,336.2	2.99	28,944.3	3.92
2	24,599.7	2.16	27,853.6	0.34
3	24,079.0	4.05	27,758.6	6.06
4	23,142.7	3.38	26,172.1	5.63
5	22,386.6	4.86	24,776.4	1.77
6	21,350.0	8.97	24,344.9	9.94
7	19,592.6	1.95	22,143.4	4.82
8	19,218.1	0.66	21,124.7	−0.70
9	19,093.0	8.23	21,273.3	3.57
10	17,641.5		20,539.1	

intercepts of the profiles in the bottom panels of figures 2.13 and 2.14 and their percentage increase relative to the intercept of the next older cohort. The "gains" from one cohort to the next seem to be higher (both in means and medians) for the middle cohorts than for the youngest and the oldest. For instance, for the two youngest cohorts, the intercept for the means rises on average by 2.1 percent, while for the next four cohorts it rises by 5.8 percent. The figures for the medians are 2.6 percent and 5.3 percent. For the three oldest cohorts, the average increase in the intercept is 2.6 percent for the means profiles and 3.6 percent for the medians.[43]

Finally, it is possible to detect some business-cycle effects:[44] for most cohorts the raw profiles increase considerably more in the years after 1982. In figure 2.15 we plot the coefficients on the time dummies estimated for the median income profile.[45]

So far we have not controlled for within-cell heterogeneity. In the next graph we look at the income-age profiles for different education groups. Mean and median income-age profiles for college graduates, high school graduates, and high school dropouts are plotted in figure 2.16. The size of the cells on which these estimates are based is relatively small, especially for college graduates and high school dropouts: this is reflected in the larger variability of these estimates, as is most evident in the graph for high school dropouts. As expected, the profiles are higher and steeper for higher education groups (notice the different scale). These profiles are going to be compared with analogous profiles for consumption and savings.

2.4.2 Components of Household Income

In this section we analyze the components of household income. We decompose total before-tax household income into interest income, labor income, pensions, and transfers. These four components exclude some minor items because their economic significance is minor and because they are not easily classifiable. Labor income is defined as wages and salaries, plus income from own business.[46] Interest income includes interest, dividends, and royalties. Interest income does not include capital gains or income for the sale of assets. Pensions are all payments of pensions. Transfers include unemployment compensation, welfare payments, food stamps, Social Security payments, alimony for child support, and other transfer income. Unlike the BLS definition, this one leaves out income or loss from taking in boarders.

In the four panels of figure 2.17, the percentage of households with positive quantities of each of the four components of income is plotted in turn against age, for each year-cohort cell.

The top two panels are not surprising. The percentage of households with

---

43. Similar results are obtained if, in smoothing the means, we do not include year dummies at all.

44. Most of the period under study is characterized by a boom: only the first few years were affected by the 1981–82 recession. Unfortunately, as we mentioned in section 2.3, the quality of the 1980–81 survey is doubtful: therefore we should be careful in comparing the means of those years with those for subsequent years. Analyzing the data for 1991 and 1992, when they become available, will be extremely interesting.

45. One should remember that these coefficients are constrained to sum to zero and to be orthogonal to a time trend. Also notice that what we call 1982 includes data referring to 1981 (see section 2.2); this is why figure 2.15 starts in 1979.

46. The inclusion of this last category is questionable. The results, however, do not change substantially.

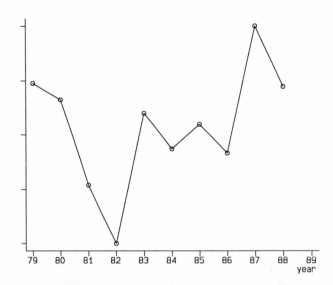

Fig. 2.15   Year effects for median cohort income

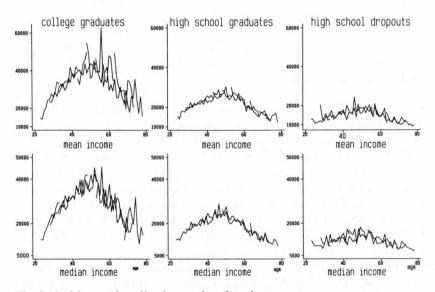

Fig. 2.16   Mean and median income by education group

positive values for labor income is very close to unity until age 50, and declines after that, when an increasing proportion of earners retire.

The evidence in the third panel (lower left) shows that the proportion of households receiving interest income increases until around age 65 and flattens out after that. At the beginning of the life cycle, this proportion is very low (around 30 percent) but reaches almost 70 percent by retirement age. Given

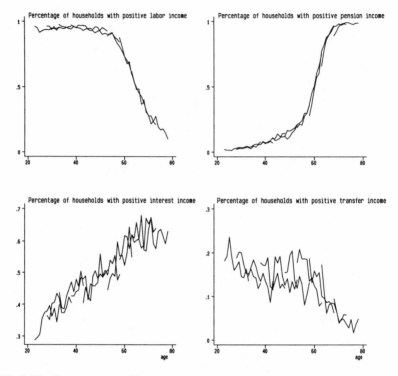

Fig. 2.17   Income composition

the amount of nonreporting that plagues this measure, this evidence indicates that a substantial proportion of households hold assets that provide income by the time the household head reaches retirement.

The last panel of figure 2.17, with the proportion of households receiving some form of transfer income, shows that this proportion is much lower and much more variable than for the other income sources. As expected, a substantial amount of fluctuation over the business cycle is evident in this graph (the figures for the early years of the sample are relatively higher than the others). In terms of life-cycle fluctuation, the proportion seems to decrease until age 40, to increase slightly after that, and to decline again.

In figure 2.18 we plot the age profile for median labor income.[47] The profile increases until around age 50 and declines steeply at retirement. There are no strong cohort effects: the profiles for overlapping cohorts are very close to each other.

Figure 2.19 plots the profile for the median and the third quartile of interest income. Both graphs, and especially that of the median, are very noisy: some

47. In this subsection, we will only look at the quantiles of income components, thus avoiding maximum likelihood estimation.

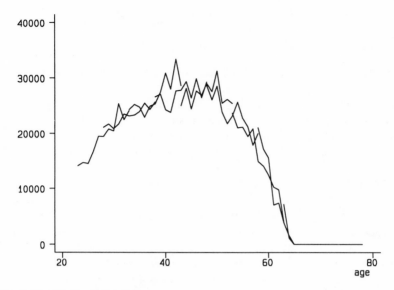

Fig. 2.18   Median labor income

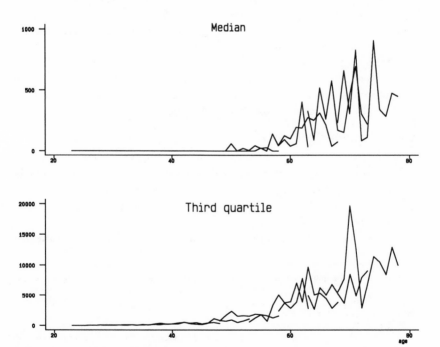

Fig. 2.19   Interest income

interesting features, however, emerge clearly. Interest income becomes somewhat important only late in the life cycle. Median interest income, for instance, is below 1 percent of median labor income at age 60 and is above 10 percent for only one of the cells. The median of the ratio of interest to labor income has a similar pattern: only for two cells it is above 10 percent, and it is always below 20 percent. On the right tail of the distribution, however, interest income is much more important. At age 60 the third quartile of interest income is above 10 percent of the third quartile of labor income, and by age 66 is 36 percent for cohort 8 and 71 percent for cohort 9.[48]

When compared to the quantiles of pension income, the quantiles of interest income exhibit a similar pattern. If we take the ratio of medians (or compute the median of the ratios), we notice that interest income is a small fraction of pension income, while, when we consider the third quartiles, it is much more important. The ratio of the medians averages 5 percent for ages above 65, while the median of the ratio averages just under 1 percent for ages above 65. The same numbers for the third quartiles are 66 percent and 18 percent.[49]

These patterns are a reflection of the fact that the inequality in the distribution of interest income is, as expected, much higher than that of labor or pension income. At age 66, the median of interest income averages at just over $300, while the third quartile averages at almost $5,000. With an average interest rate of 5 percent these figures imply assets worth $6,000 and $100,000 for the median and the third quartile of financial wealth.[50]

For the sake of completeness, in figure 2.20 we plot the age profile for median pension income and for the 90th percentile of transfer income. The 90th percentile for transfer income was chosen because the proportion of households receiving transfer income is often just above 10 percent.

2.4.3 Pension Contributions

In this section we analyze Social Security and pension contributions. The latter are divided into contributions to government pensions (including railroad retirement schemes), private pensions, and individual retirement accounts.[51] In this paper we consider pension contributions as saving, while Social Security contributions are considered as taxes.

We start with the latter. In the top left panel of figure 2.21 we plot average

---

48. Obviously the household earning the third quartile (or the median) labor income is not the same one that earns the third quartile (or the median) interest income. The third quartile of the ratio of interest income to labor income is on average 0.1 for cells with ages between 60 and 65 and 0.27 for ages between 65 and 70.

49. By age 66 almost 90 percent of the households in the sample receive pension income.

50. It should be remembered that these figures do not include capital gains and/or income from the sale of assets.

51. In 1980 and 1981 the data on Social Security and pension contributions were top-coded when any other income variable was top-coded. In subsequent years these variables were not top-coded at all. In this section we ignore the problem completely. All the figures are deflated by a cohort-specific CPI.

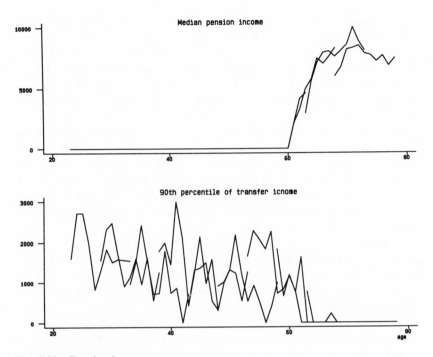

Fig. 2.20   Pension income

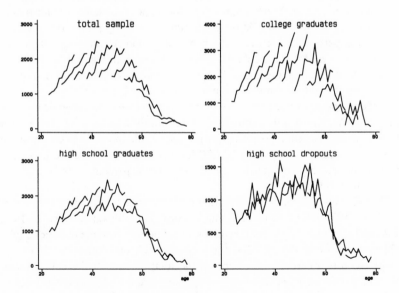

Fig. 2.21   Contributions to social security by education group

contributions to Social Security for the whole sample. The impressive feature of this picture is the steady and strong increase (for most cohorts) of the average contribution. The decline in the last part of the life cycle is explained by the decline in the percentage of households contributing to Social Security as an increasing number of individuals retire. The strong increase in the average contribution is reflected in a strong increase in the ratio of contribution to gross income.

The increase in Social Security during the 1980s is explained in part by an increase in the tax rate of Social Security, but even more important, by several increases in the taxable base. This is apparent in the remaining three panels of the figure 2.21 which plot average contributions for the three education groups considered above. Notice that the increase over time is strongest for college graduates (who perceive the highest income) and weakest for high school dropouts (note the difference in scale).

In the top panel of figure 2.22 we plot the proportion of households contributing to government pension schemes. This proportion is, as expected, fairly low. In the bottom panel we plot the average level of contributions to government pensions, conditional on positive amounts. This profile is slightly hump-shaped and peaks around $2,000.

In figure 2.23 we look at contributions to private pension schemes. As stressed in section 2.2 these include only employees' contributions (deducted from the pay) but not employers' contributions. In the top panel, we plot the proportion of households with positive contributions to private pension schemes, while in the bottom panel we plot the average annual contribution for those households with positive contributions. The top profile rises sharply in the early part of the life cycle and peaks at around .15 after age 40. Notice the sharp increase for some cohorts in the last years of the sample. The average level shows substantial increases over time for most cohorts. At the end of the sample, most middle cohorts are at a level of about $2,000.

In the top panel of figure 2.24 we plot the percentage of households contributing to IRAs, while in the bottom panel we plot the average contributions for those households with a positive contribution. While the average contribution is mostly stationary around the $2,000 level, we see that there are two large fluctuations, corresponding to 1982 and 1986, for the percentage of households contributing to IRAs.

There is now a voluminous literature on the effects that the two tax acts of 1982 and 1986 have had on IRAs and, more generally, on savings. In 1982 IRAs were given strong fiscal incentives: contributions became tax-deductible, while a limit of $2,000 ($2,500 for a couple with one earner, $4,000 for a couple with two earners) was kept on the total amount of the contribution. Most of the fiscal incentives were subsequently removed with the tax act of 1986. From the two panels of figure 2.24 it is evident that the tax incentives had a large effect on participation: the percentage of households participating jumps from below 5 percent to almost 30 percent around the tax act of 1982.

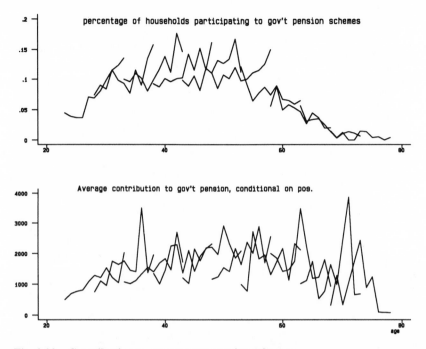

Fig. 2.22 Contribution to government pension schemes

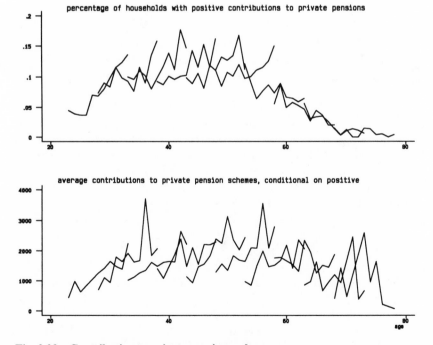

Fig. 2.23 Contribution to private pensions schemes

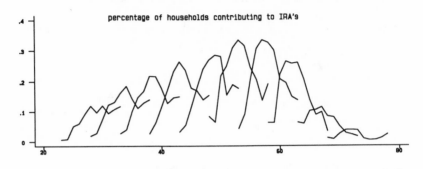

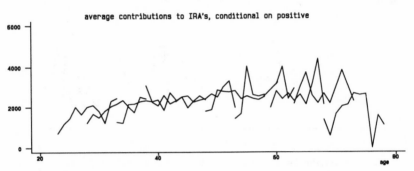

Fig. 2.24   Contribution to IRAs

This percentage drops following the tax act of 1986, but not by the same amount. Most contributions, as documented by Feenberg and Skinner (1989) were at the statutory limit of $2,000 (or $4,000). This explains the fact that the average level of the contributions in the bottom panel of the figure is stable around $2,000.

It is beyond the scope of this paper to address the main issue in the literature on IRAs, i.e., whether the tax incentives given to IRAs in 1982 increased aggregate savings. It is interesting to notice, however, that the decline in IRA participation in 1987 occurs simultaneously with an increase (for many cohorts) in the average level of private pension contributions, perhaps indicating that, after the fiscal incentives to IRAs were removed in 1987, some households moved some funds (back?) from IRAs to other pension schemes. If the movement had been symmetric, this would indicate that the IRA legislation caused a reshuffling of existing savings rather than the creation of "new" savings. Further investigation of this issue is needed.[52]

Whether Social Security contributions should be considered as a tax or as a form of saving, as we have done for pension contributions, is questionable. To give an idea of the order of magnitude of these variables, in the top panel of

52. A nonexhaustive list of papers on the effects of IRA legislation includes Venti and Wise (1990), Feenberg and Skinner (1989), and the survey by Gravelle (1991).

figure 2.25 we plot the age profile for the ratio of average total contributions (pensions and Social Security) to consumption. In the bottom panel we exclude Social Security contributions.

2.5 Consumption

2.5.1 Total Consumption Expenditure

In this section we estimate age-consumption profiles following the same steps that we used for household disposable income. The only difference is that, because consumption is not top-coded, we can use sample averages to estimate cell means.

In figures 2.26 and 2.27 we plot cohort means and medians for total consumption expenditure against age, with the same method for smoothing.

Age-consumption profiles present features similar to those of disposable income: the characteristic hump shape is, if anything, even more apparent than for income. As in the case of income, mean consumption age profiles are higher for younger cohorts. The pattern of the increase in the smoothed profiles, however, is slightly different. In table 2.18 we see that, while it is still true that the percentage increase in the intercept is smaller for the two youngest cohorts, cohorts 8 and 9 present percentage increases comparable to those of the other cohorts. The profiles for the medians, instead, are much flatter and the "cohort effects" do not present any distinguishable pattern. The difference in the dynamics of mean and median consumption indicates that there have been changes in the cross-sectional distribution of consumption, discussed below.

The similarity between income and consumption age profiles has been interpreted as evidence against the life-cycle model.[53] In these simple graphs, however, we are ignoring family composition and labor supply behavior, not to mention investment in human capital. While the specification of a structural model including flexible adult-equivalent schemes and endogenous labor supply in a dynamic framework is necessary to test the life-cycle hypothesis, it is interesting to look at the effects of some extremely simple adult-equivalent scheme. In figure 2.28 we plot mean per capita consumption (i.e., consumption divided by family size) and mean per adult-equivalent consumption (which is constructed by considering children under age 15 to be equivalent to half an adult). From this figure is evident that, while some life-cycle movements are still apparent (such as the decline in consumption corresponding to retirement), these consumption-age profiles look much flatter than in figure 2.26.

The variability of consumption and income in figures 2.13, 2.14, 2.26, and

---

53. See Carroll and Summers (1991) and the discussion on these issues in Attanasio and Browning (1992). It is interesting to notice that this same evidence has also been interpreted as evidence in *favor* (Ghez and Becker 1975) of the life-cycle model.

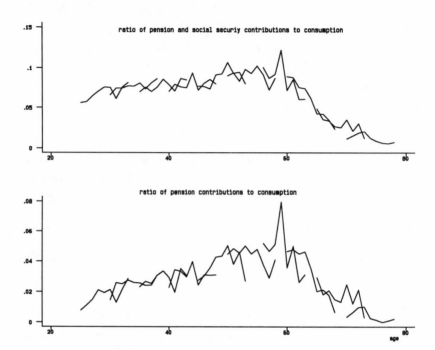

Fig. 2.25   Ratio of pension and social security to consumption

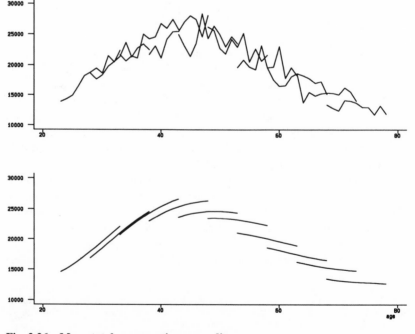

Fig. 2.26   Mean total consumption expenditure

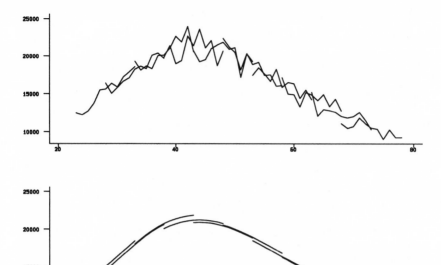

Fig. 2.27   Median total consumption expenditure

Table 2.18   Cohort Intercepts and Their Changes for Consumption Profiles

Cohort	Intercept for Medians	Percentage Increase	Intercept for Means	Percentage Increase
1	21,750.95	2.309	26,765.93	4.174
2	21,260.13	−0.501	25,693.38	1.158
3	21,367.19	3.164	25,399.34	5.214
4	20,711.78	1.507	24,140.68	7.681
5	20,404.27	−0.458	22,418.60	5.364
6	20,498.21	2.200	21,277.34	11.558
7	20,056.91	0.475	19,072.93	8.470
8	19,962.07	3.991	17,583.60	7.309
9	19,196.02	5.195	16,386.01	12.486
10	18,247.99		14,567.19	

2.27 reflects both life-cycle and business-cycle effects. In an attempt to remove life-cycle variability and cohort effects, we consider the standard error of the deviations of the cell means and medians from the smoothed profiles. According to this measure, income is more variable than consumption: in the case of means, the standard deviation of consumption around the smoothed profile is $1,277 and $1,340 for income; in the case of medians, these two figures are $926 and $1,293. This is not inconsistent with the prediction of the life-cycle model, but it might also reflect greater measurement error in income.

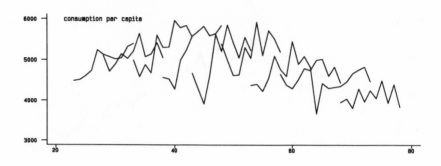

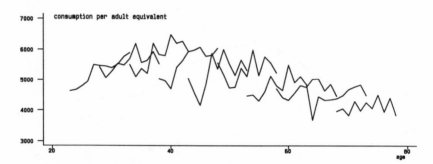

Fig. 2.28   Consumption per capita and adult equivalent

In studying inequality, consumption might be a better measure to look at than income for two reasons: first, if some version of the life-cycle permanent-income hypothesis holds, consumption should not be affected by transitory shocks that increase both the time-series and the cross-sectional variability of income; second, consumption gives a more direct measure of the resources available to a household and therefore is a better indicator of inequality.

In figure 2.29 we plot cell mean and median consumption for the three education groups considered above. The profiles of the three groups are, after rescaling, qualitatively similar. However, as in the case of income, age-consumption profiles are higher and steeper for better educated households: inequality in consumption across education groups increases with age. This similarity in the patterns of income and consumption has been interpreted by Carroll and Summers (1991) as a failure of the life-cycle model. However, as we saw with figure 2.28, these patterns could be explained by changing family composition and/or by nonseparabilities between leisure and consumption.

2.5.2   The Components of Consumption

In this section we look at various components of expenditure. There are several reasons to do so. Ideally, one would like to observe *consumption* rather than *expenditure*. Unfortunately, this is virtually impossible with the data sources currently available. It is therefore interesting to focus on components

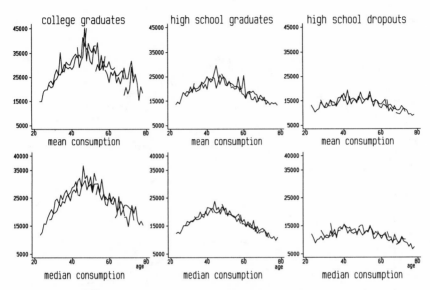

Fig. 2.29   Median and mean consumption by education group

of expenditure that are directly related to consumption. This means excluding all components of expenditure that have an element of durability, i.e., both expenditure on durable commodities and on some services whose effect (it is hoped) lasts in time, such as education and health care. Within the framework of the life-cycle model this is important because durability automatically introduces intertemporal nonseparability in the utility function.

Furthermore, we want to exclude from consumption items that are all but unmeasured for a substantial part of the sample. The obvious example here is housing: for home owners we should impute housing services from owner-occupied houses, a quantity which is very difficult to estimate with the data source available.

Finally, it might be interesting to focus on some items whose relative cost has increased considerably in the last decade, such as education and health care.

In figures 2.30 and 2.31 we plot mean and median expenditure on nondurable and service consumption. This excludes all expenditures on durables, housing, education, and health. While the overall shape of this profile is similar to that in figures 2.26 and 2.27, some important differences emerge. In particular, note that in figure 2.30 the "cohort effects" discussed for income and consumption disappear almost completely, and that in figure 2.31 they are, if anything, reversed.

The relative price of education increased tremendously during the 1980s. In addition, education expenses can be considered, to a certain extent, a form of savings. In the two panels of figure 2.32 we plot average expenditure on per-

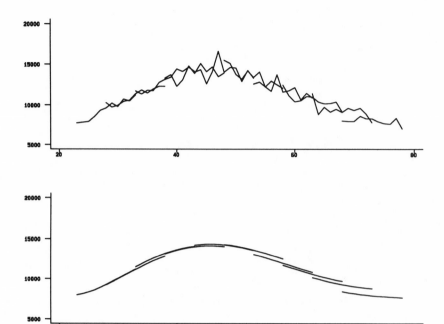

Fig. 2.30   Mean nondurable consumption

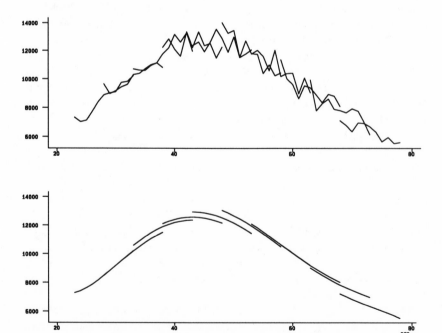

Fig. 2.31   Median nondurable consumption

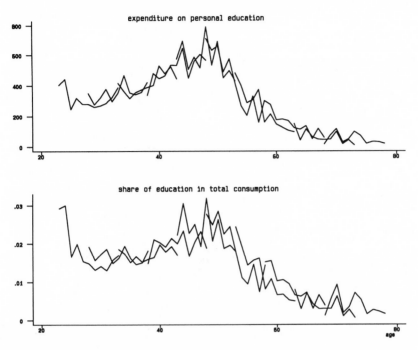

Fig. 2.32   Personal education expenditure

sonal education and its share in average total household consumption. The shape of these profiles is, as expected, correlated with the average number of children: the estimated profiles increase until around age 50 and decline rapidly afterward. Expenditure on education as a share of total consumption is much flatter than the profile of the *level* of education. In several instances, older cohorts are above younger ones, probably reflecting both the fact that education was relatively cheaper in the early 1980s than at the end of the decade and the fact that some of the middle cohorts had, on average, a higher number of children or potential students.

The other item whose relative price has increased tremendously is health care. In the two panels of figure 2.33 we plot the age profiles for health expenditure. The difference between the two panels is in the deflator used to convert current into constant dollars. In the top panel we deflate average health expenditure by a cohort-specific CPI, while in the bottom one we use a health price index. It should be remembered that the CEX data on health expenditure are out-of-pocket figures. Therefore they do not include those items that are covered by health insurance (see section 2.2.1).

The profiles increase monotonically with age. In the top panel we also notice that there are strong time effects, evident in the large spikes corresponding to the last years of the sample for most cohorts. As a consequence of the large increase in the relative price of health care, the top profile, deflated by the CPI, increases over time at a much faster rate than the bottom one.

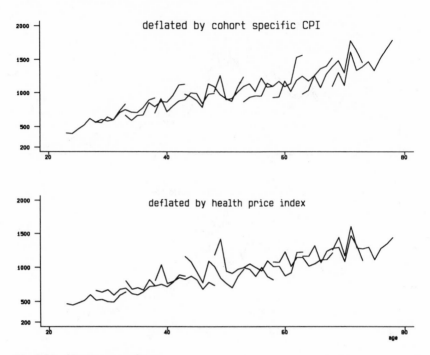

Fig. 2.33   Health expenditure

In figure 2.34 we plot the ratio of out-of-pocket health expenditure to total consumption. The ratio increases monotonically with age, reaching a level around 15 percent toward the end of the life cycle.

2.6   Saving

In this section we characterize the saving behavior of U.S. households. The analysis is similar to that in Attanasio (1993b), with two main differences: the definition of disposable income and the analysis of several consumption measures. The section is divided into three subsections. In subsection 2.6.1 we look at the age profiles for the *level* of saving. In subsection 2.6.2 we look at saving levels across education groups. Finally in subsection 2.6.3 we analyze individual *saving rates* conditional on various observable variables.

2.6.1   Saving Levels

As in section 2.3 saving is defined as disposable income minus consumption expenditure. Unlike in Attanasio (1993b), we do not consider as disposable income the BLS definition, but subtract from it contributions to Social Security. Employees' pension contributions are considered as saving because they

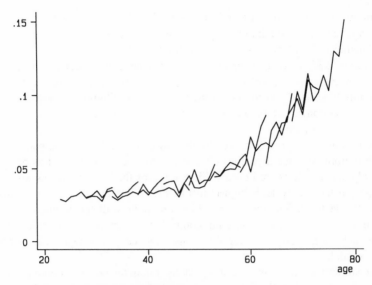

Fig. 2.34   Share of health in consumption

are not subtracted from disposable income.[54] That Social Security contributions should be considered as a tax is questionable: even if compulsory, they give the right to a stream of future income, just as pensions do.

Consumption can also be defined in different ways, since some expenditure items can be legitimately considered a form of investment. The obvious example is expenditure on durables: one should exclude it from total consumption expenditure and add instead the service flow from the stock of existing durables. Another example is expenditure on education and possibly health, which can be considered investment in human capital. Finally, mortgage payments include both service of the debt and repayment of the principal: the latter part should be considered saving.

Ideally, one would like to measure consumption, while only expenditure data are available. Unfortunately, the information available in the CEX is not sufficient to construct all the variables of interest. There is not enough information to estimate the service flow from the stock of existing durables, or the part of mortgage payments that repays the principal. Therefore we use different definitions of consumption that make, in turn, opposite and extreme assumptions: for instance, we consider cases where durable expenditure and mortgage payments are considered first as saving and then as consumption. In total, we consider five different definitions of consumption and therefore of saving. The first is the closest to the National Account definition and includes both expenditure on durables and mortgage payments. The second and third exclude ex-

---

54. As stressed in section 2.2 the CEX does not contain any information on employers' contributions to pensions.

penditure on education and health, respectively. The fourth and fifth exclude mortgage payments and durable expenditure. In a sense, in this subsection we put together the evidence presented in sections 2.4 and 2.5.

In figure 2.35 we plot the age profile for our benchmark definition of saving.[55] For each year-cohort cell we compute average disposable income by maximum likelihood and subtract from it average contributions to Social Security (as in section 2.4.1). Finally, we subtract average consumption (as in figure 2.26) to obtain saving.[56]

As in figures 2.13 and 2.26, we plot the raw cell means in the top panel, and in the bottom, smoothed profiles obtained using the same method as before. Several considerations are in order. First, it seems that saving increases in the first part of the life cycle, is highest just before retirement, and declines afterward. While these features are roughly consistent with the implications of the life cycle, given that we have not controlled for family composition, labor supply behavior, or any other variables, this evidence cannot be used in support of the model.

The smoothed age-saving profiles peak later than the corresponding profiles for disposable income: the polynomial in the bottom panel of figure 2.35 peaks around age 56, while that in figure 2.13 peaks at 50.[57]

A possible interpretation of figure 2.35, supported by the analysis of the smoothed profiles in the bottom panels of the two figures, is that the middle cohorts (cohorts 4 to 8) saved less, given their age, than the other cohorts in the sample. The only difference among the smoothed profiles of different cohorts is in the intercepts: in the second column of table 2.19 we report the ratio of the intercepts of each cohort's saving-age profile (in figure 2.35) to that of cohort 3. As a term of reference, in the first column of the same table we report the same ratio for the consumption-age profiles of figure 2.26.

The fact that the cohort-specific intercepts for the middle cohorts are lower than those for the younger ones does not necessarily reflect a behavioral change. It could conceivably be explained by the fact that we are considering saving *levels:* the intercepts of the smoothed profiles depend in an obvious way

55. In figures 2.35–2.38 we exclude data from 1980 and 1981. This was motivated by the fact that in 1980 and 1981 top-coded observations had all components of income (including Social Security contributions) top-coded. It turns out that the treatment of Social Security contributions and of top-coded observations in these two years affects substantially the shape of the estimated saving-age profiles. As a consequence we prefer to exclude these data from the analysis at this point. When considering Social Security as saving, the inclusion of 1980 and 1981 has no strong effects on the shape of the estimated profiles. The fact that cohorts are defined on a five-year band and that we have (after the exclusion of 1980 and 1981) nine years of data still leaves us with four ages of overlap between adjacent cohorts. After 1981 Social Security contributions were never top-coded.

56. Alternatively, we could have fitted a density to the cross-sectional distribution of savings with similar results.

57. If we consider Social Security contributions as a form of saving (as in Attanasio 1993b), we obtain a picture very similar to figure 2.35, except that the raw means are slightly smoother and the smoothed profiles peak earlier (around age 53).

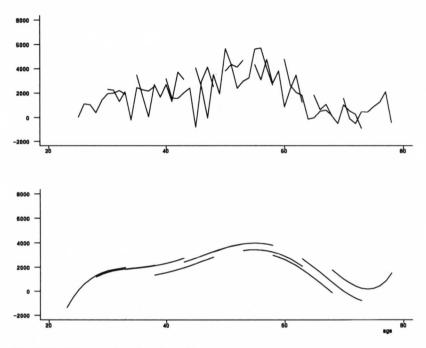

Fig. 2.35   Mean saving (benchmark)

on the amount of resources available to a given cohort. However, it is much harder to use this explanation for the fact that the intercepts for the middle cohorts are lower than those for the older cohorts, if, as we saw in the analysis of income and consumption data, cohort effects are positive and reasonably strong. Furthermore, the presence of negative cohort effects on the saving behavior of the middle cohorts is confirmed by the analysis of saving *rates* in section 2.6.3 below.

This interpretation is not uncontroversial, and it is not the only possible: an alternative would be to say that a typical saving-age profile is flat rather than bell-shaped in the middle part of the life cycle and that, therefore, the middle cohorts have *not* saved relatively less than the others. The problem is, of course, one of identification. As stressed above, it is not possible, without additional information, to identify separately age, cohort, and time effects and therefore a "pure" age profile. In this sense, the smoothing procedure used to obtain the bottom panel of figures 2.13, 2.26, and 2.35 is not neutral: to interpret the smoothed profiles as pure age profiles, one has to assume that the year effects sum up to zero over the sample period and that they are orthogonal to a linear trend. All trends in saving would then be interpreted as age effects. In Attanasio (1993b) we provide another, and maybe stronger, justification for this interpretation based on evidence from financial asset accumulation.

Table 2.19   Ratio of Cohort-Specific Age Profile Intercepts to Cohort-3 Intercept

Cohort	Consumption (1)	Saving (benchmark) (2)	Saving with Social Security (3)	Consumption Except on Education (4)	Consumption Except on Health (5)	Consumption Except on Housing (6)	Consumption Except on Durables (7)
1	1.06	1.07	1.11	1.13	1.09	1.14	1.10
2	1.01	1.02	1.03	1.05	1.04	1.06	1.03
3	1.00	1.00	1.00	1.00	1.00	1.00	1.00
4	0.94	0.67	0.82	0.72	0.71	0.86	0.79
5	0.85	0.86	0.80	0.87	0.83	0.71	0.76
6	0.77	0.85	0.86	0.82	0.78	0.59	0.66
7	0.70	0.62	0.77	0.60	0.60	0.44	0.48
8	0.63	0.50	0.79	0.51	0.46	0.31	0.41
9	0.58	0.88	1.05	0.82	0.68	0.29	0.53
10	0.51	1.32	1.29	1.18	0.93	0.28	0.68

This reading of the evidence in figures 2.35 and 2.36, i.e., that the middle cohorts saved relatively "less," could explain the decline in aggregate saving observed during the 1980s. The cohorts that were observed in that part of their life cycle when saving is highest, saved "less." This is the main explanation for the decline in aggregate personal saving given in Attanasio (1993b).

Using alternative definitions of saving we obtain figures very similar to figure 2.35, which are not reported for the sake of brevity. In table 2.19, however, we report the ratio of cohort-specific intercepts to that of cohort 3 for the definitions of saving derived by adding Social Security contributions (column [3]), and excluding from consumption expenditure on education (column [4]), health (column [5]), housing, and mortgage payments. There are no substantial changes in the pattern of these intercepts.

Figure 2.36 is analogous to figure 2.35 except in the definition of saving, which is constructed excluding from consumption expenditure on durable commodities. Unlike the other definition of saving we experimented with, we observe a quite different pattern in the shape and relative position of the age profiles. This is particularly evident if we consider the smoothed profiles in the bottom panels. The only feature that they have in common with figure 2.35 is the characteristic hump shape. The increase in the early part of the life cycle, however, is steeper: young households are more likely to buy durables than old households. In fact, the share of durables over total consumption declines monotonically with age.

What is more interesting, however, is that the pattern of cohort effects, as represented by the cohort-specific intercepts, is very different. The ratio of the cohort-specific intercepts to the intercept of cohort 3 are reported in column (7) of table 2.19. We observe that the cohort-specific intercepts increase monotonically with the year of birth of the cohort. This is consistent with the pattern of cohort effects that we saw both for income and consumption in sections 2.4 and 2.5.

2.6.2   Saving by Education Group

In section 2.6.1 we ignored within-cohort heterogeneity. Yet we know from the analysis in sections 2.4 and 2.5 that the dynamics of disposable income and consumption is very different across education groups and that most of the changes in inequality occurred across rather than within groups.

It is therefore interesting to recast the analysis of the previous section conditioning on education. The drawback of this, of course, is that we will be looking at much smaller cells than in the unconditional case.

In figure 2.37 we plot age profiles for the basic definition of saving for the three education groups. As expected, the profiles are much noisier.[58]

---

58. To obtain the smoothed profiles we used weighted OLS on the cohort means, using as weights an estimate of the standard errors of mean income. For a few cells the maximum likelihood algorithm to estimate mean income did not converge: in these cases we consider a missing value for savings for that cell.

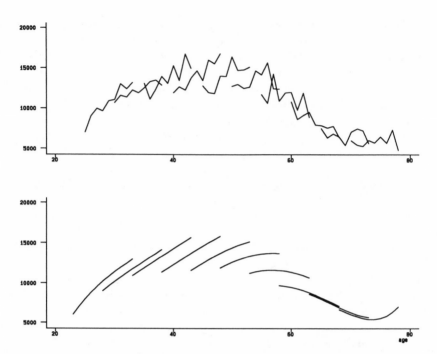

Fig. 2.36   Mean saving (excluding durable expenditure from consumption)

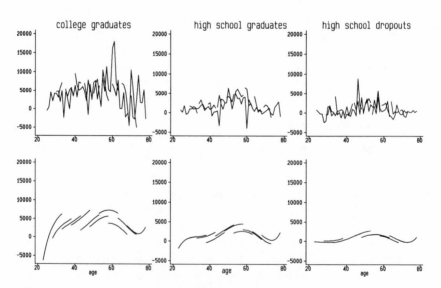

Fig. 2.37   Mean saving by eduction group

Some features, however, emerge pretty clearly. Saving is obviously higher for richer households: this could be explained simply by the larger amount of lifetime resources available to wealthier households. In the next section, where we look at saving *rates* rather than *levels,* we will come back to this problem.

The three smoothed profiles peak approximately at the same age group (55–57), but are quite different in shape, as one would expect, given the difference in the shape of income profiles.

The decline for the middle cohorts, discussed in section 2.6.1, while less evident because of the noisiness in the data, is still visible. The decline for college graduates obviously has larger aggregate effects, since they save more on average.

2.6.3 Individual Saving Rates

While the characterization of saving *levels* carried out in sections 2.6.1 and 2.6.2 can be translated directly into significant information about aggregate saving, the microeconomic behavior underlying these aggregates deserves to be analyzed further. To do so it might be more interesting to consider saving *rates.* Furthermore, both for statistical and economic reasons it might be more useful to consider measures of location other than means, in particular medians and various quantiles. The drawback, of course, is that neither ratios nor quantiles aggregate; they might provide a more interesting description of individual behavior, however.

Individual saving rates are very noisy almost by construction, as is evident by looking at their large variance and kurtosis. To deal with this problem we use two devices. First, we consider measures of location that are relatively robust to the presence of large outliers. Furthermore, instead of considering the traditional definition of saving rates (saving over income) we consider, as in section 2.3, saving over consumption.

In this section we will estimate several versions of the following equation:

$$(2) \qquad SC_t^i = \theta' X^c + f(\text{age}_t^i) + \gamma' D_t + \beta' Z_t^i + u_t^i,$$

where SC_t^i is the ratio of saving to consumption for household i observed at time t, X^c and D_t are sets of cohort and year dummies, respectively, f is a polynomial in age, the Z_t^i are household-specific variables we want to control for, the u_t^i are residuals, and β, θ, and γ are parameter vectors; the γs are constrained to have zero mean and to be orthogonal to a time trend. The first three terms are equivalent to the terms used to obtain the smoothed age profiles in sections 2.4, 2.5, 2.6.1, and 2.6.2; the Zs control for various observable variables.[59] To construct the dependent variable we use the benchmark definition of saving.

---

59. As an alternative we also substituted the cohort and year dummies and the polynomial in age with fully interacted year-cohort dummies. The results were extremely similar and are available on request.

It is important to distinguish between Zs that are time invariant (such as race, education, and region) and Zs that may vary over the life cycle (such as the number of children, home ownership, and so on). When we condition on Zs that do not vary over time, the interpretation of the results is straightforward. If we were to fully interact the year-cohort dummies with these Zs, we would get entirely different profiles for different groups; this is similar to the analysis conducted in sections 2.4, 2.5, and 2.6 for the three education groups. In equation (2) we impose more structure in that we assume that the effects of the Z are the same across cohorts and time; this kind of restriction is motivated only by the lack of a large enough data set.

When we consider Zs that vary over time, the interpretation of the results is more complicated because of two related reasons. First, it is often the case that the variables we condition on are endogenous and are planned in advance by most households (home ownership or children). Second, most of these variables have a very distinctive life-cycle pattern which is going to interact with the age polynomial and the cohort dummies. Both of these problems make it very difficult to interpret the estimated coefficients. Nonetheless, as long as we do not intend to give the parameters any structural interpretation, they can be interesting.

Finally, notice that we never condition on income. This is because income is obviously endogenous and because it includes transitory shocks that, if the life-cycle model holds, are correlated with saving rate innovations. Instead we condition on variables such as education or race, which are likely to be correlated with permanent income.

Before turning to the regression results, we plot ratios of median saving to consumption in figure 2.38.[60] As with the other graphs of this kind we also plot a smoothed version of the same graph obtained using the same technique as above. The evidence in this graph confirms the interpretation of the evidence given in section 2.6.1: the middle cohorts seem to have saved, *given age, less* than other cohorts.

Table 2.20 contains estimates of θ and β in equation (2), and of the cohort dummies, obtained by least absolute deviations.[61] This is equivalent to estimating conditional medians. The reference group is households headed by a nonblack, high school dropout, residing in the West and belonging to cohort 10.

In column (1) we condition on variables that do not vary over the life cycle: the race and education of the household head and the region of residence. Education has a positive effect on saving rates: both the dummies for college grad-

---

60. The computation of the medians is equivalent to estimating eq. (2) with only year-cohort dummies on the right-hand side.
61. In this section, we completely ignore the problem of top-coding. Given that we estimate conditional *medians*, the bias introduced should not be large. The standard errors are computed using standard formulas for least absolute deviation estimation which assume homoskedasticity and gaussian residuals.

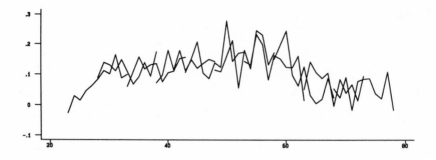

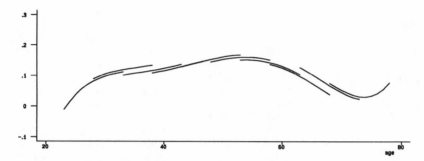

Fig. 2.38 **Median saving rates**

Table 2.20 **Saving Rate Regressions Using Least Absolute Deviations**

Variable	(1)	(2)	(3)	(4)	(5)
College graduate	0.125	0.128	0.091	0.124	0.084
	(0.008)	(0.009)	(0.009)	(0.009)	(0.008)
High school graduate	0.057	0.054	0.030	0.055	0.030
	(0.007)	(0.008)	(0.008)	(0.007)	(0.007)
Northeast	0.035	0.036	0.016	0.028	0.037
	(0.008)	(0.009)	(0.009)	(0.008)	(0.008)
Midwest	0.056	0.059	0.034	0.054	0.053
	(0.008)	(0.008)	(0.008)	(0.008)	(0.007)
South	0.022	0.025	0.011	0.021	0.014
	(0.008)	(0.008)	(0.010)	(0.008)	(0.007)
Black	−0.021	−0.029	0.002	−0.017	0.020
	(0.009)	(0.010)	(0.010)	(0.009)	(0.008)
Self-employed head		−0.127	−0.142	−0.139	−0.188
		(0.012)	(0.012)	(0.011)	(0.010)
Self-employed spouse		−0.050	−0.067	−0.057	−0.088
		(0.018)	(0.017)	(0.016)	(0.015)
Home owner			0.115		
			(0.007)		
Home owner with mortgage			0.105		
			(0.009)		
Earners					0.095
					(0.004)

(*continued*)

Table 2.20   (continued)

Variable	(1)	(2)	(3)	(4)	(5)
Retired head					-0.049
					(0.012)
Female head					-0.119
					(0.006)
Children aged 3–15				-0.031	-0.030
				(0.003)	(0.003)
Children aged 16–17				-0.051	-0.097
				(0.009)	(0.009)
Infants				-0.024	-0.017
				(0.010)	(0.009)
Adults				0.064	-0.031
				(0.003)	(0.005)
Cohort 1	-0.040	-0.026	-0.055	-0.025	0.000
	(0.046)	(0.050)	(0.050)	(0.046)	(0.043)
Cohort 2	-0.040	-0.041	-0.052	-0.021	0.003
	(0.044)	(0.049)	(0.048)	(0.045)	(0.042)
Cohort 3	-0.042	-0.039	-0.063	-0.026	-0.009
	(0.043)	(0.047)	(0.046)	(0.043)	(0.040)
Cohort 4	-0.059	-0.058	-0.071	-0.052	-0.028
	(0.040)	(0.044)	(0.044)	(0.041)	(0.038)
Cohort 5	-0.064	-0.057	-0.089	-0.069	-0.047
	(0.037)	(0.041)	(0.041)	(0.038)	(0.035)
Cohort 6	-0.046	-0.043	-0.074	-0.042	-0.023
	(0.034)	(0.037)	(0.037)	(0.034)	(0.032)
Cohort 7	-0.070	-0.065	-0.100	-0.060	-0.056
	(0.030)	(0.033)	(0.032)	(0.030)	(0.028)
Cohort 8	-0.074	-0.082	-0.094	-0.070	-0.048
	(0.024)	(0.026)	(0.026)	(0.024)	(0.023)
Cohort 9	-0.021	-0.018	-0.048	-0.027	-0.012
	(0.019)	(0.021)	(0.021)	(0.019)	(0.018)

Notes: The dependent variable is the ratio of saving to consumption. The regression also includes a fifth-order polynomial in age and year dummies constrained to sum to zero and to be orthogonal to a linear trend. Numbers in parentheses are standard errors. The regression uses 47,647 observations. Year dummies are excluded from the specification in col. (4) because of convergence problems.

uates and high school graduates are very strongly significant and significantly different from one another. The higher saving rates for more educated households might indicate differences in tastes and/or economic opportunities, probably related to the higher level of permanent income of better educated households.

The regional dummies are statistically significant and positive, indicating that households living in the West have the lowest saving rates. The highest saving rates prevail in the Midwest.

The dummy for black household heads is negative and significant. Again, a variable likely to be related to households' permanent income takes a sign that implies a positive relationship between permanent income and saving rates.[62]

Finally, the pattern of the cohort dummies is consistent with the evidence presented in section 2.6.1: cohorts 5 to 8 seem to be those with the lowest conditional median saving rates. This is true for all the columns in table 2.20.

In column (2) we add two dummies to the previous specification, dummies that equal one if the household head or the spouse is self-employed. These variables have received some attention in the precautionary saving literature (see, e.g., Skinner 1988) because it is believed that self-employed individuals face riskier income. Consistent with that literature, the measured effect of self-employed status on the conditional median of saving rates is negative and strongly significant. One should treat these results with care: as we saw in section 2.3, there are strong variations in the proportion of self-employed individuals over both the life cycle and the business cycle. This indicates that assuming self-employed status is probably correlated with various economic variables and therefore with variations in labor income. In addition, it is likely that less risk-averse individuals will select into riskier occupations. Finally, income is likely to be underreported and consumption overreported for self-employed individuals. The coefficients on the other variables do not change substantially.

In column (3) we control for the effect of home ownership by introducing two dummies that equal one if the household owns its place of residence without and with a mortgage, respectively. Both dummies are positive and strongly significant. The interpretation of these results is difficult because of the life-cycle pattern that characterizes home ownership. It is likely that the positive sign of the coefficients reflects a correlation with individuals' permanent income.

Column (4) adds to the specification of column (2) the number of children between ages 3 and 15, the number between ages 16 and 17, the number of infants, and the number of adults. Not surprisingly, all the children variables are negative and strongly significant, probably indicating that a given level of consumption will produce different levels of utility depending on the number of children present, while the same children have, for the most part, no effects on income. The coefficient on the number of adults is positive and strongly significant.

Finally, in column (5) we add to the specification of column (4) the number of earners, a dummy for retired individuals, and a dummy for a female household head. While the first variable is strongly positive, the other two, perhaps not surprisingly, are negative and significant. The other noticeable features of

---

62. It might be interesting to note that one of the facts that was discussed in the early literature on the permanent-income hypothesis, namely, that black households save *more* for each income level than nonblack households, holds true in the CEX sample.

this specification are that the dummy for black household heads is no longer significant and that the coefficient on the number of adults is now negative, probably indicating that the positive sign in column (4) picked up the correlation between the number of adults and the number of earners.

2.7 Financial Wealth Accumulation

In this section we look briefly at one of the most investigated issues in the life-cycle literature: the accumulation of wealth over the life cycle. In what follows, we analyze the main features of the wealth data in the CEX: the focus, however, is not the issue of asset decumulation by the elderly. Most of the results in this section are taken from Attanasio (1993a).

As described in section 2.2, the CEX provides some information on financial asset holdings. This information is only collected in the last interview: as a consequence of the fact that some households do not reach the fourth interview and that some households that have valid information on consumption and income do not respond to the questions on assets, in this section of the paper we use a reduced sample of 32,050 observations.

We divide financial wealth into two components: the first, defined as liquid assets, includes savings and checking accounts; the second includes U.S. savings bonds and other bonds and equities. In figure 2.39 we plot mean and median total financial wealth age profiles.[63] These means and medians are calculated by fitting a distribution that has a mass point at zero (to take into account households reporting zero assets, who constitute approximately 15 percent of the sample) and is given, for households with positive assets, by the mixture of two log-normal densities.

The main features of these graphs are by and large consistent with what is found in the literature: financial wealth increases with age at decreasing rates until retirement. After retirement average and median wealth seem to have little tendency to decline. In Attanasio (1993a) we discuss why this does not necessarily contradict the life-cycle model: failure to observe a decline in assets at the end of the life cycle could be caused by changes in preferences, the failure to control properly for retirement (see Hurd 1989), the correlation between mortality and wealth (see Shorrocks 1975; Attanasio and Hoynes 1993), or uncertainty.

In figure 2.40 we plot the proportion of households with positive quantities of nonliquid assets. A first observation is that this proportion is extremely low. In the whole sample, only 25 percent of households report positive quantities of nonliquid assets. If we look at this proportion in the year-cohort cells we see that it increases rapidly until age 40 and then flattens out well below 40 percent. In the last part of the life cycle it declines, even though it is not clear

---

63. These graphs are reproduced from Attanasio (1993a).

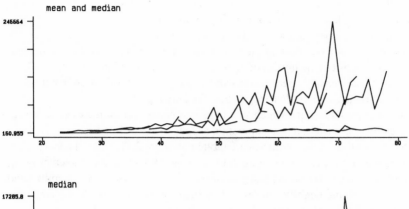

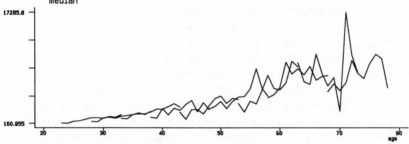

Fig. 2.39   Mean and median total financial assets

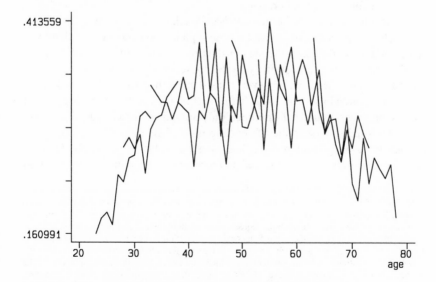

Fig. 2.40   Percentage of households with positive nonliquid assets

whether this is a sign of asset decumulation or a reflection of the fact that older cohorts were less likely to hold nonliquid financial assets.

Given that the sample we use to study financial assets is considerably smaller than the one used in the rest of the paper and that less than 30 percent of it holds positive quantities of nonliquid assets, the maximum likelihood estimates of the density's parameters exhibited a great deal of variability in many cells and often take implausible values. We only report the sample 90th percentile for nonliquid assets, which should give us consistent estimates of the corresponding parameters in the population as long as the top-coding level is above that percentile. These estimates are plotted in figure 2.41, and tell a story similar to that of the median in figure 2.39: nonliquid financial assets keep growing until around age 60. In the last part of the life cycle, asset levels stabilize and possibly decline slightly: unfortunately the estimates are much noisier in the last part of the sample, partly because of the smaller size of those cells.

Probably the most important feature that emerges from these data is that a large number of households hold (at least directly) very small quantities of financial assets. The ratio of the stock of financial assets to annual total consumption expenditure averages only 0.57 for the whole sample.[64] This average, however, is somewhat misleading because of the strong skewness of the ratio: its median is only 0.08, and even its third quartile is below the mean (0.43).[65]

These figures hide large differences across the education groups we considered in the previous sections: the median of the ratio of financial assets to consumption is 0.21 for college graduates, 0.07 for high school graduates, and below 0.01 for high school dropouts.

The low level of assets for most households does not necessarily mean that their behavior is irrational or that they are liquidity constrained.[66] It should be remembered that the assets we are considering do not include two of the most important assets in the portfolio of U.S. households: real estate and pension wealth. This low level is, however, consistent with the evidence on interest income presented in section 2.4.2. In that section we saw, however, that interest income becomes somewhat important only around retirement age. It is therefore interesting to look at the life-cycle profile of the ratio of financial assets to consumption, as in figure 2.42. The most noticeable feature of the figure is probably the sharp increase just before retirement: the median ratio goes from

64. We prefer to use the ratio of financial assets to consumption rather than to income for two reasons. First, under the life-cycle permanent-income hypothesis, consumption is less affected than income by temporary fluctuations: consumption should be related to permanent rather than current income. Second, in the present data set, consumption is better measured than income. Furthermore, consumption unlike income is not top-coded; this allows us to determine at least the sign of the bias introduced by the observations which have top-coded financial wealth. The results are not affected dramatically, however, if income rather than consumption stands in the denominator.

65. The ratio of average financial assets to average consumption in the sample is about 0.6.

66. Deaton (1991) constructs a model of optimizing behavior with liquidity constraints in which agents hold (optimally) very small amounts of assets.

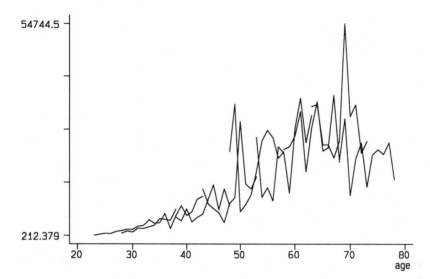

Fig. 2.41   90th percentile of nonliquid financial assets

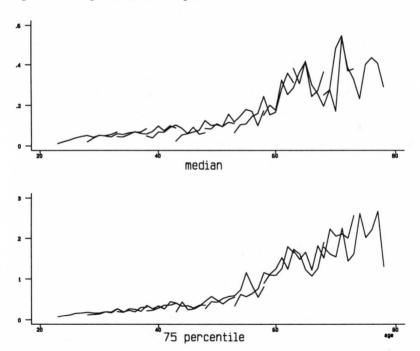

Fig. 2.42   Ratio of financial wealth to consumption

around 0.17 at age 60, to around 0.4 at age 65, to around above 0.5 at age 71; the third quartile goes from around 1.1 at age 60 to around 1.45 at age 65.

2.8 Conclusions

This paper presents a detailed analysis of the only U.S. microdata set that contains complete and exhaustive data on consumption, as well as information on income, wealth, labor supply, and a variety of other demographic and socioeconomic variables. While the quality of the data is far from perfect, the data set gives a unique opportunity to study savings at the individual level, as is essential for understanding the recent dynamics of aggregate saving rates.

The model we use as a benchmark and frame of reference is the life-cycle theory of consumption. The paper, however, is descriptive in nature: we estimate and characterize age profiles for a variety of variables directly or indirectly relevant to savings. We think of this as an essential first step which should be followed, in the future, by a more structural analysis. The descriptive statistics are very suggestive but, without additional structure, are consistent with numerous and diverse interpretations.

The main features that emerge from the analysis are as follows:

1. Both the income and consumption age profiles are hump-shaped, though without a model of household production and of joint consumption and labor supply decisions, this cannot be taken as evidence against the life-cycle model. There are fairly strong cohort effects, probably reflecting productivity growth, as younger cohorts appear "wealthier" than older ones.

2. Profiles of savings by age are hump-shaped. This is roughly consistent with the life-cycle model, and it is true across education groups, but especially for more highly educated individuals.

3. A possible interpretation of the evidence presented on savings is that the middle cohorts (roughly, the households headed by individuals born between 1925 and 1940) saved less than the other cohorts, keeping age constant. This is consistent with the decline in aggregate savings during the 1980s, because those cohorts were in that part of the life cycle when savings are the highest.

4. When we consider alternative definitions of savings to take into account the fact that some expenditure items have an important element of savings, a different pattern emerges for the definition that excludes durable consumption from consumption.

5. A regression analysis of saving rates shows that savings are higher for better educated individuals, nonblacks, and households residing in the Midwest.

6. Very few households hold financial assets directly (we do not have information on pension wealth and how it is invested); furthermore, the median level of financial assets is very low. Very few households, especially in the low

tail of the distribution, receive substantial amounts of interest income, at least until retirement age. Interest income is much more skewed than labor income.

7. There is little evidence of asset decumulation by the elderly.

8. Real estate is one of the principal means by which U.S. households hold wealth.

9. There are large differences in the dynamics of consumption, income and savings across education groups.

Several issues are left for future research. We think that there are four areas of research that are particularly promising. First, we think it necessary to develop, estimate, and test a structural model which considers consumption and labor supply decisions jointly. It seems obvious that saving and consumption choices cannot be considered separately from labor supply decisions; however no systematic evidence yet exists on this issue. Second, it is important to understand the effects of changing family composition on consumption and saving. This is only possible with the help of a structural model which allows for flexible adult-equivalent schemes. Third, it is important to gather more data on real estate wealth, as it is clear that it is one of the most important assets in the portfolio of U.S. households. The new data sets released by the BLS since 1988 seem the right ones to use. Fourth, it is important to study the implications of the dynamics of income and consumption inequality for aggregate savings.

References

Attanasio, O. P. 1993a. An analysis of life-cycle accumulation of financial assets. *Ricerche economiche* 47.

——. 1993b. A cohort analysis of saving behavior by US households. NBER Working Paper No. 4454. Cambridge, Mass.: National Bureau of Economic Research.

Attanasio, O. P., and M. Browning. 1992. Consumption over the life cycle and over the business cycle. NBER Working Paper No. 4453. Cambridge, Mass.: National Bureau of Economic Research.

Attanasio, O. P., and H. W. Hoynes. 1993. Differential mortality and wealth accumulation. In preparation.

Bosworth, B., G. Burtless, and J. Sabelhaus. 1991. The decline in saving: Evidence from household surveys. *Brookings Papers on Economic Activity,* no. 2.

Browning, M. J., A. S. Deaton, and M. Irish. 1985. A profitable approach to labor supply and commodity demands over the life-cycle. *Econometrica* 53:503–44.

Carroll, C. D., and L. H. Summers. 1991. Consumption growth parallels income growth: Some new evidence. In *National savings and economic performance,* ed. B. D. Bernheim and J. B. Shoven. Chicago: University of Chicago Press.

Curtin, R. T., F. T. Juster, and J. N. Morgan. 1987. Survey estimates of wealth: An assessment of quality. In *The measurement of saving, investment and wealth,* ed. R. E. Lipsey and H. S. Tice. Chicago: University of Chicago Press.

Deaton, A. 1985. Panel data from time series of cross sections. *Journal of Econometrics* 30:109–26.

———. 1991. Saving and liquidity constraints. *Econometrica* 59:1221–48.

Deaton, A., and C. Paxson. 1992. Aging and consumption in Taiwan. Princeton University. Mimeograph.

Feenberg, D., and J. Skinner. 1989. Sources of IRA savings. In *Tax policy and the economy 1989,* ed. L. H. Summers. Cambridge: MIT Press.

Friedman, M. 1957. *A theory of the consumption function.* Princeton, N.J.: Princeton University Press.

Friend, I. 1954. *Individuals' saving.* New York: Wiley.

Friend, I., and R. Jones, eds. 1960. *Proceedings of the conference on consumption and saving.* Philadelphia: University of Pennsylvania.

Ghez, G. R., and G. S. Becker. 1975. *The allocation of time and goods over the life cycle,* New York: Columbia University Press.

Gieseman, R. 1987. The Consumer Expenditure Survey: Quality control by comparative analysis. *Monthly Labor Review* 108.

Goldsmith, E. 1956. *A study of saving in the US.* Princeton, N.J.: Princeton University Press.

Gravelle, J. G. 1991. Do individual retirement accounts increase savings? *Journal of Economic Perspectives* 5:133–48.

Heckman, J. J., and R. Robb. 1987. Using longitudinal data to estimate age, period and cohort effects in earnings equations. In *Cohort analysis in social research,* ed. W. M. Mason and S. E. Fienberg. New York: Springer-Verlag.

Hurd, M. 1989. Mortality risk and bequest. *Econometrica* 57:779–813.

Jianakoplos, N. A., P. L. Menchik, and F. O. Irvine. 1987. Using panel data to assess the bias in cross-sectional inferences of life-cycle changes in the level and composition of household wealth. In *The measurement of saving, investment and wealth,* ed. R. E. Lipsey and H. S. Tice. Chicago: University of Chicago Press.

Juster, T. F. 1966. *Household capital formation and financing.* New York: Columbia University Press.

Kimball, M. 1990. Precautionary saving in the small and in the large. *Econometrica* 58:53–73.

King, M. A., and L. D. L. Dicks-Mireau. 1982. Asset holdings and the life cycle. *Economic Journal* 92:247–67.

Kotlikoff, L., and L. Summers. 1981. The role of intergenerational transfers in aggregate capital accumulation. *Journal of Political Economy* 86:706–32.

———. 1988. The contribution of intergenerational transfers to total wealth: A reply. In *Modelling the accumulation and distribution of wealth,* ed. D. Kessler and A. Masson. Oxford: Clarendon.

MaCurdy, T. E., and T. Mroz. 1990. Measuring macroeconomic shifts in wages from cohort specifications. Stanford University. Mimeograph.

Modigliani, F. 1988. Measuring the contribution of intergenerational transfers to total wealth: Conceptual issues and empirical findings. In *Modelling the accumulation and distribution of wealth,* ed. D. Kessler and A. Masson. Oxford: Clarendon.

Modigliani, F., and R. Brumberg. 1954. Utility analysis and the consumption function: An interpretation of cross section data. In *Post Keynesian economics,* ed. K. K. Kurihara. George Allen and Unwin.

Moffitt, R. 1991. Identification and estimation of dynamic models with a time series of repeated cross sections. Brown University. Mimeograph.

Paulin, G., M. Boyle, R. Branch, and R. Cage. 1991. Comparison of 1987–1988 CEX integrated survey and PCE annual estimates. Washington, D.C.: Bureau of Labor Statistics. Mimeograph.

Shorrocks, A. F. 1975. The age-wealth relationship: A cross-section and cohort analysis. *Review of Economics and Statistics* 57:155–63.

Skinner, J. 1988. Risky Income, life cycle consumption and precautionary savings. *Journal of Monetary Economics* 22:237–55.

Slesnick, D. T. 1992. Aggregate consumption and saving in the postwar United States. *Review of Economics and Statistics* 74:585–97.

Venti, S. F., and D. A. Wise. 1990. Have IRA's increased US saving? Evidence from consumer expenditure surveys. *Quarterly Journal of Economics* 105:661–98.

3   Household Saving Behavior in Japan

Noriyuki Takayama and Yukinobu Kitamura

3.1 Introduction

This chapter presents a brief survey of microdata sources and microdata descriptions of the nature of household behavior and, in particular, saving behavior in Japan. For those who are interested in Japanese saving behavior on the microlevel, this chapter is intended to play the role of an introductory guided tour.

It has been widely recognized that the level of aggregate household savings in Japan is quite high by international standards. To identify who actually saves in Japan, it is necessary to analyze microdata and to investigate the wealth formation process over the life cycle. In so doing, it is not sufficient to observe the age profile of saving behavior from cross-sectional data alone. Life-cycle behavior can be identified only when changes in wealth by the same cohort over time can be fully traced.

We will make our argument more concrete. In Japan, it is true that a high proportion of household financial assets are held by the elderly. But this static fact alone cannot tell us how the elderly have accumulated their wealth from the time when they were much younger. With information on the composition of wealth increases by the same cohort, the wealth formation process over the

Noriyuki Takayama is professor of economics at Hitotsubashi University. Yukinobu Kitamura is an economist at the Institute for Monetary and Economic Studies of the Bank of Japan and a research associate of Hitotsubashi University.

The authors are grateful for comments from the conference participants, in particular, from Martin Feldstein and Takatoshi Ito. We are also very grateful to Fumiko Arita (Toyo Eiwa Women's University) and Saibi Saito (Bank of Japan) for statistical assistance and to Miki Seno and Miho Yamaguchi (Bank of Japan) for data collection and editorial assistance. Calculations using the 1989 NSFIE tapes were performed at Hitotsubashi University. Data on the 1979 and 1984 NSFIE are heavily based on the work of a research project in the Economic Planning Agency, the Government of Japan, headed by N. Takayama.

life cycle becomes clearer. For instance, we find that households, when young, obtain their wealth partly through their own finance (via loans) and partly through intergenerational transfers from their parents, while, as they get older, their wealth is accumulated through capital gains. After age 60, these households, in turn, start leaving bequests (intergenerational transfers) to their children.

Along with playing the role of tour conductor, we present sufficient materials and a new method to analyze life-cycle, as well as cohort, effects by combining different data points in time. In fact, this chapter presents the first clearcut and probably the most definitive picture of microeconomic household saving behavior in Japan to date.

This chapter is organized as follows. Section 2 explains the available microdata sources on household behavior in Japan. The statistical comparability of the National Survey of Family Income and Expenditure with the Annual Report on National Accounts and with the Flow of Funds Accounts is also discussed at some length. Section 3 gives a detailed data analysis of the NSFIE. Special emphasis is placed on saving and wealth formation behavior over the life cycle. Section 4 examines the age-contribution and age-recipient pattern of social security and retirement pensions, with regard to household saving behavior. A brief conclusion is given in section 5.

3.2   Microdata Sources on Household Behavior in Japan

Several large-sample microsurveys concerning Japanese household behavior are conducted regularly by the government.[1] With advances in sampling survey technique, the data sources cover wide-ranging aspects of household behavior. Major aspects include (1) consumer behavior, (2) asset accumulation, (3) labor supply, and (4) time allocation. These data sources are used for the statistical adjustment of national income accounts, the construction of the consumer price index, and forecasts of business activities, among other things.

Each data source has pros and cons. For example, the Family Income and Expenditure Survey (FIES) has the following characteristics: (1) because it is used to construct the consumer price index, a special emphasis has been placed on time-series comparability; (2) expenditures are accounted by a daily bookkeeping (diary) method; (3) because housewives normally keep records, expenditures made by other members are likely to be underestimated. In particular, the consumption behavior of those who live with their parents is not

1. The major surveys include the Family Income and Expenditure Survey (Designated Statistics, no. 56), Family Saving Survey (Approved Statistical Report), National Survey of Family Income and Expenditure (Designated Statistics, no. 97), Comprehensive Survey of Living Conditions of the People on Health and Welfare (Designated Statistics, no. 116) and Survey on Time Use and Leisure Activities (Designated Statistics, no. 114). For more information on these surveys, see Statistics Bureau (1991). Note, however, that the Japanese government does not collect "panel data" on household behavior.

captured fully. Nevertheless the reported data are, in general, known to be reliable. A major statistical problem lies in the declining response rate such that households in the randomly selected sample often refuse to participate in data collection. In fact, it is said that the response rate dropped from 69.9 percent in 1955 to 55.0 percent in 1990 (see Mizoguchi 1992, 62). This would distort the sample distribution. Those who refuse to participate are quite likely to fall in the categories of self-employed workers, merchants, unemployed workers by occupation, elderly by age, and wealthier and poorer households by income class.[2] In the case of the National Survey of Family Income and Expenditure (NSFIE), according to the Statistics Bureau the response rate for the 1989 survey was about 85 percent which was substantially higher than for the FIES.

The NSFIE reports much lower per household financial assets than do the Flow of Funds Accounts (FFA) and Annual Report on National Accounts (SNA). In 1984, the FFA estimated 10.35 million yen on average, and the SNA 8.8 million yen, while the NSFIE reported 6.2 million yen. In 1989, the FFA reported 16.45 million yen, the SNA 16.90 million yen, and the NSFIE 10.30 million yen. The gap between the FFA and the SNA is relatively small (i.e., SNA/FFA was 0.850 in 1984 and 1.027 in 1989), compared with that between the NSFIE and the FFA (or between the NSFIE and the SNA) (i.e., NSFIE/FFA was 0.600 in 1984 and 0.626 in 1989; NSFIE/SNA was 0.705 in 1984 and 0.609 in 1989). These facts imply that, although the gap between the SNA and the FFA (less than 15 percent) can be explained in terms of differences in statistical coverage (e.g., private nonprofit institutions and health insurance funds are included in the FFA but not in the SNA), the approximately 40 percent difference between the NSFIE and the FFA (or between the NSFIE and the SNA) must go beyond the usual explanations of differences in statistical coverage and reporting months. Three explanations can be made: First, as was discussed above, there exists a sample selection bias due to refusals among wealthier households to participate in the survey. Consequently, the mean asset holdings in the NSFIE are lower than in the SNA or the FFA. Second, the difference may be affected by underreporting by self-employed households. Although both the NSFIE and the FFA (and the SNA) include self-employed households, those in the NSFIE seem to report financial assets only for personal use and exclude those for business purposes. Third, it should be noted that the SNA data are constructed from value added in the production sector and that, with the commodity flow method, the household sector is treated as a residual. Thus, in general, household sector accounts (e.g., savings) are sub-

---

2. A similar tendency is found in the United Kingdom, according to Pudney (1989, 62): "The responding and non-responding households were compared in terms of a number of general household characteristics. Significant differences were found for the age of the head of household (younger households being more likely to co-operate), for the number of children (the more children, the greater the likelihood of response), for employment status (much lower response for the self-employed), for household size (better response for large households) and for wealth holdings (wealthier and higher-spending households are less likely to respond)."

ject to statistical (measurement) errors.[3] Note, however, because the data on financial assets in the SNA are based on the FFA, no discrepancy between the two should exist.

Table 3.1 summarizes the data content of the major microsurveys on household behavior. As no survey collects all behavioral variables, an appropriate data source must be selected for a specific purpose. A basic reason why no single survey can collect all variables is that a comprehensive survey would impose too heavy a burden on participants, who would have to keep books for several months. In other words, there is certainly a trade-off between the completeness of the survey and the burden on participants. With the response rate declining, seeking more completeness may not be a realistic option.

Among the available microsurveys, the NSFIE covers nearly all saving and consumption data, except intergenerational transfers (bequests) and education, as is evident from table 3.1. Detailed comparisons of the NSFIE with other data sources in Takayama et al. (1989, chap. 3) indicate that the NSFIE captures a fairly accurate and unbiased picture of household behavior in Japan. All in all, we conclude that the NSFIE is one of the most reliable sources of information (though we admit that it contains possible reporting errors). For this reason, throughout the chapter, the NSFIE is used to identify household behavior in Japan. In addition, fortunately we are able to use three different NSFIE data points in time, i.e., the 1979, 1984, and 1989 surveys. Although these are not panel data, intertemporal comparisons among three data points in time can be made to approximate actual life-cycle behavior.[4]

3.3   Data Analysis of the NSFIE

This section draws a general picture of household behavior in Japan and, in particular, of savings and wealth accumulation over a lifetime. In so doing, we mostly present descriptive statistics from the NSFIE.[5]

3. A statistical error could occur when inventories of consumer goods pile up or when these are increasingly consumed by other sectors of the economy (e.g., the corporate sector).

4. The statistical surveys by the government are published regularly in highly summarized forms. Although these summaries contain valuable information and are accessible to everyone, detailed data analysis can not be made without using the original microdata tapes. According to laws governing the use of these statistics, researchers must apply to use these original tapes and give sound reasons. Only after obtaining permission from the government can researchers use the data tapes, in which individual identities are carefully disguised.

5. Several economists have used NSFIE data. Ando, Yamashita, and Murayama (1986), using the 1979 NSFIE, argue that the extended life-cycle hypothesis holds when the behavior of the elderly living with younger families is carefully distinguished from that of the independent elderly. Hayashi, Ando, and Ferris (1988) conclude from the 1984 NSFIE that a large amount of wealth is being transferred within extended families. Ando et al. (1992), with the 1979 NSFIE, propose an explanation for the lack of dissaving by very young households based on the hypothesis of consumption lumping. Takayama and Arita (1992a, 1992b) make clear the economic profile of elderly couples and singles in the 1989 NSFIE and find that a substantial portion of the elderly can be considered wealthy. Takayama (1992a, 1992b) extensively utilizes the 1979 and 1984 NSFIE and discusses broad issues in household consumption and savings, public pension programs, and tax reform proposals among others. As to saving behavior, he rejects the simple life-cycle hypothesis and the public finance neutrality proposition.

Table 3.1   **Microdata Sources on Household Behavior**

	Microdata Source						
Information	(1)	(2)	(3)	(4)	(5)	(6)	(7)
Household attributes							
Annual income	*	*	*	*	*	*	*
No. of household members	*	*	*	*	*	*	*
Work status	*	*	*	*		*	*
Type of household	*		*	*	*	*	*
Financial assets/liabilities		*	*				*
Head of household							
Sex and age	*	*	*	*	*	*	*
Occupation (industry type)	*	*	*	*	*	*	*
Education				*		*	
Housing							
Structure	*		*		*	*	*
Ownership	*	*	*	*	*	*	*
Size of house (no. of rooms)	*		*		*	*	*
Area of housing lot			*		*		
Rent	*		*		*		
Other member of household							
Sex and age	*		*	*		*	*
Occupation (industry type)	*		*	*		*	*
Education				*		*	

Source: Mizoguchi (1992, 72, table 4.4).

Notes: An asterisk (*) implies availability of data. Microdata sources are (1) Family Income and Expenditure Survey, (2) Family Saving Survey, (3) National Survey of Family Income and Expenditure, (4) Basic Survey on Wage Structure, (5) Housing Survey, (6) Survey on Time Use and Leisure Activities, and (7) Comprehensive Survey of Living Condition of the People on Health and Welfare.

The NSFIE has been conducted every five years since 1959 to reveal levels of income, consumption, and household assets, and their structure and distribution, as well as their differences among regions, through the investigation of family income and expenditure and assets and liabilities in Japanese households. This survey is designed to sample over 50,000 households (to be more precise, 53,000 in 1979, 54,000 in 1984, and 59,100 in 1989). Survey items include (1) family income and expenditure, (2) annual income, financial assets, and liabilities, (3) major durable goods, and (4) attributes of households and their members, including housing conditions.

With a large sample size and wide coverage in items, the NSFIE is indeed a mine of information. It enables us to make detailed analyses according to various household characteristics.

3.3.1   Disposable Income

In the NSFIE, gross yearly income includes wages and salaries, income through business and work at home, returns from assets, social security benefits, donations, and consumption in kind. The amount left over after deducting nonconsumption expenditures such as taxes and social security contributions is disposable income. After subtracting consumption expenditures from disposable income, we obtain savings on the flow base.

The definitions of disposable income and consumption in the system of national accounts differ from those of the NSFIE in the treatment of imputed rents from housing and depreciation of housing structures. It will be useful to list here characteristic features and shortfalls of the disposable income concept used in this chapter (except in subsection 3.3.6, where further statistical adjustments are made). These are as follows:

1. Remittances to other family members or relatives are treated as part of "other consumption expenditures." On the other hand, remittances from relatives are counted as a source of yearly income of receiving households. Intergenerational transfers within extended families are not reported separately and are counted in consumption expenditures.

2. Medical benefits in kind are excluded.

3. Imputed rent from housing is excluded from income.

4. The flow of services from consumer durables is not reported. Expenditure on consumer durables is counted as consumption.

5. Capital gains or losses on stocks, equity in one's own home, and equity in consumer durables are not included.

6. The annual tax burden is not reported. Income and resident taxes are to be estimated. Annual social security contributions are also not reported in the NSFIE, while annual social security benefits are reported.

7. Interest on loans is included in income and is also treated as part of nonconsumption expenditures.

8. Interest and dividends are underreported.[6]

In sum, this chapter intends to use raw data without arbitrary statistical adjustments; therefore, it does not seek full comparability with the SNA.[7]

Figure 3.1 and table 3.2 present the hump-shaped age profile of disposable income. Regardless of the survey years, disposable income peaks at ages 50–54. The often discussed seniority wage system in Japan is valid until ages 50–54, except for those who are promoted to executive at ages over 55.

3.3.2 Consumption Expenditure

The NSFIE definition of consumption expenditure includes medical expenditures in cash and purchases of consumer durables. Remittances to other family members and intergenerational transfers in the form of gifts are also included.

---

6. Around 70 percent of households in the NSFIE do not report any amount of interest or dividends. With such a low awareness of capital income, the value of the real interest rate seems to be hardly recognized by households.

7. In order to obtain full international comparability, it is necessary to use a common accounting framework such as the system of national accounts. Statistical adjustments are, however, not easy to make in different microdata sources. A preliminary trial was made for the 1984 NSFIE and reported in Takayama (1992a, 1992b).

Table 3.2   **Disposable Income (10,000 yen)**

Year and Age	All Households		Employees Households		Self-Employed Households	
	Mean	Median	Mean	Median	Mean	Median
1979						
0–24	243	223	241	221	273	257
25–29	283	257	284	258	268	236
30–34	307	287	307	290	304	268
35–39	347	323	349	330	340	287
40–44	379	353	384	363	366	310
45–49	410	384	420	398	387	336
50–54	448	420	454	435	434	378
55–59	427	391	455	429	395	338
60–64	366	319	406	377	348	288
65–69	359	295	421	386	340	259
70–74	350	263	411	347	342	252
75–79	273	214	321	260	271	209
80+	274	176	375	414	273	174
Average	367	331	370	341	361	300
1984						
0–24	275	256	279	260	242	221
25–29	336	315	341	317	294	275
30–34	383	359	388	364	362	320
35–39	431	407	444	420	392	342
40–44	475	453	492	471	430	370
45–49	508	486	532	514	463	402
50–54	535	508	574	555	483	422
55–59	528	491	587	559	496	425
60–64	467	403	502	456	509	441
65–69	413	339	466	433	482	402
70–74	378	314	511	407	440	381
75–79	366	297	486	393	469	372
80+	300	229	183	183	460	386
Average	458	419	476	442	456	387
1989						
0–24	320	302	318	298	412	421
25–29	384	350	381	349	433	374
30–34	446	409	442	409	483	411
35–39	508	471	506	474	526	455
40–44	562	527	563	533	560	487
45–49	631	601	629	612	643	559
50–54	685	646	693	673	680	597
55–59	658	618	684	653	660	589
60–64	538	467	578	530	614	538
65–69	482	394	595	508	577	482
70–74	463	356	539	503	604	512
75–79	428	309	491	421	653	513
80+	385	289	512	380	567	499
Average	558	506	564	522	610	524

Note: Figures for jobless households are included in those for self-employed households only for 1979.

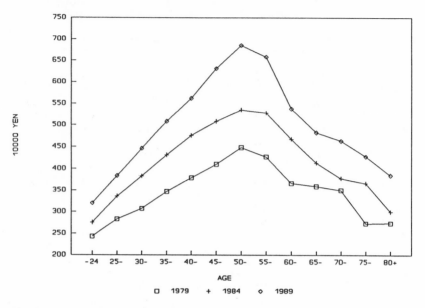

Fig. 3.1   Age profile of disposable income (for all households)
Source: NSFIE for 1979, 1984, and 1989.

In the NSFIE, monthly average household income and expenditures are obtained only for three months, namely, September through November. For our
analysis, it is necessary to convert monthly data to yearly data. If the monthly
average consumption of the three months September through November is simply multiplied by 12, a bias is very likely to result due to the existence of
seasonal fluctuations. Using the FIES, seasonal adjustment ratios for 10 major
expenditure items are calculated to obtain an annual conversion factor (see
table 3.3). In addition, it is known that a substantial number of the sample
households may omit reporting purchases of large durables such as cars.

Consumption Smoothing or Lumping?

The age-consumption profile is not smooth over the life cycle. Like the age
profile of disposable income, it reaches its peak at ages 50–54 (see fig. 3.2
and table 3.4). Although detailed data are not presented in this chapter, the
composition of consumption items also changes over time. Furthermore, this
age profile remains robust, regardless of survey years and employment status.
It corresponds exactly to the age-income profile of the heads of households. In
addition, household composition[8] and the ages of household members may
evolve over time and so affect the shape of the age-consumption profile.

These facts cast serious doubt on the plausibility of the permanent-income
life-cycle hypothesis at the microlevel. This is not a partial refutation of the

8. Note that equivalence scale adjustment is outside the scope of this chapter.

Table 3.3   **Month-to-Year Consumption Conversion Ratio**

Items	1979/1984	1989
Food	12.240	12.028
Housing	12.252	11.845
Fuel, light, and water charges	13,476	12,790
Housing, furniture, and household appliances	11.952	11.328
Clothes and footwear	12.960	12.361
Medical care	11.808	11.948
Transportation and communication	12.120	12.173
Education	12.900	11.942
Recreation	13.008	12.914
Other	13.092	13.511

Source: FIES for 1984 and 1989.
Note: For the 1979 and 1984 adjustments, the conversion ratios are calculated from the 1984 FIES.

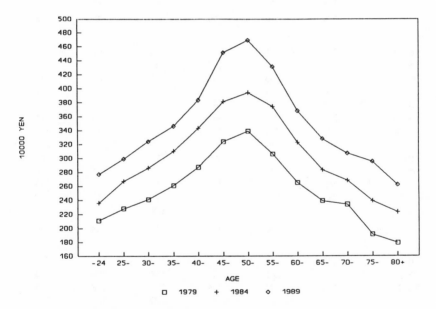

Fig. 3.2   Age profile of consumption (for all households)
Source: NSFIE for 1979, 1984, and 1989.

hypothesis of consumption smoothing, as has often been argued by economists (e.g., Hall and Mishkin 1982)—that is, that a small part of the population is subject to liquidity constraints or myopia while the rest broadly follow the permanent-income life-cycle hypothesis. Using the NSFIE, Takayama (1992a, chap. 5 and app. 6A) presents econometric evidence that Japanese household consumption behavior displays various socioeconomic characteristics which are much more complex than those assumed by the simple permanent-income

Table 3.4   **Consumption Expenditure (10,000 yen)**

Year and Age	All Households		Employee Households		Self-Employed Households	
	Mean	Median	Mean	Median	Mean	Median
1979						
0–24	211	186	208	186	249	195
25–29	228	209	228	211	227	198
30–34	241	219	241	221	241	212
35–39	261	243	260	244	267	235
40–44	287	265	284	266	296	261
45–49	324	291	324	295	321	279
50–54	339	299	345	309	327	275
55–59	306	265	316	280	295	240
60–64	265	219	279	234	258	212
65–69	239	201	252	216	236	197
70–74	234	188	248	219	232	183
75–79	191	168	223	153	190	168
80+	179	137	247	166	178	133
Average	279	248	279	251	278	236
1984						
0–24	236	211	236	215	261	174
25–29	267	249	268	250	265	234
30–34	286	266	287	271	280	249
35–39	310	289	315	293	295	271
40–44	343	321	346	325	334	305
45–49	381	346	394	361	359	313
50–54	394	350	4231	380	357	302
55–59	374	314	409	359	346	272
60–64	323	268	360	297	325	268
65–69	283	241	310	267	305	256
70–74	268	222	317	284	296	245
75–79	239	206	322	240	282	249
80+	223	173	608	608	306	249
Average	333	297	344	310	328	280
1989						
0–24	277	239	277	236	295	274
25–29	299	266	299	266	296	268
30–34	324	294	326	297	308	265
35–39	346	322	350	327	331	296
40–44	383	354	387	359	372	329
45–49	451	407	459	419	435	375
50–54	469	405	487	430	438	351
55–59	431	365	456	388	405	331
60–64	368	310	397	335	370	306
65–69	328	276	385	324	333	280
70–74	307	254	349	289	340	288
75–79	295	310	277	219	400	301
80+	262	194	192	232	354	251
Average	385	335	397	350	384	320

Note: Figures for jobless households are included in those for self-employed households only for 1979. Consumer durables are included.

life-cycle hypothesis. As Ando et al. (1992) argue, each household climbs up and down the socioeconomic ladder, thus changing social status. Along the way, it becomes acquainted with new people, observes new life-styles and discovers new consumption patterns. The age-consumption profile cannot be as smooth as the inherently static life-cycle hypothesis predicts.

Housing-related Issues

The acquisition of a house is probably the most significant consumption decision each household makes over the life cycle. Therefore, saving behavior is quite likely to be affected by the housing purchase decision (see, e.g., Horioka 1988; Hayashi, Ito, and Slemrod 1988). Table 3.5 presents the age profile of the home-ownership rate. Regardless of the survey years, the rate starts rising at around ages 30–34 and reaches a steady-state level (i.e., about 90 percent) at ages 55–59, just before retirement. This steady-state level seems quite high by international standards.

Noguchi (1990) reports that, among residents of the Greater Tokyo area in 1988, 67.6 percent of houses and 57.4 percent of housing lots (land) were acquired completely by their own finance. Others obtained them with the financial help of their parents, presumably through gifts and inheritance. Noguchi also estimates the share of life-cycle wealth (50.9 percent) and intergenerationally transferred wealth (49.1 percent) in total wealth holdings among the sample households.[9] He concludes that, up until the early 1980s, the majority of Japanese households obtained their home out of their own income, but after 1986, homeownership tended to be transferred increasingly through bequests.

Seko (1992) provides interesting information on the composition of home purchase down payments in Japan. For first-time house buyers, a down payment of around 30–33 percent of the total payment is required for households below age 50. As the head of household gets older, the down-payment ratio is raised from 39 percent to 100 percent. Because housing prices went up in the late 1980s, the absolute amount of required down payment also went up substantially, even though the ratios remained, more or less, constant. In practice, as Seko notes, it has become virtually impossible for first-time buyers of a house in the suburbs of Tokyo and Osaka to save substantial financial assets equivalent to down-payment requirements without transfers from their parents or other relatives.

Medical Expenditure and Benefits

As the proportion of the population over age 65 is increasing, medical expenditures are expected to increase, especially among the elderly. Table 3.6 shows the age profile of medical expenditures and benefits. Expenditures in

---

9. Note that households in rural areas may enjoy lower housing prices along with a higher possibility of receiving intergenerational transfers. Location of housing plays a crucial role in accelerating the inequality of wealth distribution, chiefly because of different rates of capital gains in different locations.

Table 3.5   Age Profile of Home Ownership Rates (%)

Age	1979	1984	1989
0–24	20.8	20.6	15.9
25–29	33.0	29.5	27.1
30–34	47.5	48.9	45.0
35–49	64.1	66.1	64.6
40–44	71.4	76.7	76.5
45–49	79.1	82.9	83.2
50–54	83.9	85.3	85.6
55–59	85.5	90.4	89.1
60–64	85.7	89.0	91.3
65–69	85.2	88.1	90.4
70–74	88.2	90.3	90.4
75–79	87.3	89.2	86.9
80+	80.0	88.5	88.0
Average	68.3	74.2	75.6

Sources: NSFIE for 1979, 1984, and 1989.

Table 3.6   Age Profile of Health and Medical Costs in 1984 (1,000 yen)

Age	Expenditure in Cash	Benefits in Kind
0–24	65	210
25–29	75	233
30–34	76	276
35–39	70	308
40–44	69	342
45–49	65	490
50–54	72	536
55–59	83	534
60–64	96	506
65–69	85	590
70–74	83	952
75–79	59	1,024
80+	70	1,044
Average	74	433

Source: National Survey of Medical Expenditures for 1984.

cash among different age groups are, more or less, equal, whereas benefits in kind go mostly to the elderly, over age 70. It is evident that medical benefits in kind are used as a public instrument of intergenerational transfer.

As to the source of social security medical benefits, general revenue from the government covered 35.3 percent in 1979, 34.5 percent in 1984, and 31.4 percent in 1989. Contributions to social health insurance programs provided 53.0 percent in 1979, 53.7 percent in 1984, and 56.1 percent in 1989. User charges (expenditures in cash) accounted for only 11.7 percent in 1979, 11.9 percent in 1984, and 12.5 percent in 1989. In Japan, uninsured medical expenditures have been kept minimal, overall. However, there are growing anxieties about who will provide nursing care or terminal care services. Due to these anxieties, households are very likely to save before retirement and probably even after retirement, as well.

3.3.3   Age-Saving Profile

Flow savings are obtained by subtracting seasonally adjusted yearly consumption expenditure from annual disposable income. In this respect, flow savings are defined by a residual concept.

Using disposable income and consumption expenditure as discussed in the previous sections, 3.3.1 and 3.3.2, flow savings are calculated in table 3.7, table 3.8, and figure 3.3.

Figure 3.3 shows a slightly deformed hump-shaped age profile of savings over the life cycle, with its peak at ages 55–59. It is important to notice that elderly households keep saving a substantial amount even at the very end of their lives (i.e., over age 80). This fact, however, cannot be straightforward evidence to refute the life-cycle hypothesis. Hayashi, Ando, and Ferris (1988, 453), in fact, argue that "many Japanese workers retire just before 60 and they tend to merge with younger households, presumably their children. Those who are remaining independent over the age of 60, and therefore enter the NSFIE sample, tend to be those who are wealthy or remain active in their income earning activities, or both. Therefore, there exists a serious possibility of sample selection biases being present in our estimates." They then distinguish between nuclear families and extended families and analyze them separately, attempting to extract as much information as possible on the behavior of older persons living with younger families. However, their prototypical view of Japanese family formation has been increasingly weakened by the recent trend. For example, the percentage of the population over age 65 who are living with their children decreased rapidly in the 1980s. In the near future the elderly living with their children will become a minority in Japan. In addition, the 1986 Comprehensive Survey of Living Conditions of the People on Health and Welfare indicates that, overall, 44 percent of the elderly are living as household heads and 17 percent as spouses of household heads. Specifically, 30 percent of the elderly living with their married sons or daughters are heads or spouses of heads, and nearly 70 percent of those living with their unmarried children are living as heads or spouses of heads (see, for more details, Takayama 1992a, 43–49). In subsection 3.3.6, we will discuss whether Hayashi, Ando, and Ferris's distinction is crucial and show an alternative approach to identifying the trend and quantity of wealth accumulation of the elderly.

Tables 3.7 and 3.8 provide information on who saves when and how much. Several interesting facts crop up. First, both in 1979 and in 1984, employee households save more than self-employed households, while the reverse is the case in 1989. As is evident from table 3.2, disposable income of self-employed households exceeded that of employee households for the first time in 1989. It is also evident that disposable income of self-employed households does not

Table 3.7   **Savings (10,000 yen)**

Year and Age	All Households		Employee Households		Self-Employed Households	
	Mean	Median	Mean	Median	Mean	Median
1979						
0–24	32	33	33	33	23	25
25–29	55	53	56	54	41	39
30–34	66	66	67	68	64	43
35–39	85	79	89	84	73	45
40–44	92	85	100	93	70	43
45–49	87	86	95	95	66	48
50–54	109	105	110	116	107	79
55–59	121	104	139	123	100	76
60–64	101	77	127	102	90	63
65–69	119	73	169	165	105	57
70–74	116	68	163	130	109	61
75–79	82	36	98	54	81	33
80+	95	32	127	249	95	32
Average	89	77	91	84	83	54
1984						
0–24	38	37	43	39	−19	−33
25–29	69	66	74	70	29	23
30–34	97	89	101	93	82	59
35–39	122	114	129	122	97	73
40–44	132	127	146	142	96	68
45–49	127	122	139	137	104	82
50–54	140	139	153	156	127	110
55–59	154	144	178	177	150	124
60–64	144	112	142	128	184	144
65–69	130	88	156	146	177	129
70–74	110	74	194	129	144	105
75–79	127	74	164	168	187	117
80+	77	34	122	122	155	104
Average	125	111	132	123	128	97
1989						
0–24	43	58	40	57	117	118
25–29	85	86	82	86	137	82
30–34	122	112	116	111	175	136
35–39	162	147	156	147	194	146
40–44	179	170	176	173	188	153
45–49	180	172	171	176	208	155
50–54	216	206	206	207	242	213
55–59	227	212	228	225	254	221
60–64	170	132	181	162	244	200
65–69	154	107	210	172	244	168
70–74	156	99	190	214	264	191
75–79	133	66	214	263	254	205
80+	123	90	320	148	213	197
Average	173	150	167	157	226	177

Note: Figures for jobless households are included in those for self-employed households only for 1979.

Table 3.8   **Savings by Housing Type (10,000 yen)**

Year and Age	Home-Owning		Tenant		Household Head Working		Household Head Nonworking	
	Mean	Median	Mean	Median	Mean	Median	Mean	Median
1979								
0–24	62	63	24	25	32	33	131	131
25–29	91	79	37	42	55	53	1	29
30–34	90	85	45	50	66	66	35	30
35–39	101	94	57	57	86	79	38	18
40–44	104	96	62	57	92	85	−7	−5
45–49	94	95	59	55	88	87	−12	−4
50–54	116	116	73	69	111	108	−9	11
55–59	127	111	82	80	133	116	−12	−2
60–64	107	87	67	37	128	105	18	20
65–69	129	89	63	28	173	133	25	21
70–74	127	75	28	23	177	123	40	27
75–79	90	46	22	25	111	70	56	32
80+	113	54	25	15	185	74	29	15
Average	105	94	53	50	92	80	21	19
1984								
0–24	87	78	25	30	39	38	4	−22
25–29	109	107	52	53	70	67	−24	−27
30–34	130	123	66	65	98	90	−14	−12
35–39	145	138	75	74	122	115	−23	−31
40–44	148	144	78	78	133	128	−56	−40
45–49	137	134	77	69	128	123	−13	−19
50–54	150	150	83	79	142	140	−34	−32
55–59	161	153	87	81	165	155	17	20
60–64	154	124	58	45	170	135	48	46
65–69	140	100	54	38	173	133	41	36
70–74	118	80	30	30	150	110	44	40
75–79	137	86	43	13	186	124	66	33
80+	85	44	14	8	154	112	26	15
Average	144	133	69	66	131	117	38	32
1989								
0–24	39	109	44	50	43	58	33	−30
25–29	138	135	66	73	86	86	42	47
30–34	170	152	83	82	122	112	31	72
35–39	191	177	108	104	162	147	94	41
40–44	200	190	111	108	179	170	210	241
45–49	196	189	99	95	180	173	135	48
50–54	227	223	148	120	217	208	119	98
55–59	237	225	140	119	238	223	52	40
60–64	178	141	88	67	218	182	53	50
65–69	160	113	98	52	235	170	43	43
70–74	161	103	106	47	252	197	59	47
75–79	144	80	59	10	251	205	52	36
80+	128	102	84	64	215	197	73	64
Average	196	177	99	91	184	161	58	47

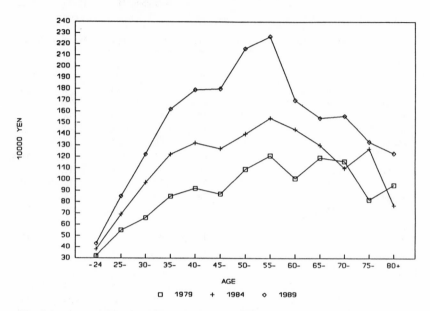

Fig. 3.3   Age profile of savings (for all households)
Source: NSFIE for 1979, 1984, and 1989.

decrease as fast as that of employee households, as they get older. Second, owner-occupied households save much more than tenant households, regardless of the survey years. If, as is often argued, high savings are motivated chiefly by housing purchase, other things being equal, tenant households must save at least as much as owner-occupied households, considering that a certain amount of the savings of owner-occupied households are counted as repayment of housing loans. However, as far as table 3.8 is concerned, this does not seem to be the case throughout the age profile.[10] This is probably because tenant households earn less income than owner-occupied households. It is also clear that households keep saving even after paying back their housing loans at ages over 70. Thus, savings do not seem to be motivated primarily by housing purchase. Third, savings made when the head of household is not working are much lower than those made when he or she is working. However, savings remain broadly positive, except for younger households in 1984. Positive savings by nonworking elderly households are possible because of generous public pension benefits and huge lump-sum retirement severance payments.

Differences in saving behavior between families with and those without children cannot be fully identified by the NSFIE, because the NSFIE surveys only those children who actually live with their parents or who depend on their

10. Note, however, that as table 3.8 does not control for income and other socioeconomic characteristics, the difference in savings between tenant households and owner-occupied households may reflect something other than the motivation for housing purchase.

parents. When children get married and form new households, the NSFIE can no longer trace them.[11]

3.3.4 Saving Rates by Age and Income Class

This section presents the main results of this chapter, namely, the saving rates by different household characteristics. In order to identify stylized facts about household saving behavior in Japan, a new dimension of income class is added. The results are reported in tables 3.9–3.15 and figures 3.4–3.7.

First stylized fact: *What really matters with the saving rate is income rather than the age profile.* Variations of saving behavior across different income classes are much wider than those over the age profile within the same income class (see figs. 3.5–3.7). Indeed, no stylized pattern in saving rates over the age profile across income classes is found.[12]

Second stylized fact: *The households in the highest income class save at increasingly high rates over the age profile.* As income grows and wealth accumulation increases, the richer households depart from the pattern of the life-cycle hypothesis and follow what the intergenerational transfer hypothesis would suggest (see subsection 3.3.6 below). As society in general becomes wealthier, average households behave more the way richer households do (see fig. 3.4).

Third stylized fact: *The elderly households in the middle and higher income classes save at significantly positive rates.* Diversity of saving behavior among elderly households is much wider than among younger households, as their employment status, home ownership, and financial asset holdings differ substantially.

Let us look at each table in turn. About table 3.9, two observations can be made. One is that, within the same survey year, only the poorest quarter of households (I) experience negative saving rates. The other is that, as income grows over the years, even the poorest quarter of households increasingly save positive sums (note that the average saving rate of the poorest quarter becomes positive in 1989. For the second and third quarters of households, the age profiles of saving rates are, more or less, hump-shaped over the life cycle, with positive rates even over age 80 for the third quarter for all years and for the second quarter for 1989. For the richest quarter (IV), the age profile of saving rates is somewhat different from those of the other quarters. It keeps rising until over age 70 and ends with a very high rate (above 40 percent) over age 80. The picture of average saving rates in all households shown in figure 3.4

---

11. The Comprehensive Survey of Living Conditions of the People on Health and Welfare includes rich information on children; however, it has a drawback in relatively weak information on savings.

12. Note, however, that many households move across different income classes over the life cycle. It is not surprising to find no stylized relationship between the saving rate and the age profile across income classes. The saving rate over the age profile can be fully analyzed when the actual income-earning profile over the life cycle is identified. See Creedy (1992).

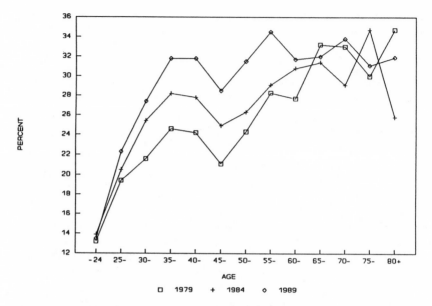

Fig. 3.4   Age profile of saving rates (for all households)
Source: NSFIE for 1979, 1984, and 1989.

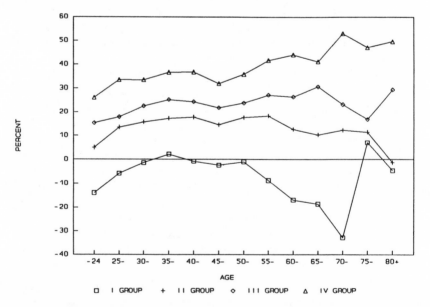

Fig. 3.5   Age profile of saving rates by income class in 1979
Source: NSFIE for 1979.

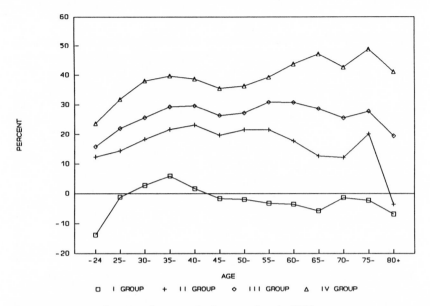

Fig. 3.6   Age profile of saving rates by income class in 1984
Source: NSFIE for 1984.

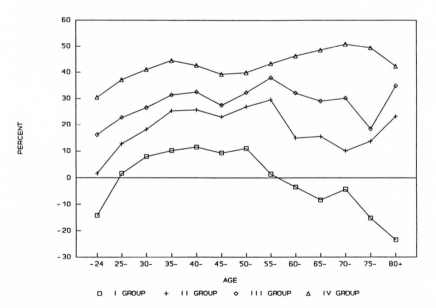

Fig. 3.7   Age profile of saving rates by income class in 1989
Source: NSFIE for 1989.

Table 3.9   **Saving Rates of All Households by Income Class (%)**

	Income Class				
Year and Age	I	II	III	IV	Mean
1979					
0–24	−14.0	5.0	15.3	26.1	13.2
25–29	−5.8	13.4	17.8	33.5	19.4
30–34	−1.4	15.7	22.5	33.4	21.6
35–39	2.2	17.2	25.2	36.6	24.6
40–44	−0.8	17.7	24.3	36.7	24.2
45–49	−2.4	14.5	21.8	31.9	21.1
50–54	−1.0	17.6	23.8	35.8	24.3
55–59	−8.7	18.3	27.2	41.7	28.3
60–64	−16.9	12.6	26.4	44.0	27.7
65–69	−18.6	10.3	30.6	41.1	33.2
70–74	−32.8	12.2	23.2	53.0	33.0
75–79	7.0	11.4	16.8	47.1	30.0
80+	−4.6	−1.3	29.4	49.6	34.7
Average	−2.7	16.3	23.5	36.6	24.1
1984					
0–24	−13.8	12.3	15.8	23.6	13.9
25–29	−1.2	14.4	22.0	31.8	20.5
30–34	2.7	18.3	25.6	38.0	25.4
35–39	5.9	21.6	29.3	39.7	28.2
40–44	1.6	23.1	29.6	38.7	27.8
45–49	−1.7	19.7	26.3	35.5	24.9
50–54	−2.0	21.5	27.1	36.3	26.3
55–59	−3.3	21.5	30.8	39.3	29.1
60–64	−3.6	17.7	30.7	43.7	30.8
65–69	−5.8	12.6	28.6	47.1	31.4
70–74	−1.4	12.1	25.5	42.6	29.1
75–79	−2.3	20.1	27.7	48.8	34.7
80+	−6.9	−3.6	19.4	41.1	25.8
Average	−0.6	19.4	28.5	38.1	27.2
1989					
0–24	−14.2	1.6	16.1	30.4	13.5
25–29	1.7	12.7	22.8	37.1	22.3
30–34	7.9	18.1	26.5	41.0	27.4
35–39	10.2	25.3	31.3	44.4	31.8
40–44	11.5	25.7	32.5	42.6	31.8
45–49	9.3	23.0	27.5	39.3	28.5
50–54	11.0	26.9	32.3	39.9	31.5
55–59	1.4	29.6	37.9	43.3	34.5
60–64	−3.5	14.9	32.1	46.2	31.7
65–69	−8.3	15.5	29.1	48.5	32.0
70–74	−4.3	10.1	30.2	50.8	33.8
75–79	−15.2	13.7	18.4	49.4	31.1
80+	−23.4	23.2	34.8	42.3	31.9
Average	4.6	22.9	31.5	42.1	31.0

Note: Income classes I–IV are yearly income quartile groups.

traces the same trend. It never fits with the picture the simple life-cycle hypothesis would draw.

Table 3.10 presents the saving rates of households that own their homes. This table again shows that it is income class that mainly differentiates saving rates. The general characteristics of saving behavior overlap with those of all households. A noticeable aspect in table 3.10 is that home-owning households with little, if any, saving motivation for housing purchase keep high savings, except for the very poor elderly households. As mentioned before, a substantial part of their savings can be counted as repayments of housing loans. In addition, savings for home reconstruction every 15 to 20 years cannot be negligible. Another reason for high savings is simply that home-owning households earn relatively high income. Table 3.11 shows that the saving rates of tenant households are, in general, lower than those of home-owning households. Judging from the average saving rates in all households, tenant households seem to be concentrated in the first three quarters (I, II, and III) of the income distribution of all households. Thus even the highest income quarter (IV) of tenant households save smaller amounts than the highest quarter (IV) of all households. Nevertheless, it should be noted that only the poorest quarter (I) dissaves.

The general characteristics in table 3.12 of households with a working head also overlap with those in table 3.9. Table 3.13 implies that the saving rate goes down substantially when the household head is not working. Households in the first two quarters (I and II) in table 3.13 dissave quite heavily and save very little, if any. These facts might imply that households whose heads are not working receive very low income flows.

In the case of the employee households (table 3.14), virtually every household saves. The age profile of saving rates is common to all income classes; it keeps rising over the life cycle. This might reflect the fact that the income of employee households is, more or less, guaranteed to increase because the seniority wage system prevails. Table 3.15 exhibits the saving behavior of self-employed households. Income flows of self-employed households, on the other hand, fluctuate a great deal as the saving rates vary from negative for the first quarter (I) to significantly positive for the fourth quarter (IV). In fact, the fourth quarter (IV) of self-employed households seems to be the highest savers, probably with the highest income, in society.

3.3.5 Age-Wealth Profile

Net worth is calculated as a sum of net financial assets, net housing assets, and consumer durables (i.e., total durables minus golf club membership certificates). According to the NSFIE, net worth increases over the life cycle without a substantial decrease after retirement (see fig. 3.8). Net housing assets increase as a share of total worth holdings as housing prices go up. In the 1979 NSFIE, 58.1 percent of total net worth was accounted for by housing assets, in the 1984 NSFIE, 65.8 percent, and in the 1989 NSFIE, 71.8 percent (see tables 3.16–3.18).

Table 3.10   **Saving Rates of Home-Owning Households by Income Class (%)**

Year and Age	Income Class				Mean
	I	II	III	IV	
1979					
0–24	5.5	3.3	22.7	29.2	19.4
25–29	3.7	20.6	28.6	39.7	28.0
30–34	5.1	20.8	26.0	38.3	26.6
35–39	6.4	21.8	28.3	38.5	27.6
40–44	2.7	20.5	25.9	37.9	26.1
45–49	−2.7	16.5	24.0	32.1	22.0
50–54	0.4	17.9	25.3	36.2	24.9
55–59	−6.0	20.3	27.1	42.3	28.8
60–64	−15.5	14.5	26.5	44.5	28.2
65–69	−21.5	11.5	33.7	52.1	34.1
70–74	−26.9	12.8	23.5	54.5	34.5
75–79	7.2	7.8	23.5	47.1	31.2
80+	−8.5	−5.3	29.2	54.9	37.7
Average	0.1	19.5	25.8	38.2	26.4
1984					
0–24	5.4	13.0	19.4	44.2	26.8
25–29	5.1	22.9	31.0	39.6	29.0
30–34	11.0	23.4	31.3	42.2	31.0
35–39	11.6	25.3	33.2	42.0	31.7
40–44	6.5	25.0	31.4	40.2	29.9
45–49	1.9	21.3	27.4	36.1	26.1
50–54	0.0	22.9	28.5	36.6	27.3
55–59	−4.2	22.4	31.5	40.1	29.7
60–64	−3.1	19.8	32.4	44.4	31.9
65–69	−2.7	13.4	31.7	47.3	32.6
70–74	0.6	14.0	26.2	44.5	30.5
75–79	0.4	21.3	29.2	49.6	35.7
80+	−13.9	7.2	19.1	41.6	27.1
Average	3.2	23.3	30.5	39.5	29.5
1989					
0–24	20.9	−58.6	13.0	37.1	10.3
25–29	3.6	26.2	35.3	41.4	31.2
30–34	14.9	30.2	35.7	44.1	34.7
35–39	15.8	28.4	34.8	47.1	35.2
40–44	16.0	28.5	34.5	43.8	34.0
45–49	12.5	24.6	29.3	40.0	30.0
50–54	11.9	28.6	33.4	39.8	32.2
55–59	2.6	31.1	38.2	43.8	35.2
60–64	−3.6	15.7	34.1	46.3	32.2
65–69	−7.7	15.7	29.6	48.9	32.3
70–74	−4.9	11.5	29.7	51.2	33.9
75–79	−13.1	19.0	21.1	48.4	32.0
80+	−21.0	27.7	32.3	42.3	31.9
Average	7.9	26.3	33.8	43.1	33.0

Note: Income classes I–IV are yearly income quartile groups.

Table 3.11   **Saving Rates of Tenant Households by Income Class (%)**

Year and Age	Income Class				
	I	II	III	IV	Mean
1979					
0–24	−18.6	2.3	16.8	23.6	10.9
25–29	−6.8	8.5	14.8	26.2	14.2
30–34	−7.0	10.5	18.3	27.3	16.1
35–39	−2.9	12.2	18.9	31.0	18.4
40–44	−5.6	11.8	19.3	31.6	18.6
45–49	−8.5	13.1	16.1	28.5	16.9
50–54	−9.1	12.9	24.1	30.3	20.2
55–59	−17.0	17.5	20.5	38.7	24.2
60–64	−22.3	1.1	22.2	43.5	23.6
65–69	−18.2	−1.2	21.4	44.0	25.3
70–74	−39.6	0.7	5.7	29.0	13.6
75–79	−23.4	19.2	5.0	28.6	14.4
80+	−0.5	21.6	n.a.	13.1	14.2
Average	−8.9	11.0	17.9	30.3	15.6
1984					
0–24	−17.3	9.5	19.3	13.1	9.7
25–29	−7.5	12.4	18.8	26.6	16.3
30–34	−4.4	15.1	19.6	30.4	19.0
35–39	−1.6	14.2	20.1	31.4	19.8
40–44	−9.9	14.6	22.5	30.3	19.4
45–49	−16.3	10.2	19.1	31.0	18.0
50–54	−7.4	8.9	21.8	29.5	19.0
55–59	−5.5	12.7	18.0	34.4	21.4
60–64	−10.9	7.1	16.7	30.9	17.9
65–69	−34.9	6.7	19.9	33.3	18.3
70–74	−29.4	10.0	19.9	13.6	10.9
75–79	−27.5	16.5	1.5	38.4	19.8
80+	−50.6	−2.0	10.9	23.4	8.0
Average	−7.3	11.7	19.4	29.9	18.7
1989					
0–24	−16.2	4.9	17.3	30.2	14.2
25–29	−2.9	11.8	18.8	31.2	18.2
30–34	3.6	12.3	18.5	34.5	20.2
35–39	3.4	18.4	26.7	36.2	24.3
40–44	−0.7	16.7	26.6	33.9	23.1
45–49	−3.4	15.4	18.4	29.1	19.1
50–54	10.0	16.7	24.8	37.8	26.6
55–59	−12.3	23.4	29.0	37.7	27.3
60–64	−9.0	16.0	19.9	35.9	22.7
65–69	−4.6	8.9	28.3	43.4	27.4
70–74	−12.5	8.9	29.4	51.6	32.2
75–79	−37.4	−11.9	17.8	48.1	22.1
80+	−90.5	12.8	28.9	55.1	31.7
Average	0.0	15.0	22.5	33.9	22.4

Note: Income classes I–IV are yearly income quartile groups.

Table 3.12   Saving Rates of Households with Working Head by Income Class (%)

Year and Age	Income Class				
	I	II	III	IV	Mean
1979					
0–24	−14.2	5.0	15.3	26.0	13.2
25–29	−5.9	13.5	17.9	33.5	19.5
30–34	−1.2	15.6	22.6	33.4	21.6
35–39	2.3	17.2	25.2	36.5	24.7
40–44	−0.4	18.1	24.3	36.6	24.3
45–49	−1.6	14.6	21.9	32.0	21.3
50–54	0.3	18.3	24.6	35.8	24.6
55–59	−1.8	21.6	28.6	42.6	29.9
60–64	−6.2	20.4	29.1	46.7	31.8
65–69	−1.4	25.8	40.2	52.9	39.8
70–74	−39.4	28.1	28.1	58.7	39.6
75–79	4.9	9.1	12.1	54.8	31.6
80+	−7.1	27.1	22.0	66.3	46.5
Average	−0.1	16.9	24.0	36.7	24.6
1984					
0–24	−11.1	11.4	15.8	23.6	14.1
25–29	0.2	14.4	22.1	31.8	20.8
30–34	2.9	18.3	25.7	38.1	25.5
35–39	6.7	21.5	29.2	39.9	28.3
40–44	2.3	23.4	29.6	38.7	28.0
45–49	−1.0	19.4	26.6	35.5	25.0
50–54	−1.1	21.9	27.3	36.3	26.5
55–59	2.8	22.2	32.3	39.8	30.3
60–64	3.5	22.0	34.5	45.0	33.6
65–69	−0.5	23.8	36.3	48.4	36.1
70–74	11.9	14.9	31.5	45.3	33.4
75–79	20.4	20.6	37.1	51.1	39.5
80+	3.7	21.8	21.8	49.3	33.7
Average	2.7	20.7	28.8	38.3	27.8
1989					
0–24	−13.9	1.6	15.8	30.4	13.5
25–29	0.1	12.7	22.8	37.1	22.3
30–34	8.3	18.2	26.5	41.0	27.4
35–39	10.6	25.3	31.2	44.4	31.9
40–44	11.9	25.6	32.4	42.4	31.8
45–49	9.8	22.9	27.4	39.2	28.5
50–54	11.7	26.9	32.3	39.8	31.6
55–59	6.4	31.1	38.0	43.5	35.3
60–64	6.5	25.1	36.0	48.7	36.4
65–69	13.9	28.3	38.2	52.6	40.5
70–74	9.7	29.4	40.4	55.4	42.5
75–79	0.1	11.5	40.5	54.4	39.1
80+	−11.0	31.8	32.3	50.7	38.0
Average	8.5	24.6	32.3	42.3	31.9

Note: Income classes I–IV are yearly income quartile groups.

Table 3.13   **Saving Rates of Households with Nonworking Head by Income Class (%)**

	Income Class				
Year and Age	I	II	III	IV	Mean
1979					
0–24	37.3	n.a.	n.a.	n.a.	37.3
25–29	−104.2	−0.3	22.7	9.8	1.1
30–34	−48.6	15.7	24.1	24.2	16.2
35–39	−13.2	8.8	9.4	34.1	18.4
40–44	−160.8	−22.3	16.2	21.5	−3.9
45–49	−73.9	−3.5	11.9	−4.0	−5.6
50–54	−55.5	−14.6	−24.4	21.6	−4.3
55–59	−52.2	−31.9	7.6	8.0	−5.0
60–64	−35.2	−2.6	1.3	25.6	7.3
65–69	−25.7	−13.8	3.7	33.0	11.0
70–74	−22.4	4.4	15.0	32.4	17.3
75–79	−2.8	12.6	17.8	44.9	27.5
80+	−3.6	−7.6	22.5	25.4	16.0
Average	−26.7	−10.5	5.6	27.1	9.2
1984					
0–24	n.a.	n.a.	−15.4	22.1	2.7
25–29	−0.4	−74.1	−38.4	−10.2	−22.9
30–34	−100.9	−11.9	−21.1	11.8	−9.3
35–39	−103.6	−28.9	−3.0	4.6	−16.8
40–44	−135.3	−56.3	−46.1	5.2	−31.3
45–49	−92.1	−6.7	−17.0	19.4	−6.2
50–54	−46.1	−52.1	−10.0	5.6	−14.4
55–59	−63.7	−15.1	4.9	28.5	5.5
60–64	−10.9	0.6	11.0	29.3	14.8
65–69	−13.8	8.9	8.2	28.5	14.6
70–74	−9.2	7.3	11.2	32.1	16.9
75–79	−20.9	11.1	19.8	43.3	25.4
80+	−5.1	−31.7	25.2	28.3	13.5
Average	−21.5	2.7	9.7	28.1	13.4
1989					
0–24	−101.0	−33.7	41.1	n.a.	16.9
25–29	19.0	−45.6	20.0	62.4	18.7
30–34	−288.8	20.4	25.0	60.7	9.6
35–39	−120.9	−2.3	43.7	48.6	25.3
40–44	−116.4	16.1	55.8	50.3	39.2
45–49	−80.4	−17.8	28.9	51.2	28.4
50–54	−74.1	16.8	20.0	47.5	27.1
55–59	−50.3	−9.2	4.3	39.4	13.4
60–64	−11.1	−4.5	10.1	30.9	13.7
65–69	−27.9	1.3	10.9	30.9	12.5
70–74	−7.0	9.5	2.5	36.7	18.0
75–79	−12.8	5.0	17.6	34.2	18.6
80+	−26.2	18.9	36.4	34.5	25.5
Average	−22.0	3.0	9.7	34.9	16.2

Note: Income classes I–IV are yearly income quartile groups.

Table 3.14   **Saving Rates of Employee Households by Income Class (%)**

| Year and Age | Income Class | | | | |
	I	II	III	IV	Mean
1979					
0–24	−14.1	4.3	17.4	26.6	13.6
25–29	−2.1	14.1	18.5	33.1	19.9
30–34	2.9	15.9	22.9	32.5	21.7
35–39	9.4	20.2	26.3	35.3	25.5
40–44	9.9	20.8	25.8	36.0	26.0
45–49	7.4	17.9	23.1	31.3	22.7
50–54	9.0	19.2	24.1	32.6	24.1
55–59	9.7	25.6	30.0	39.8	30.5
60–64	3.6	27.7	28.0	42.6	31.3
65–69	17.6	35.9	42.1	46.5	40.1
70–74	−9.1	25.6	34.6	54.2	39.6
75–79	24.9	30.8	31.4	30.9	30.5
80+	n.a.	−3.7	n.a.	60.0	34.0
Average	6.0	19.9	24.8	33.9	24.6
1984					
0–24	−9.2	11.7	17.3	25.2	15.4
25–29	1.2	14.9	22.2	33.1	21.6
30–34	7.3	19.6	25.4	37.8	25.9
35–39	13.4	23.3	29.8	38.7	29.1
40–44	13.8	26.4	31.0	37.6	29.7
45–49	10.7	23.9	26.5	33.2	26.1
50–54	13.3	23.6	27.7	32.4	26.6
55–59	17.8	22.4	31.5	38.1	30.3
60–64	14.1	19.7	27.0	37.5	28.3
65–69	16.6	31.6	33.9	39.4	33.5
70–74	36.3	18.1	39.1	45.0	38.0
75–79	34.5	−2.8	49.2	37.3	33.7
80+	n.a.	n.a.	n.a.	66.8	66.8
Average	11.4	23.1	29.0	35.2	27.7
1989					
0–24	−13.6	1.6	16.2	28.7	12.7
25–29	0.5	12.8	23.6	35.1	21.6
30–34	9.2	17.6	26.6	38.9	26.3
35–39	14.0	26.1	30.3	41.7	30.8
40–44	16.8	26.4	32.4	39.8	31.3
45–49	15.3	23.4	26.3	35.3	27.2
50–54	15.6	26.6	30.5	36.4	29.8
55–59	14.4	31.1	36.8	38.2	33.3
60–64	9.6	21.5	33.6	41.1	31.4
65–69	21.1	32.3	31.4	43.2	35.4
70–74	31.0	37.3	33.3	37.7	35.3
75–79	1.8	54.3	42.3	49.9	43.5
80+	38.9	n.a.	83.2	n.a.	62.5
Average	12.1	24.9	30.8	37.4	29.6

Note: Income classes I–IV are yearly income quartile groups.

Table 3.15   **Saving Rates of Self-Employed Households by Income Class (%)**

| Year and Age | Income Class | | | | |
	I	II	III	IV	Mean
1979					
0–24	−17.2	14.3	3.6	17.0	8.6
25–29	−28.8	2.0	11.4	35.8	15.2
30–34	−27.2	6.1	16.6	42.6	20.9
35–39	−24.3	4.2	17.9	41.4	21.4
40–44	−24.8	3.0	15.8	38.7	19.1
45–49	−29.5	0.3	18.5	33.3	17.0
50–54	−24.3	8.0	23.1	42.0	24.6
55–59	−30.8	8.1	24.4	42.7	25.3
60–64	−23.0	1.8	24.8	44.9	25.7
65–69	−25.3	2.3	23.9	51.3	30.7
70–74	−33.1	10.1	24.0	51.0	32.0
75–79	5.5	11.5	16.1	47.7	30.0
80+	−6.8	−0.1	26.8	50.6	34.7
Average	−25.1	5.1	19.3	41.7	23.0
1984					
0–24	−26.3	−15.4	−12.3	1.8	−7.7
25–29	−26.2	7.7	13.5	18.0	9.8
30–34	−21.4	7.4	23.9	40.2	22.6
35–39	−19.7	9.8	23.9	44.2	24.8
40–44	−26.7	7.2	22.0	41.6	22.3
45–49	−28.5	9.6	22.3	40.1	22.4
50–54	−19.8	13.4	26.6	41.8	26.2
55–59	−16.1	18.9	34.6	41.3	30.3
60–64	−4.5	24.9	37.3	48.6	36.2
65–69	−7.0	21.1	36.6	50.9	36.8
70–74	9.3	13.6	32.8	43.9	32.6
75–79	19.5	22.1	36.0	52.2	39.9
80+	0.5	21.8	21.8	49.3	33.6
Average	−16.7	12.8	28.6	43.6	28.0
1989					
0–24	−23.0	8.9	43.0	56.3	28.4
25–29	−8.3	13.8	20.2	60.4	31.6
30–34	1.6	23.7	33.2	53.5	36.3
35–39	−7.3	20.2	37.5	54.9	37.0
40–44	−5.6	21.0	32.1	50.6	33.5
45–49	−8.8	20.4	30.6	48.4	32.3
50–54	1.0	25.9	39.5	45.7	35.6
55–59	−6.4	29.1	40.5	51.4	38.6
60–64	3.6	27.8	39.3	52.3	39.7
65–69	12.6	25.8	41.3	55.3	42.3
70–74	5.5	27.0	42.2	57.6	43.7
75–79	2.0	7.9	40.3	54.9	38.8
80+	−11.0	31.5	32.3	50.1	37.6
Average	−0.7	22.9	37.5	51.1	37.1

Note: Income classes I–IV are yearly income quartile groups. Figures for jobless households are included in 1979.

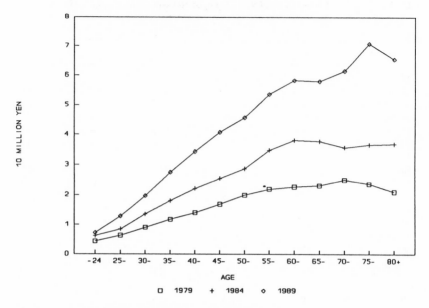

Fig. 3.8   Age profile of net worth (for all households)
Source: NSFIE for 1979, 1984, and 1989.

Wealth distribution also became more imbalanced in the 1980s. In particular, net worth holdings became increasingly distorted between home owners
and tenants (see table 3.16). For example, the ratio of net worth holdings by
tenants to those of home owners, on average, decreased from 19.0 percent in
1979, to 15.4 percent in 1984, and, further, to 11.9 percent in 1989. In other
words, home owners were 8.4 times as rich as tenants in 1989, while they had
been 5.3 times as rich in 1979.[13]

Figure 3.9 exhibits net worth held by cohorts over the period of 1979–89.
Net worth increases substantially in the period between 1984 and 1989, which
corresponds to the bubble economy period in Japan. In the 1989 survey, those
born in 1905–14 may not reflect the distribution of the same cohort in the
previous surveys, because of disproportional increases in wealth in the 1984–
89 period. Apart from this problem, each cohort increases its wealth holdings
over time. Figure 3.10 illustrates net financial assets held by cohorts over the
same period. Those who reach ages 60–64 seem to have the largest holdings of
financial assets. This would certainly reflect the fact that employee households
receive lump-sum retirement severance payments at around age 60.

The share of small savers among those who reach retirement age is shown
in table 3.19. Considering the amount of average annual expenditure by the
elderly (e.g., for ages over 80, 2.2 million yen in 1984 and 2.6 million yen in

---

13. In Japan net worth holdings classified by income class and employment status are less significantly distorted than classified by home ownership.

Table 3.16   **Net Worth by Home Ownership (10,000 yen)**

Year and Age	Total Mean	Total Median	Home-Owning Mean	Home-Owning Median	Tenant Mean	Tenant Median
1979						
0–24	438	201	1,379	1,160	190	166
25–29	636	355	1,373	1,213	273	237
30–34	899	559	1,538	1,343	320	286
35–39	1,177	961	1,625	1,427	375	321
40–44	1,399	1,152	1,790	1,500	422	352
45–49	1,687	1,368	2,017	1,645	434	369
50–54	1,995	1,607	2,276	1,835	526	419
55–59	2,192	1,732	2,458	1,988	624	469
60–64	2,269	1,804	2,543	1,986	631	415
65–69	2,310	1,856	2,630	2,138	473	334
70–74	2,495	1,769	2,759	2,030	516	292
75–79	2,365	1,715	2,654	2,004	381	242
80+	2,103	1,629	2,559	2,155	285	227
Average	1,483	1,142	1,994	1,610	378	303
1984						
0–24	625	243	2,174	1,806	223	196
25–29	845	407	2,055	1,826	339	304
30–34	1,352	798	2,319	2,004	428	368
35–39	1,804	1,361	2,496	2,102	453	405
40–44	2,211	1,832	2,731	2,286	494	422
45–49	2,543	2,097	2,946	2,430	592	473
50–54	2,870	2,379	3,253	2,695	649	492
55–59	3,478	2,813	3,775	3,034	691	473
60–64	3,807	3,041	4,192	3,395	681	504
65–69	3,772	3,095	4,185	3,440	723	543
70–74	3,569	2,944	3,882	3,257	658	457
75–79	3,656	2,953	4,044	3,173	459	384
80+	3,683	2,777	4,071	3,041	705	330
Average	2,456	1,916	3,141	2,537	483	388
1989						
0–24	726	242	3,128	2,073	271	203
25–29	1,283	442	3,761	2,368	361	328
30–34	1,964	804	3,786	2,441	485	419
35–39	2,747	1,544	3,939	2,565	578	476
40–44	3,431	2,149	4,288	2,831	650	496
45–49	4,070	2,641	4,747	3,213	723	504
50–54	4,569	2,913	5,203	3,455	829	520
55–59	5,366	3,306	5,894	3,740	954	594
60–64	5,829	3,746	6,287	4,093	993	648
65–69	5,799	3,574	6,326	4,022	913	566
70–74	6,148	3,591	6,730	3,926	764	643
75–79	7,079	3,789	8,046	4,847	782	505
80+	6,548	4,171	7,364	4,868	691	334
Average	4,025	2,349	5,129	3,262	611	444

Table 3.17   **Net Financial Assets by Home Ownership (10,000 yen)**

Year and Age	Total		Home-Owning		Tenant	
	Mean	Median	Mean	Median	Mean	Median
1979						
0–24	137	70	296	150	95	62
25–29	203	133	260	159	175	126
30–34	272	195	305	212	243	178
35–39	340	249	357	260	308	225
40–44	425	300	449	320	364	254
45–49	527	360	566	380	378	270
50–54	640	433	674	455	466	332
55–59	778	507	816	525	555	401
60–64	772	492	810	522	549	316
65–69	759	479	823	521	390	250
70–74	871	485	929	530	442	220
75–79	761	421	825	470	324	201
80+	677	310	785	377	245	200
Average	470	291	546	342	305	204
1984						
0–24	157	82	396	167	95	70
25–29	226	159	287	200	200	143
30–34	353	247	397	275	311	223
35–39	447	315	483	339	375	277
40–44	544	380	575	401	442	308
45–49	640	430	667	445	509	360
50–54	747	485	780	500	554	388
55–59	979	609	1,018	637	607	393
60–64	1,066	681	1,124	727	600	405
65–69	987	643	1,035	670	633	430
70–74	932	598	969	607	590	380
75–79	913	509	978	590	380	300
80+	876	500	910	578	620	269
Average	620	390	728	449	388	252
1989						
0–24	194	70	458	163	144	60
25–29	326	201	512	283	257	170
30–34	464	329	532	356	409	310
35–39	626	438	666	456	553	402
40–44	778	534	820	560	641	440
45–49	975	635	1,029	671	709	455
50–54	1,091	675	1,135	713	834	452
55–59	1,359	829	1,412	890	920	546
60–64	1,660	1,040	1,725	1,097	968	588
65–69	1,659	1,000	1,743	1,090	882	530
70–74	1,631	910	1,728	967	729	594
75–79	1,466	830	1,574	939	759	490
80+	1,561	840	1,687	966	662	315
Average	999	580	1,139	670	568	360

Table 3.18   **Net Housing Assets (10,000 yen)**

Year and Age	Total		Home-Owning	
	Mean	Median	Mean	Median
1979				
0–24	188	0	929	772
25–29	303	0	954	842
30–34	487	0	1,069	912
35–39	688	528	1,103	937
40–44	820	658	1,173	956
45–49	999	790	1,279	1,002
50–54	1,186	929	1,424	1,103
55–59	1,250	982	1,468	1,148
60–64	1,347	1,008	1,574	1,195
65–69	1,421	1,062	1,669	1,266
70–74	1,502	1,056	1,702	1,227
75–79	1,493	1,048	1,710	1,214
80+	1,335	1,066	1,670	1,303
Average	862	638	1,282	1,012
1984				
0–24	325	0	1,592	1,312
25–29	445	0	1,547	1,291
30–34	815	0	1,708	1,447
35–39	1,163	807	1,796	1,457
40–44	1,467	1,194	1,941	1,576
45–49	1,691	1,371	2,054	1,658
50–54	1,902	1,544	2,239	1,801
55–59	2,274	1,783	2,522	1,956
60–64	2,544	1,951	2,862	2,193
65–69	2,614	2,106	2,969	2,352
70–74	2,482	1,944	2,751	2,194
75–79	2,604	2,038	2,921	2,274
80+	2,673	1,980	3,020	2,193
Average	1,616	1,235	2,197	1,725
1989				
0–24	385	0	2,487	1,699
25–29	801	0	3,057	1,657
30–34	1,359	0	3,092	1,758
35–39	1,987	844	3,124	1,787
40–44	2,519	1,321	3,323	1,925
45–49	2,950	1,668	3,564	2,123
50–54	3,326	1,814	3,907	2,277
55–59	3,859	1,982	4,327	2,301
60–64	4,045	2,103	4,433	2,386
65–69	4,041	2,160	4,480	2,430
70–74	4,428	2,182	4,907	2,561
75–79	5,538	2,361	6,391	3,086
80+	4,919	2,365	5,604	3,167
Average	2,890	1,407	3,846	2,124

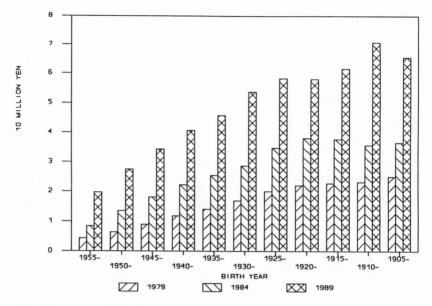

Fig. 3.9   Net worth by birth year (for all households)
Source: NSFIE for 1979, 1984, and 1989.

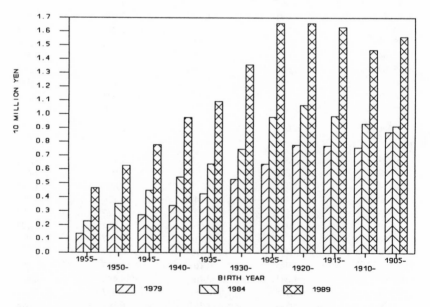

Fig. 3.10   Net financial assets by birth year (for all households)
Source: NSFIE for 1979, 1984, and 1989.

Table 3.19   **Share of Small Savers in the Elderly Population (%)**

Year and Age	Financial Assets Less Than 1 Million Yen			Financial Assets Less Than 3 Million Yen		
	Total	Home Ownership		Total	Home Ownership	
		Owner	Tenant		Owner	Tenant
1979						
55–59	11.1	10.6	13.9	32.3	31.2	39.1
60–64	10.3	9.0	17.7	32.9	30.6	46.3
65–69	10.8	8.9	21.5	33.2	29.1	56.6
70–74	10.9	8.2	31.3	36.5	33.6	57.9
75–79	15.0	13.0	29.4	39.4	34.3	74.0
80+	13.3	13.1	14.0	45.4	39.9	67.1
1984						
55–59	10.3	9.5	18.2	27.5	25.9	42.2
60–64	9.1	8.0	18.1	25.1	23.1	41.4
65–69	9.6	8.4	18.2	25.9	24.5	35.9
70–74	12.3	10.6	28.2	30.1	28.5	45.4
75–79	11.4	10.2	21.1	30.0	27.6	49.5
80+	17.7	16.9	23.2	41.2	39.4	55.1
1989						
55–59	8.6	7.3	19.1	20.3	18.4	36.4
60–64	6.0	5.3	13.6	14.8	13.7	26.8
65–69	4.7	4.1	10.8	15.4	14.1	27.5
70–74	5.2	4.4	12.1	16.9	15.5	30.8
75–79	6.7	5.1	17.5	19.8	17.6	33.9
80+	8.1	4.5	35.0	20.8	17.0	48.6

1989), financial assets of less than 3 million yen are by no means sufficient. In particular, a substantial portion of tenant households fall into the category with financial assets below 3 million yen. For those households, social security pension benefits are the major source of income. We will discuss this issue, in detail, in section 3.4.

3.3.6 Intergenerational Transfers

Increase in net worth over the life cycle of the cohort would draw a different picture from that of the age profile, from cross-sectional data, in figure 3.8. As discussed before, Hayashi, Ando, and Ferris (1988) argue that the prevalence of extended families makes the analysis of increase in net worth over the life cycle extremely difficult. The existence of extended families implies that there are two categories of older people: those still maintaining independent households (the independent elderly) and those living with children (the dependent elderly). It is the independent elderly only that enter the NSFIE sample. This creates sample selection bias. Hayashi, Ando, and Ferris (1988) present an innovative method to delete this bias by using only one data point in time (i.e., the 1984 NSFIE). In their method, increase in net worth brought about by the presence of older generations (intergenerational transfers) is inferred by the difference in income, consumption, and wealth between extended and nuclear families in the same age bracket (cohort).

We present an alternative method to infer intergenerational transfers by combining three data points in time (i.e., the 1979, 1984, and 1989 NSFIEs). Our method uses the following identity of wealth stock for cohort a at the end of year t:

(1) $W(a,t) = S(a,t) + TR(a,t) + (1 + \phi)W(a,t-1)$,

where W = wealth stock, S = flow savings on an asset increment basis,[14] TR = intergenerational transfers, and ϕ = the capital gains rate. Note that all capital income, such as interest and dividends, is included in disposable income, while capital gains are not included in the NSFIE. Note also that aggregate intergenerational transfers at the macroeconomic level cancel out to zero because they are mere transactions among the household sector. Rearranging equation (1) yields

(2) $TR(a,t) = dW(a,t, t-1) - S(a,t) - \phi W(a,t-1)$,

where $dW(a,t, t-1)$ = wealth stock change from year $t-1$ to year t. Given a fixed composition of wealth stock with respective capital gains rates and its change over years, intergenerational transfers can be calculated as a residual, if accumulated savings are obtained.

Suppose that the flow savings of each cohort grow at $100g$ percent per annum. Given the actual flow savings in the five-year interval, the annual growth rate (g) can be calculated as follows:

(3) $g = \frac{1}{5}[\log(S(a, t)) - \log(S(a, t-5))]$.

The five-year accumulated savings (A) are then given, using g from equation (3), by

(4) $A(a,t) = S(a,t-5)[(1 + g) + (1 + g)^2 + (1 + g)^3 + (1 + g)^4 + (1 + g)^5]$.

Reformulating equation (2) in terms of the five-year transfers,

(5) $TR(a,t, t-5) = dW(a, t, t-5) - A(a,t) - \phi W(a,t-5)$.

Equation (5) is the formula used for calculating intergenerational transfers. A positive value of TR means that, on average, the household receives wealth from other members of the family or from someone else, and a negative value

14. In order to estimate intergenerational transfers as accurately as possible, the concept of savings used here is statistically adjusted in the sense that service flows and depreciation of consumer durables, interest payments on loans, etc., are taken into account (see case 7 in Takayama 1992a, 173).

means that, on average, the household transfers wealth to other members of the family or to someone else.[15]

The results are reported in figures 3.11 and 3.12. As is evident from figure 3.11, the growth of net worth peaks at around ages 55–59, just before retirement, at which point transfers (receipts) from other generations start declining and transfers (by gifts or bequests) to younger generations increase. A similar story holds in figure 3.12, even though the growth of net worth peaks once at ages 55–59, then reaches a second peak at ages over 70. The second peak could be the result of strong sample bias.[16] Nevertheless, as for 1979–84, for 1984–89 intergenerational transfers become negative at around age 60. A noticeable feature in figure 3.12 is that wealth increases are made mainly through capital gains in this period. The younger generations around age 45 start receiving intergenerational transfers, although these remain small until around age 60.

Our method does not try to adjust sample selection bias[17] as discussed by Hayashi, Ando, and Ferris (1988). On the other hand, we combine three NSFIE data points in time; in so doing, increases in net worth over an extended period of time can be directly inferred. What we show, then, is that even independent elderly households, on average, transfer wealth to younger generations at ages over 60. The merged dependent elderly households would transfer more, as shown by Hayashi, Ando, and Ferris (1988). Our result can, therefore, be considered a complement to Hayashi, Ando, and Ferris (1988). In addition, considering the high level of wealth holdings at ages over 70 and the comparatively lower intergenerational transfers, the bulk of intergenerational transfers must take the form of bequests. This point is also made by Hayashi, Ando, and Ferris (1988) and supported by our empirical findings.

3.4 Social Security and Retirement Pensions

3.4.1 Social Security Pensions: Background

Public pensions are provided under six different programs in Japan. However, the benefit structures have all been similar since the most recent fundamental amendments became effective on April 1, 1986. Japan currently has a

---

15. It should be borne in mind that lump-sum retirement severance payments (which are transfers from employers) at around age 60 could be counted in intergenerational transfers because they are not treated as disposable income in the NSFIE. Unfortunately, the NSFIE cannot isolate lump-sum retirement severance payments from the wealth stock either, so intergenerational transfers could be, more or less, overestimated in our calculation at around age 60. However, this fact enforces, rather than offsets, our point that elderly households, in fact, transfer more wealth (in the form of gifts or bequests) to the younger generations than would appear to be the case from the values calculated from eq. (5).

16. We could not eliminate this bias by omitting samples as outliers when they are distributed outside 4σ (four times the standard deviation). The samples within 4σ seem to contain the elderly households with relatively high capital gains.

17. Takayama, Arita, and Kitamura (1994) discuss the problems arising from sample selection bias and the omission of single-person households from the sample.

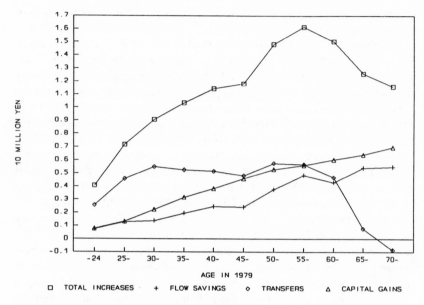

Fig. 3.11 Wealth increases from 1979 to 1984
Source: NSFIE for 1979 and 1984.

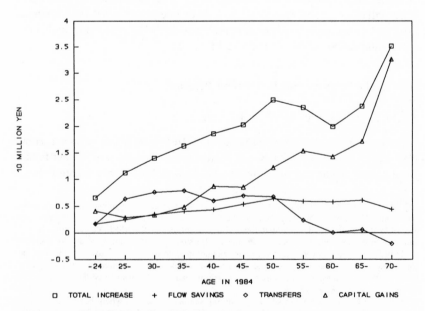

Fig. 3.12 Wealth increases from 1984 to 1989
Source: NSFIE for 1984 and 1989.

two-tier system of public pensions; the first tier, flat-rate basic benefits, covers all residents including self-employed and jobless persons. The second tier, earnings-related benefits, applies only to employees.

The full old-age pension is payable after 40 years of contributions. The maximum flat-rate basic benefit for the 1992 fiscal year was about 60,000 yen per month. The pension may be claimed at any age between 60 and 70. It is subject to actuarial reduction if claimed by self-employed or jobless persons before age 65 or to actuarial increase if claimed after age 65. The benefit is indexed automatically each fiscal year (as of April 1) to reflect changes in the consumer price index of the previous calendar year.

Earnings-related benefits are given to all employees. Under the KNH (Kosei Nenkin Hoken, the principal program for private-sector employees), the accrual rate for the earnings-related component of old-age benefits is 0.75 percent per year, in principle. Thus, 40-year contributions will earn 30 percent of the career average monthly real earnings. The full pension is payable starting at age 60 to an employee who is fully retired. From age 60, he or she can receive the full amount of benefits, including the flat-rate component, without any reductions. An individual who has reached age 60 but has not fully retired can receive a reduced pension. The earnings test is applicable only to those under age 65.

At present, KNH old-age benefits for the newly awarded "model" retiree (with an average salary earned for the average 35 years of coverage) and his dependent spouse (full-time housewife) were about 206,000 yen per month in 1991, replacing 68 percent of the average *monthly* earnings of currently active male workers.

In Japan, employees usually receive semiannual bonuses which typically amount to four or five months' salary, although in small companies they are often much smaller. Since these bonuses are not included in the earnings base for both public pension contributions and benefits, the replacement rate for the above-mentioned "model" retiree will be considerably lower, about 50 percent of the average *annual* earnings.

Needless to say, the labor income replacement rate varies with different income levels. The highest rate will be 180 percent (not the 68 percent stated above) for the minimum-salary earners (80,000 yen per month in 1992), while it will be the lowest, 53 percent, for employees at the earnings ceiling covered by the KNH (currently 530,000 yen per month in 1992).

Under the KNH, equal percentage contributions are required of employees and their employers. The total percentage in effect in 1991 was 14.5 percent.[18] The contribution rate of the KNH was initially set at 6.4 percent in 1942 and in 1944 was raised to 11.0 percent; it was reduced to 3.0 percent in 1948. The relatively low rate of 1948 has been gradually increased, and the current

18. The contribution rate of the KNH was 9.1 percent in 1979, 10.6 percent in 1984, and 12.4 percent in 1989.

contribution rate is expected to rise by 2.5 percent every five years, although this is not legally fixed.

Independent workers, the self-employed, and the jobless between ages 20 and 59 make flat-rate individual contributions to social security pensions. The rate as of April 1994 is 11,700 yen per month. It is scheduled to rise each fiscal year by 500 yen plus the increase in the consumer price index from the previous calendar year.[19]

3.4.2 Age-Contribution and Age-Recipiency Patterns of Social Security Pensions

Table 3.20 presents the age-contribution and age-recipiency patterns of social security pensions of Japan in 1984. It indicates that the mean and median of social security benefits per annum were about 1.40 million yen in 1984. Note that these figures include self-employed and jobless persons.

Figure 3.13 shows the 1989 distribution of annual public pension benefits for elderly couples only. The majority of them were retired salaried workers. On average, they were receiving benefits of about 2.4 million yen per annum. The present value of their total lifetime benefits would be near 60 million yen. Public pension benefits are the major source of income for the elderly and, overall, form a little over 50 percent of total income, though the share of public pension benefits in income varies with the current employment status of the household head and with his or her age (see table 3.21).[20]

3.4.3 Private Pensions

About 90 percent of private companies and institutions in Japan have occupational retirement benefit plans. Their benefits are usually paid as a lump sum. The average benefits paid to benefit-eligible male retirees were 20–24 million yen in large firms and 10–13 million yen in smaller ones in 1989.

Occupational retirement benefits in Japan are largely financed on a pay-as-you-go basis, and in general no contributions are required from employees.

Table 3.22 shows the marginal accrual rate of lump-sum retirement benefits and the labor income replacement rate in terms of final monthly salaries, too. It shows that the typical replacement rate is about 40 months for those with a lifetime of continuous employment.

The 90 percent coverage of occupational retirement benefit plans has remained unchanged. A growing number of contracted-out plans (e.g., Kosei Nenkin Kikin, employee pension funds) are rapidly being set up, which finance part of their retirement benefits on a fully funded basis.[21]

19. The contributions per month for nonemployees were 3,300 yen in 1979, 6,220 in 1984, and 8,000 in 1989. See Takayama (1992a, chap. 1) for a general description of public pension programs in Japan and Takayama (1994) for the 1994 government reform plan of the public pension system.
20. See Takayama and Arita (1992a, 1992b) and Takayama (1992a, chap. 2; 1993) for an economic profile of the elderly in current Japan.
21. Takayama (1993) gives a brief explanation of occupational pensions in Japan.

Table 3.20   **Annual Amount of Public Pension Benefits and Contributions (10,000 yen)**

	Benefits		Contributions	
Year and Age	Mean	Median	Mean	Median
1984				
0–24	5	0	13	12
25–29	7	0	15	14
30–34	10	0	16	15
35–39	12	0	17	16
40–44	12	0	19	17
45–49	12	0	20	19
50–54	14	0	22	22
55–59	41	0	22	22
60–64	110	80	78	7
65–69	142	140	6	0
70–74	144	131	6	0
75–79	146	136	6	0
80+	122	108	6	0
Average	32	0	17	16

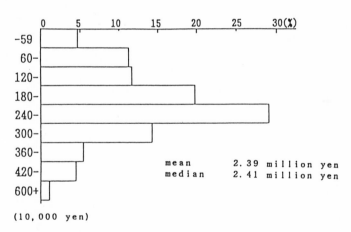

Fig. 3.13   Household distribution of annual public pension benefits
Source: NSFIE for 1989.
Notes: Figures for elderly couples only.

Private individual pensions have also been growing in Japan, though their coverage is still very small. This growth is mainly due to recent reforms in the tax treatment of individual pensions and to the introduction of the Kokumin Nenkin Kikin, a new scheme of individual pensions giving extremely generous tax advantages to nonemployee persons.[22]

22. See Ito and Kitamura (1994) for more details.

Table 3.21   Household Distribution by the Share of Public Pension Benefits in Income

	Share of Benefits in Annual Income (%)						Average Benefits	Average Annual Income
	0–19.9	20–39.9	40–59.9	60–79.9	80–99.9	100		
Age								
60–64	11.4	15.5	17.3	18.8	19.2	17.8	238	448
65–69	9.8	12.0	14.9	17.5	24.1	21.8	243	447
70–74	6.2	12.3	14.6	15.7	25.4	25.7	245	436
75+	5.1	9.4	14.4	14.8	23.4	32.8	226	346
Total	8.9	12.8	15.6	17.2	22.6	22.9	239	430
Average benefits	102	183	228	261	296	260	–	–
Average annual income	941	600	458	373	328	260	–	–
Head of household working	20.2	25.5	27.1	16.2	8.4	2.6	202	572
Nonworking couples	0.8	2.8	5.9	15.3	33.8	41.4	269	322

Source: NSFIE for 1989.

Notes: Figures are for elderly couples only. Units: average benefits and average annual income (10,000 yen), others (%).

Table 3.22   Marginal Accrual Rate of Lump-Sum Retirement Benefits

Continuing Years of Service	Lump-Sum Retirement Benefits (MSE)	Continuing Period of Service (years)	Marginal Accrual Rate (months)
Senior High School Graduates			
5	3.4	0–5	0.68
10	7.3	5–10	0.78
15	12.4	10–15	1.02
20	19.0	15–20	1.32
25	26.8	20–25	1.56
30	34.2	25–30	1.48
35	39.8	30–35	1.12
37	42.3	35–37	1.25
College and University Graduates			
5	3.2	0–5	0.64
10	7.2	5–10	0.80
15	12.2	10–15	1.00
20	18.8	15–20	1.32
25	26.4	20–25	1.52
30	34.3	25–30	1.58
33	38.2	30–33	1.30

Source: Central Labor Relation Board, 1991.

Notes: MSE = monthly salary equivalent. The survey from Central Labor Relation Board covers large employers with 1,000 or more employees.

There will probably be a big change in the Japanese public pension system in 1994. The social security wealth of each individual will be reduced by raising the normal retirement age (from 60 to 65) and/or by decreasing real levels of monthly benefits (by introducing *net* wage indexation in place of current *gross* wage indexation). These reforms will encourage household savings through private retirement saving programs, including occupational pensions.

3.5 Conclusion

This chapter presents a broad survey of microdata sources and microdata descriptions of the nature of household saving behavior in Japan. As the three NSFIE data sets are mines of information, the statistical materials we provide in this chapter are a very small portion of all the information available. It should be noted, however, that the NSFIEs are not free from statistical and conceptual difficulties. Nevertheless, all the chapters in this volume use the same definitions of income, consumption, and savings. International comparisons among the different countries can be done without further statistical adjustments.

In the course of data analysis, several interesting features of household saving behavior in Japan became clear:

1. Variations in saving behavior across different income classes are much wider than those over the age profile within the same income class.

2. As income grows and wealth accumulation increases, richer households save at increasingly high rates over the age profile.

3. Diversity of saving behavior among elderly households is much greater than among younger households, as their employment status, home ownership, and financial asset holdings differ substantially. The richer elderly households keep saving at significantly positive rates.

4. The above findings do not imply that intergenerational transfers occur only at the death of elderly household heads. With a careful analysis of the increase in net wealth by the cohort over time, the wealth formation process over the life cycle emerges clearly. The growth of net wealth peaks at ages 50–59, just before retirement (for 1984–89, the samples at ages over 70 include uncontrollable bias). At the same time, receipts of intergenerational transfers start declining and transfers of wealth to the next generation increase.

5. According to Noguchi (1990), thus far in Tokyo, those who have obtained their housing assets through bequests are small in number compared with those who have financed such purchases by themselves. The strong propensity of Japanese households to purchase their houses at an early stage of accumulated wealth has resulted in unexpected capital gains on home equity, thereby increasing their wealth holdings to quite high levels. As a result, inequality in wealth holdings between home owners and tenants and/or between home owners in high capital gain areas and those in low capital gain areas has worsened.

6. As society experiences a growing proportion of people over age 65, the

personal burden of medical costs is expected to increase and social security benefits to be reduced in coming years. Whether they like it or not, households will have to prepare for their expenditures after retirement. As far as the NSFIEs are concerned, dissavings by the elderly are unlikely to happen in Japan until the final stage, just before death, as is evident in this chapter.

Economic behavior over the life cycle can be analyzed directly by panel data. However, household panel data does not exist in Japan. The second-best approach, the one we have taken, is to combine different microsurveys in time and to examine the cohort effect. The more data points in time are available, the more detailed the cohort analysis can be. In particular, effects of structural changes over time, such as financial liberalization and the demographic change discussed by Takahashi and Kitamura (1994), can be analyzed by the microsurvey data both in cross section and in cohort time series, if the surveys can be combined over sufficiently long periods. In the case of the NSFIE, we have to accumulate survey data for the coming decades. Alternatively, we can combine the FIES with the NSFIE as a benchmark because, since the FIES is surveyed every year, the missing data for years between the NSFIE surveys can be filled. In any case, we believe that this type of approach can apply to various empirical and policy issues in future research.

References

Ando, A., L. Guiso, D. Terlizzese, and D. Dorsainvil. 1992. Saving among young households: Evidence from Japan and Italy. *Scandinavian Journal of Economics* 94(2): 233–50.

Ando, A., M. Yamashita, and J. Murayama. 1986. Analysis of the life cycle hypothesis of consumption and saving behavior (in Japanese). *Keizai Bunseki*, no. 101: 25–114.

Creedy, J. 1992. *Income, inequality and the life cycle.* Hampshire: Edward Elgar.

Hall, R. E., and F. S. Mishkin. 1982. The sensitivity of consumption to transitory income: Estimates from panel data on households. *Econometrica* 50(2): 461–81.

Hayashi, F., A. Ando, and R. Ferris. 1988. Life cycle and bequest savings: A study of Japanese and U.S. households based on data from the 1984 NSFIE and the 1983 Survey of Consumer Finances. *Journal of the Japanese and International Economies* 2:450–91.

Hayashi, F., T. Ito, and J. Slemrod. 1988. Housing finance imperfections, taxation, and private saving: A comparative simulation analysis of the United States and Japan. *Journal of the Japanese and International Economies* 2:215–38.

Horioka, C. Y. 1988. Saving for housing purchase in Japan. *Journal of the Japanese and International Economies* 2:351–84.

Ito, T., and Y. Kitamura. 1994. Public policies and household saving in Japan. In *Public policies and household saving,* ed. J. M. Poterba, 133–60. Chicago: University of Chicago Press.

Mizoguchi, T. 1992. Modern issues in national statistics of Japan (in Japanese). Tokyo: Iwanami Shoten.

Noguchi, Y. 1990. Household wealth and inheritance (in Japanese). In *The Japanese system of political economy,* ed. Contemporary Economy Study Group. Tokyo: Nihon Keizai Shinbun.

Pudney, S. 1989. *Modelling individual choice.* Oxford: Blackwell.

Seko, M. 1992. The stock economy and housing (in Japanese). In *Analysis of wealth accumulation in the Japanese economy,* ed. T. Ito and Y. Noguchi. Tokyo: Nihon Keizai Shinbun.

Statistics Bureau. 1991. *Japan statistical yearbook 1991.* Tokyo: Management and Co-ordination Agency.

Takahashi, W., and Y. Kitamura. 1994. Consumer behaviour in Japan under financial liberalisation and demographic change. In *The structure of the Japanese economy,* ed. M. Okabe, 135–67. London: Macmillan.

Takayama, N. 1992a. *The greying of Japan: An economic perspective on public pensions.* Tokyo: Kinokuniya; Oxford: Oxford University Press.

———. 1992b. *The stock economy* (in Japanese). Tokyo: Toyo-Keizai Shinposha.

———. 1993. Personal savings for retirement in Japan. Paper presented at the NBER-TCER Conference on Social Security and the Economic Well-Being of the Elderly at Hakone, Kanagawa, Japan, September.

———. 1994. The 1994 reform bill for public pensions in Japan: Its main contents and related discussion. Paper presented at the Seminar on Pension Reform and Social Vision of the Future for Japan and Sweden, Tokyo, Japan, April.

Takayama, N., F. Funaoka, F. Ohtake, M. Sekiguchi, and T. Shibuya. 1989. Household assets and the saving rate in Japan (in Japanese). *Keizai Bunseki,* no. 116 (September).

Takayama, N., and F. Arita. 1992a. Income, consumption and wealth of elderly singles in Japan (in Japanese). *Hitotsubashi Review* 107(6): 16–34.

———. 1992b. Income, consumption and wealth of elderly couples in Japan (in Japanese). *Keizai Kenkyu* 43(2): 158–78.

Takayama, N., F. Arita, and Y. Kitamura. 1994. Factors contributing to the wealth increase of the Japanese households (in Japanese). *Keizai Kenkyu* 45(1): 16–30.

1. The major surveys include the Family Income and Expenditure Survey (Designated Statistics,

4   Household Saving Behavior in the United Kingdom

James Banks and Richard Blundell

4.1 Introduction

The issues dealt with in this paper relate to the level and composition of savings among U.K. households over the past 20 years. Our previous paper (Banks and Blundell 1994) presented a detailed review of the incentives to save and the related policy experiments that occurred over this period. The intention of this study is to supplement that discussion with an assessment of the actual patterns of behavior.

Over this period different individuals have experienced quite different incentives and opportunities for saving, as well as different lifetime expectations and needs. To understand and reliably document saving behavior in the United Kingdom over the last two decades we therefore turn to microdata sources. However, we will assess the reliability of these sources by drawing on aggregate evidence to supplement the microanalysis wherever possible. Individual household data allow us to discriminate between the level and composition of saving according to type of individual or household. By using a long time series of survey data we are able to document saving profiles by different date-of-birth cohorts over this period and therefore capture the differing trends

James Banks is a program manager at the Institute for Fiscal Studies. Richard Blundell is research director at the Institute for Fiscal Studies and professor of economics at University College, London.

The authors are grateful for helpful discussions with many colleagues at the Institute for Fiscal Studies. The authors would particularly like to acknowledge Midge Clayton, Paul Johnson, Hamish Low, Costas Meghir, and Edward Whitehouse and the comments of Jonathan Skinner and the participants of the NBER conference on International Comparisons of Household Saving. Thanks are also due to NOP Corporate and Financial for use of the FRS data and the Department of Employment for use of the FES. Any errors or views expressed are entirely attributable to the authors. The support of the Economic and Social Research Council (ESRC) is gratefully acknowledged. The work is part of the programme of the ESRC Research Centre for Fiscal Policy (reference no. W100 28 1002).

in behavior mentioned above while avoiding the bias that is inherent in single cross-section analysis. Auerbach, Cai, and Kotlikoff (1990), among other studies, have emphasized the importance of cohort effects and the evolution of demographic profiles on savings projections. Our aim here is more modest and is simply to provide a description of the impact of these observed characteristics on observed consumption and saving behavior.

Our particular concern is to highlight the impact of changes in demographic status, retirement, and other aspects of labor market status on savings profiles and assess these in relation to standard life-cycle predictions. Evidence for strong interactions between savings, pensions, labor market status, and other characteristics can be found in a number of recent empirical studies. For example, Attanasio and Browning (1992) note the importance of demographic changes in models of consumption growth. This is also highlighted in the study of the consumption costs of children over the life cycle in Banks, Blundell, and Preston (1994). Labor market status is found to be a critical interaction in the Blundell, Browning, and Meghir (1994) study of nonretired households in the United Kingdom. Indeed its inclusion in a generalization of the standard Hall (1978) Euler equation of consumption and savings was shown to be sufficient to eliminate excess sensitivity to earned income.

When we include households with retired heads in the results reported below, there is a significant fall in consumption around the time of retirement. We find this can be partly explained by the anticipated fall in consumption costs associated with leaving the labor market. However, the fall in consumption more than matches the fall in income so saving remains positive. Hence the saving behavior of the retired is, on face value, somewhat puzzling. Carroll and Summers (1991) provide a catalogue of evidence suggesting that consumption tracks income more closely than the life-cycle model would predict. Our data analysis also picks out a rather close tracking for households around the time of retirement. The results suggest this cannot be attributed to anticipated changes in circumstances.

Skinner (1988, 1992) has provided some evidence for the United States that the degree of precautionary saving, especially in the 1970s, could explain the apparently myopic behavior of many households. Evidence on this topic for the United Kingdom is scarce and is beyond the scope of this paper, but the preliminary results in Banks, Blundell, and Brugiavini (1994) point to important effects of income uncertainty on consumption growth over the last two decades.

In summary then, as well as describing consumption, income, and saving patterns at the household level we will seek to answer a number of particular questions. These concern the degree to which perceived hump-shaped consumption and saving age profiles are caused by changes in demographic composition and a failure to account adequately for effects of the date of birth of the household when using time-series data. In addition we will investigate life-cycle profiles in household asset ownership and look in detail at how asset holdings change at or around the time of retirement. One area in which we will not be able to say too much, however, is the extent to which the consideration of housing and durable consumption can alter the conclusions drawn from microdata.

4.1.1   Data Sources

There is no single data source that collects all the information we require on asset levels, pension contributions, income sources, and consumption expenditures over this period, and we are forced to combine information from several data sources in this paper. However, our principal database—the U.K. Family Expenditure Survey—is able to document asset income, some pension income (and some contributions), consumption levels, and earnings levels for a detailed breakdown of household types. Moreover, it has been the centerpiece for a number of important studies of savings and consumption (see, e.g., Browning, Deaton, and Irish 1985; Attanasio and Weber 1989). At IFS it has also been the subject of a number of analyses concerning changes in individual pensions (see, e.g., Disney and Whitehouse 1992) as well as the focus for the study of the evolution of the income distribution and its relation to changes in the structure of the tax, welfare, and social security system. Its reliability in relation to both accuracy of records and aggregate grossing-up is also well documented in a number of studies (e.g., Kemsley, Redpath, and Holmes 1980; Atkinson, Micklewright, and Stern 1982). Section 4.2 provides a more detailed description of the data sources available in this area and presents some summary statistics regarding cross-sectional patterns of saving observed in a single year of Family Expenditure Survey data for comparability with the other papers of this volume.

In section 4.3 we deal with income and then expenditure profiles by age, paying particular attention to understanding how life-cycle demographic change may influence the resulting shapes.[1] In addition, we deal with issues regarding saving and wealth, particularly at and around the time of retirement; we talk specifically about retirement income in the United Kingdom in section 4.4. Section 4.5 concludes.

4.2   Cross-Sectional Patterns in Household Saving

The emphasis in this paper will be on a microeconomics-based savings analysis, and, for the United Kingdom as for most countries, complete household level data are less easily available than aggregate level data. However, in the United Kingdom, information on household consumption and incomes, at least, is good, although data on wealth and asset holdings are more difficult to obtain.

---

1. The interested reader should note that all values are expressed in 1987 prices unless otherwise stated and a description of our main data set—the cohort aggregated FES is given in Appendix A.

4.2.1   The Family Expenditure Survey

The Family Expenditure Survey (FES) is the primary U.K. microeconomic data source—providing detailed information on the characteristics, expenditures, and incomes of about 7,000 households per year. The FES has been collected on a (reasonably) consistent basis since 1969, and in much of what follows we will use the full 22 years (over 150,000 observations) to identify life-cycle patterns in consumption and income. Consumption information is collected by a two-week diary covering all purchases; there is information on usual earnings and last monthly earnings as well as on tax payments and benefit levels. There is no top-coding in the survey but a number of studies (e.g., Atkinson and Micklewright 1983; Pissarides and Weber 1989) have found that the reporting of incomes by both high-earning households and the self-employed can be unreliable. For this reason many studies trying to look into the income distribution in the United Kingdom (and indeed the official statistics on incomes) have matched income data from the Survey of Personal Incomes (SPI) for the top half-percentile (see Giles and Webb 1993; Department of Social Security [DSS] 1992).

A further household-level survey provides detailed information about particular aspects of household decision making. As such the General Household Survey (GHS) can provide detailed information on retirement or health, for example, for one year only in addition to a small core of questions relating to income consumption and demographics that facilitate linking the GHS to other years and other surveys (see Office of Population Censuses and Surveys [OPCS] 1992).

To supplement our discussion of pensions and asset wealth around the point of retirement we use the Retirement Survey (see Bone et al. 1992), which was carried out in 1988 and interviewed only individuals at or around retirement age. The survey covers just over 3,500 individuals between the ages of 55 and 69 and provides detailed coverage of pensions, work histories, saving, and health that we will refer to in section 4.5 below.

The FES has no serious top-coding or censoring problems apart from the above-mentioned underrepresentation of high-income households. The extent of this has varied from year to year and has affected the way in which the FES totals match aggregate figures themselves. Attanasio and Weber (1992) show that in the late 1980s income growth in the FES is greater than that in the national accounts, while both series exhibit consumption growth. Thus the FES does not display the large drop in the saving ratio that is thought to have occurred in the United Kingdom between 1986 and 1989. The reason given for this is an increase in the representation of high-income households in the survey, generating high average income growth from one year to the next but not being reflected in equivalent increases in consumption.[2] In the past, FES num-

---

2. Indeed the representation of high incomes in 1987–88 was such that from 1988 to 1989 there was no observed average income growth in the FES.

bers have typically been grossed-up to national totals with regard to household types only. The above scenario suggests that some kind of income distribution grossing-up factors could be important in recent years. Given the nature and scope of this paper, however, we choose not to pursue the issue of grossing-up any further. Instead in the cross-sectional analysis that follows we concentrate on sample statistics that are unadjusted for the prevalence of either demographic groups or income groups in the U.K. population as a whole.

In contrast to the above, wealth data at the household level are scarce in the United Kingdom. Indeed, apart from some questions regarding wealth at time of retirement in the retirement survey, no public-use data exist that facilitate household-level analysis of total (either housing or nonhousing) wealth. An analysis by Saunders and Webb (1988) utilized a private survey of financial wealth of U.K. households. We have managed to obtain a summary of the microdata from this survey for the period 1988–92 and will give some brief evidence of financial wealth profiles from this data set for 1990. The Financial Research Survey (FRS)[3] is a cross-sectional survey of about 40,000 individuals per year which asks detailed questions regarding holdings of financial assets. Of these individuals, approximately 10 percent are called back to answer questions regarding the value of their asset holdings. It is this "value data" sample (7,162 households in 1990) that we will draw on briefly in this paper.

In most of what follows we will use the FES from 1969 to 1990 to describe income and consumption profiles by age—occasionally drawing on other data sources for comparison. We construct a time series of cross sections from 1969 to 1990 FES data to estimate "pseudocohort" models for consumption. This model uses over 152,000 household observations over the 22-year period to identify age and cohort effects in life-cycle profiles. We construct annual averages over cohorts defined by the date of birth of the head of the household (falling in five-year bands). See the appendix for details of the cohort aggregation.

4.2.2   Cross-Sectional Saving Patterns in 1990

In the following section we present cross-sectional saving profiles from the most recent year of FES data available for comparison with similar data from the other countries in this volume. Tables 4.1 and 4.2 present medians of income, expenditure, and saving by age of the head of the household and by income quartile, respectively. Income is defined as total net-of-tax weekly income of the household (1990 prices), not including any imputed income from owner occupation of housing or capital gains on financial assets; our definition of expenditure (for this section at least) relates to all purchases, including durable and housing expenditures. Saving is defined as the residual between income and expenditure, and in addition we provide two measures of the saving rate—using both income and expenditure as the denominator.

---

3. The FRS is carried out privately by National Opinion Polls (NOP) Corporate and Financial.

Table 4.1   Median Saving by Age (£ per week, 1990 prices)

Age of Head	Income	Expenditure	Saving	Saving/ Income	Saving/ Expenditure	N
<25	164.64	172.92	2.70	0.02	0.02	346
25–29	244.81	208.37	16.24	0.08	0.09	658
30–34	251.62	226.76	14.91	0.08	0.08	686
35–39	273.45	238.24	30.27	0.12	0.14	672
40–44	317.29	285.08	28.17	0.12	0.13	676
45–49	326.43	288.02	32.13	0.11	0.13	567
50–54	295.62	258.33	18.54	0.10	0.11	491
55–59	239.92	209.33	22.04	0.13	0.15	514
60–64	181.24	176.68	7.02	0.06	0.06	537
65–69	131.10	141.71	1.25	0.02	0.02	603
70+	91.21	90.55	7.30	0.09	0.10	1,292
All	217.01	195.44	12.28	0.09	0.09	7,042

Source: FES for 1990.

Table 4.2   Median Saving by Income Quartile (£ per week, 1990 prices)

Quartile of Income	Income	Expenditure	Saving	Saving/ Income	Saving/ Expenditure	N
1	75.45	91.78	−7.88	−0.10	−0.09	1,765
2	190.32	172.40	4.53	0.03	0.03	1,760
3	281.89	229.10	28.68	0.13	0.15	1,763
4	441.90	332.27	97.93	0.24	0.32	1,754
All	217.01	195.44	12.28	0.09	0.09	7,042

Source: FES for 1990.

As one might expect there are systematic differences in saving, both by income and by age. Median saving is negative for the bottom quartile of income but rises to a rate of 24 percent of income in the top quartile. Median saving in the whole sample is 9 percent of income (some 12 pounds per week). The corresponding ratio from the aggregate statistics for 1990 was 9.9 percent for the period January–June and 7.6 percent for July–December. When broken down by age, the main feature of this cross-sectional data is the hump-shaped profile of both income and earnings. Median saving, however, is positive in all old-age bands despite the fact that income falls rapidly for retired households. These profiles also present a rather surprising feature. The "very old" households (ages 70+) save more than the households of around retirement age. We will return to this later to establish whether this is purely a date-of-birth cohort effect or a more general life-cycle pattern of saving in the United Kingdom. Saving rates fall to 2 percent at retirement age and then rise to 9 or 10 percent for those households over age 70.

The size of the FES sample also facilitates a more detailed breakdown of the three measures of saving—by age and income simultaneously. In tables 4.3, 4.4, and 4.5 we construct quartiles of income conditional on the age band of the head of the household and compute cell medians for the level of saving and the saving rate. The broad income and age trends apparent in the single-variable breakdown above are maintained even with this more disaggregate analysis. Saving increases for the oldest households in all quartiles. Indeed it is only in the 70+ age group that households in the (age-conditional) bottom quartile of income actually have a positive median saving rate.

Table 4.3   **Median Saving by Quartile of Income, Conditional on Age**

	Quartile of Household Income				
Age of Head	1	2	3	4	Quartile Cell Size
<25	−15.27	−3.48	10.66	58.02	86
25–29	−22.41	12.24	65.71	122.94	164
30–34	−17.16	1.88	40.36	139.88	170
35–39	−15.14	14.00	60.99	138.66	168
40–44	−16.71	16.84	62.03	147.94	168
45–49	−7.12	22.06	50.67	120.13	141
50–54	−8.28	27.43	29.19	139.12	122
55–59	−7.32	5.05	55.37	137.95	128
60–64	−6.09	−3.95	29.39	93.15	134
65–69	−3.94	−6.38	−4.06	47.40	150
70+	1.84	0.39	9.79	46.75	323
All	−7.88	4.53	28.68	97.93	1,754

Source: FES for 1990.

Table 4.4   **Median Saving/Income by Quartile of Income, Conditional on Age**

	Quartile of Household Income				
Age of Head	1	2	3	4	Quartile Cell Size
<25	−0.25	−0.03	0.06	0.18	86
25–29	−0.25	0.06	0.23	0.32	164
30–34	−0.19	0.00	0.15	0.31	170
35–39	−0.13	0.06	0.19	0.29	168
40–44	−0.11	0.06	0.18	0.25	168
45–49	−0.07	0.08	0.13	0.20	141
50–54	−0.06	0.11	0.09	0.25	122
55–59	−0.09	0.03	0.20	0.28	128
60–64	−0.08	−0.03	0.12	0.23	134
65–69	−0.07	−0.06	−0.03	0.17	150
70+	0.04	0.00	0.09	0.19	323
All	−0.10	0.03	0.13	0.24	1,754

Source: FES for 1990.

Table 4.5   **Median Saving/Expenditure by Quartile of Income, Conditional on Age**

Age of Head	Quartile of Household Income				
	1	2	3	4	Quartile Cell Size
<24	−0.20	−0.03	0.06	0.22	86
25–29	−0.20	0.06	0.31	0.46	164
30–34	−0.16	0.00	0.17	0.44	170
35–39	−0.12	0.07	0.24	0.41	168
40–44	−0.10	0.06	0.21	0.33	168
45–49	−0.07	0.09	0.15	0.24	141
50–54	−0.05	0.12	0.10	0.34	122
55–59	−0.08	0.03	0.25	0.39	128
60–64	−0.07	−0.03	0.13	0.30	134
65–69	−0.07	−0.06	−0.03	0.21	150
70+	0.04	0.00	0.10	0.24	323
All	−0.09	0.03	0.15	0.32	1,754

Source: FES for 1990.

Evidence about household wealth accumulation (both financial assets and housing wealth) is scarce. Indeed, in the absence of mandatory tax returns for basic-rate tax payers, even official statistics at the aggregate level are sparse and computed under very specific assumptions. In what follows we use the FRS for the calendar year 1990 to provide the age and income profiles corresponding to those above from the FES. The FRS data contain asset values for all individual holdings in banded values. Although we hope to use these data extensively in the future, in the current paper we are simply able to give some idea of the extent of wealth holdings by presenting median asset value bands by age, income, and housing tenure. It is beyond the scope of this paper to attribute expected values of holdings to individuals conditional on the band in which they are observed, but we do provide some initial evidence regarding some important financial assets.

Tables 4.6, 4.7, and 4.8 show how holdings and values of three widely held financial assets change with income, age, and household tenure type, respectively, in the 1990 FRS cross section. Building society accounts are by far the most widely held of these three instruments, with almost 70 percent of the survey holding an account. Such accounts always pay interest, although there are a range of interest rate–liquidity combinations available from most building societies. Bank deposit (or "time") accounts are less common, although the take-up rate is still about one-third. Consequently the median values for all households (not conditional on holding the asset) are zero in all age and income groups. This is also the case for equity, which is held only very sparsely in U.K. households (despite the attempts to promote wider share ownership in the late 1980s). It is important to emphasize that it is not possible to add up across asset holdings for each income (or age) band since the median band is

Table 4.6   **Median Asset Value Bands by Band of Household Income**

Income Band (thousand £)	Building Society Account (1)	(2)	(3)	Bank Deposit Account (1)	(2)	(3)	Equity (1)	(2)	(3)
None	67.9	1–100	501–1,000	35.1	0	201–500	14.2	0	101–200
<2.5	58.3	1–100	501–1,000	38.5	0	201–500	8.3	0	101–200
2.5–4.5	58.2	1–100	501–1,000	33.9	0	101–200	10.1	0	1–100
4.5–6.5	62.2	1–100	501–1,000	30.1	0	201–500	11.5	0	101–200
6.5–7.5	69.8	201–500	501–1,000	30.6	0	201–500	14.2	0	101–200
7.5–9.5	67.1	101–200	501–1,000	35.6	0	201–500	17.7	0	1–100
9.5–11.5	69.0	101–200	501–1,000	31.7	0	201–500	15.9	0	101–200
11.5–13.5	72.7	201–500	501–1,000	29.5	0	201–500	17.7	0	1–100
13.5–15.5	72.1	201–500	501–1,000	30.3	0	201–500	18.4	0	101–200
15.5–17	76.2	201–500	501–1,000	32.8	0	501–1,000	19.1	0	101–200
17–25	79.5	201–500	501–1,000	34.0	0	201–500	22.8	0	101–200
25+	78.6	501–1,000	501–1,000	36.5	0	501–1,000	32.3	0	201–500
Refused	65.2	101–200	501–1,000	33.2	0	201–500	12.9	0	101–200
All	69.7	101–200	501–1,000	33.6	0	201–500	16.9	0	101–200

Source: FRS for 1990.
Note: Col. (1) for each asset gives the proportion of the group holding at least one of that asset. Col. (2) gives the median asset band for all individuals in the group. Col. (3) gives the median asset band for those individuals that hold the asset. All values are in 1990 prices.

Table 4.7   **Median Asset Value Bands by Age Band**

Age Band	Building Society Account (1)	(2)	(3)	Bank Deposit Account (1)	(2)	(3)	Equity (1)	(2)	(3)
<25	67.5	1–100	101–200	33.3	0	101–200	8.4	0	1–100
25–29	72.0	1–100	201–500	27.2	0	101–200	12.2	0	101–200
30–34	72.2	101–200	201–500	27.3	0	201–500	16.2	0	101–200
35–39	72.0	101–200	201–500	31.1	0	201–500	18.9	0	201–200
40–44	71.3	201–500	501–1,000	36.8	0	201–500	17.8	0	101–200
45–49	65.8	201–500	501–1,000	38.7	0	201–500	20.6	0	101–200
50–54	68.0	201–500	1,000–2,000	38.3	0	501–1,000	22.1	0	101–200
55–59	68.5	201–500	1,000–2,000	38.1	0	501–1,000	24.6	0	101–200
60–64	72.6	501–1,200	2,000–5,000	37.5	0	501–1,000	22.8	0	101–200
65–69	68.2	501–1,200	2,000–5,000	34.7	0	501–1,000	21.1	0	101–200
70+	65.0	201–500	1,000–2,000	35.0	0	501–1,000	13.5	0	101–200
All	69.7	101–200	501–1,000	33.6	0	201–500	16.9	0	101–200

Source: FRS for 1990.
Note: See table 4.6 note.

Table 4.8   Median Asset Value Bands by Tenure Type

Tenure Type	Building Society Account			Bank Deposit Account			Equity		
	(1)	(2)	(3)	(1)	(2)	(3)	(1)	(2)	(3)
Other	58.3	1–100	201–500	34.6	0	101–200	7.6	0	1–100
Mortgage	72.0	101–200	501–1,000	31.8	0	201–500	18.7	0	101–200
Owner	73.1	501–1,000	1,000–2,000	37.1	0	501–1,000	22.3	0	101–200
All	69.7	101–200	501–1,000	33.6	0	201–500	16.9	0	101–200

Source: FRS for 1990.
Note: See table 4.6 note.

computed conditional on the income (or age) band and will not in general correspond to the same individual for any two types of assets.

The major feature of table 4.6 is the increasing presence of equity in the portfolios of rich households, as might be expected. Another feature, however, is that, for those households that hold a building society account, the amount in the account does not appear to depend very heavily on income. The increase in the overall median band (col. [2]) is accounted for instead by an increasing proportion of individuals holding the asset. Table 4.7 shows different patterns of these asset balances by age. The median value band of building society accounts increases with age, but in this case it is the value, not the incidence, which increases as households get older.

Table 4.7 could be seen as presenting some (albeit cross-sectional) evidence for dissaving as households retire. Both holdings and values of building society accounts decline in the last two age bands, and holdings of equity also fall rapidly for older individuals.

The final breakdown of assets is by household tenure and presented in table 4.8. Unsurprisingly this shows the high correlation between owning a house and holding financial assets—with owner-occupiers without mortgages having the highest incidence and the highest values of all three asset types.

In this section we have presented cross-sectional profiles for saving and asset holdings in the United Kingdom in 1990. The main features that emerged were a distinct hump-shaped pattern in both income and expenditure, and a peculiar savings puzzle for retired households. In many age groups behavior appears to be as one might expect, with the exception of those households well into their retirement who have higher saving than we might expect. In terms of asset holdings, although we presented banded data for a single cross section, these data show distinct patterns both over age and income for the extensive and intensive margins for a number of different financial assets. The extent to which these patterns remain once cohort effects are separated from life-cycle effects can only be assessed with data that display both time-series and cross-sectional variation, to which we turn in the next section.

4.3   Evidence from a Time Series of Cross Sections

4.3.1   Income

In this section we present age profiles of real household income. The nature of earnings profiles for the United Kingdom is quite well known—we present results for completeness from a pooled cross section. Capital income and pension contribution/income profiles are less readily available, and we will need to draw on other resources to identify household-level effects.

Earnings

At the household level we can construct cohort earnings patterns using the time series of FES data. (A description of the cohort definitions and cell sizes used throughout this report is given in the appendix.) Figure 4.1 shows log earnings for the head and second adult, combined over the life cycle. The figure plots cohort cell medians[4] against the average age of the head of household, joining each cohort with a separate line (alternately thick and thin). As we have 22 years of data there are some ages at which we observe four different cohorts. This allows us, to some extent, to distinguish visually between cohort, age, and business-cycle effects. At any particular age a vertical difference between two lines shows a "cohort" or generational effect—different cohorts experience differing circumstances at the same stage in their lives. If we follow one line, however, we can see the time series for that particular cohort—this path will indicate a combination of business-cycle and life-cycle effects. A macroshock that hits everybody equally will show up at the same point on each cohort profile, i.e., not at the same age.

The high earnings/income growth in the FES since 1987 is clearly evident—with successive cohorts becoming significantly richer than their predecessors. It is also clear that, despite this, the single cross-section patterns tabulated in section 4.2 are strongly affected by cohort effects—the last point on each line in figure 4.2 corresponds to the 1990 Age-Earnings Profile in the FES. However, for each cohort, earnings do not fall over the lifetime until people in the cohort begin to retire. Hump-shaped earnings profiles are artificially generated by looking at a single year of data. Indeed, from now on we will use the full 22-year FES data set to identify profiles, since we believe it is necessary to control for cohort effects in almost all the analyses that follows.

Capital Income

The best estimate we are able to make of household capital income comes again from the FES. We construct the sum of rent from property, interest from

4. Given the discussion of income growth and the matching of national aggregates in the FES in the late 1980s we have used median earnings by age and cohort in this figure to try and reduce the impact of outlying observations. In all the other figures that follow, we present cell means.

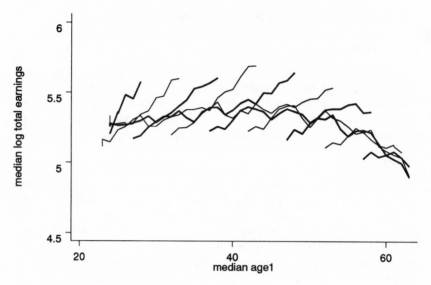

Fig. 4.1　Earnings by age and cohort

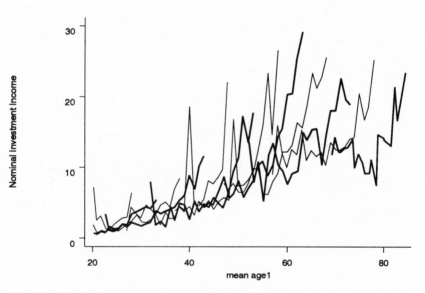

Fig. 4.2　Nominal investment income by age and cohort

savings accounts, interest and dividends from stocks, gilts, and shares (gross), and bank/building society interest (again gross). These data display both life-cycle and cohort effects as seen in figure 4.2.

In an extremely ad hoc way we try to index these gains to inflation,[5] since for much of the first half of our sample there were negative real interest rates in the United Kingdom. Figure 4.3 shows an approximate measure of real capital income by cohort and age. The older cohorts made capital losses in the 1970s—when U.K. households were saving despite the (ex post) adverse conditions. This is particularly the case for the oldest three cohorts who were at or around retirement age at this time and had, possibly, larger amounts of wealth than at other times in their life cycle. Younger cohorts have experienced rising positive capital incomes. It is worth remembering that these incomes are still incomes before tax since we have used a "gross" interest rate—the three-month Treasury Bill rate—to construct these asset income profiles.

In the absence of a panel-data survey, and given the exact nature of the financial questions in the FES, there is very little way of adding to these figures an estimate of realized capital gains, since we can never reliably know the purchase value of the asset in question.

Pensions

The analysis of pension contributions and payments is complicated in the United Kingdom by the number of regimes in which employees can choose to be. If employees take no action at all regarding pensions they will, by default, pay National Insurance contributions which will entitle them to the basic state pension plus an earnings-related element (through SERPS—the State Earnings Related Pension Scheme). In this sense many pension contributions are simply proportional to earnings (subject to the upper and lower earnings limit), and pension receipts are also proportional in some way to earnings (although again there is a fixed basic minimum). However, employees can choose to "contract out" of SERPS, in which case these profiles will change. These contracts can be occupational pension schemes or (since 1986) private pension plans, or both. Occupational schemes have had a coverage of about one-half the working population over our entire sample period and are the most relevant to this study. Personal pensions, while having had an enormously rapid take-up (see Disney and Whitehouse 1992) are really too new to facilitate reliable analysis of contribution structures (it is, of course, much too early to model payment profiles, as the majority of schemes will not begin to be redeemed until at least 2015). At the present time the take-up of personal pensions in the United Kingdom is well documented, but values and contributions remain to

5. For the purpose of this exercise we simply impute capital values as income divided by nominal interest rate (we use the three-month treasury bill rate) and then recalculate them by the same interest rate indexed by a Stone price index calculated at the household level. We use the Stone deflator throughout, although similar results are obtained using the standard aggregate price index (RPI).

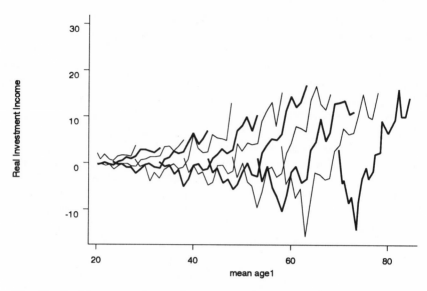

Fig. 4.3   Real investment income by age and cohort

be analyzed (although Personal Pension Plan contributions are included in the FES from 1991 onward).

While the number of individuals with occupational pensions has remained roughly constant over the last 20 years, contributions to such pension funds are proportional to income, so trends in contributions may be apparent. In addition, the majority of occupational pensions in the United Kingdom are such that the employee has little or no choice over whether to contract out and what proportion of their income to put into the scheme. However, there are no data from a single source that can reliably shed light on such issues, so in what follows we prefer to cite the work of Richard Disney and Edward Whitehouse who have concentrated on the detailed merging of all available household-level information on pensions in the United Kingdom.

Table 4.9 shows proportions of individuals currently contributing into occupational pension schemes by age and decile of earnings. Data are for all males and females and are drawn from the 1990–91 GHS. The overall take-up rate of occupational pensions is 49.86 percent, and as might be expected, the incidence of contributions rises uniformly, both with earnings and age. Occupational pensions, however, are not portable, and consequently contributions now will not always imply a significant stream of postretirement benefits for that individual. Indeed there appears to be evidence of a substantial "expectations gap" for U.K. households as they approach retirement. Disney and Whitehouse (1993) have linked 22 years of FES data to the GHS and data from the Government Actuary to estimate accrued occupational pension rights in the United Kingdom in 1987. They computed the expected value of the pension at the

Table 4.9   **Occupational Pensions by Age and by Earnings**

	Proportion Contributing (%)
Age	
20–24	28.23
25–29	48.67
30–34	53.73
35–39	52.35
40–44	56.13
45–49	57.70
50–54	58.50
55–59	55.89
60–64	61.76
Decile	
1	4.63
2	14.14
3	23.93
4	40.30
5	51.88
6	62.95
7	67.33
8	73.80
9	79.22
10	80.45

Source: GHS for 1990–91.

normal (scheme-specific) retirement age conditional on the individual's expected duration within the scheme (calculated from a job tenure model). These results are presented in table 4.10 (values are discounted to 1987 prices). The table shows clearly that current occupational pension contributions for young men and especially women will not lead to large flows of retirement income due to the high probability of a change in job tenure. Such a change in job tenure would lead to the accumulation in the fund being frozen until retirement (although in the United Kingdom such preserved benefits are indexed at least with inflation by law).

A recent study by Johnson (1992) explored many issues concerning the incomes of those in retirement. Occupational pension *receipts* by cohort and sex are reproduced as table 4.11. This evidence (also calculated from the 1970–90 FES and reported at 1989 prices) shows clear cohort effects on pension receipts for men and single women. Additionally, Johnson (1992) documents the distribution of payments by year; both the 25th percentile and the median have risen—from £9 to about £13 and from £25 to £35, respectively—but there has been a massive increase in the upper quartile point from £50 to £90 per week. A good deal of the increase in the average occupational pension by cohort is therefore attributed to rapid growth in the largest pensions, while many occupational pension payments have remained quite low.

Table 4.10   Accrued Pension Rights by Age and Sex, 1987

	Men			Women		
Age	Number (million)	Amount (billion £)	Average (£)	Number (milion)	Amount (billion £)	Average (£)
< 24	0.57	3.0	5,200	0.70	2.3	3,400
24–34	1.86	23.6	12,700	1.11	11.2	10,120
34–44	1.95	61.0	31,300	0.84	13.1	15,710
45–54	1.65	66.5	40,300	0.78	20.2	26,010
55–65	0.92	37.6	40,900	0.26	10.1	39,100

Source: Disney and Whitehouse (1993).

Table 4.11   Average Occupational Pension Receipts by Cohort and Sex
                            (£ per week)

Date of Birth	Men	Married Women	Single Women
1990–04	40	–	–
1905–09	45	34	30
1910–14	44	29	36
1915–20	57	29	35
1920–24	65	29	40
1925–29	–	29	47

Source: Johnson (1992).

4.3.2   Consumption

In this section we start by constructing consumption (or more specifically expenditure) profiles for all goods and for all goods excluding housing and durables. Both total expenditure and nondurable expenditure display hump-shaped profiles, and age effects seem to be far more important than cohort effects in determining the profiles from FES data. As visual evidence of this figure 4.4 presents age profiles of the log of nondurable expenditure. The life-cycle pattern appears to be extremely well defined for all date-of-birth cohorts. Business-cycle effects (or any noise in the data) seem to be much less prevalent than in our previous earnings plots. (On this basis we will follow many studies and try to infer as much as possible about saving behavior from consumption information and demographics alone.)

With an apparent absence of strong cohort effects we can also present raw means by age band of the 22 years of real expenditure data for both total expenditure and nondurable nonhousing expenditure. Both expenditure profiles display humps by age, with the maximum being 136 percent of the mean for total expenditure and 140 percent for nondurable expenditure. Nondurable expenditure as a proportion of total expenditure by age band varies from 73 to 76 percent for the nonretired; this ratio varies between 70 and 73 percent for retired age groups.

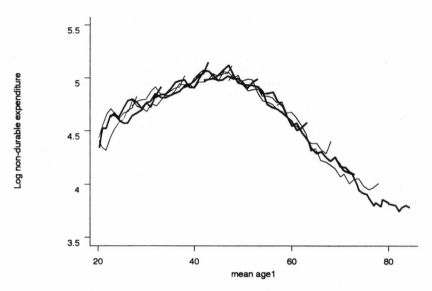

Fig. 4.4   Nondurable expenditure by age and cohort

In table 4.12 we use the adult-equivalence scales for children of McClements (1977)[6] to construct the "equivalized" expenditure columns. These profiles prove to be significantly flatter (rising to only 117 percent of the mean at their highest point). This finding (see Banks, Blundell, and Preston 1994 for more detail) is indicative of the theme of much of the recent literature on microeconomic consumption behavior in the United Kingdom—that demographics (especially children and labor market status) explain a large proportion of the life-cycle hump in consumption. Blundell, Browning, and Meghir (1994) find these variables to be particularly important in determining the intertemporal elasticity of substitution or a consumption Euler equation for 1970–86 data. We summarize the effect of equivalizing expenditure graphically in figure 4.5.

This figure corresponds exactly to figure 4.4 apart from the fact that we have plotted equivalent nondurable expenditure over the life cycle. As the two graphs are on the same scale, it can be clearly seen that equivalizing raises the incomes of young households and significantly smooths out the hump-shaped profile. However, cohort effects begin to become apparent at the end of the sample (this is even more the case when using housing and durable expenditures as well), and this reflects strong cohort effects in the demographics by which we are equivalizing expenditures (see fig. 4.9 below).

Incidentally these cohort plots can also show the series of expenditures over time rather than age of the head (although these patterns are fundamentally

---

6. These scales, although far from uncontroversial, are those used in the official statistics on poverty and income distribution. Under these sets of adult/child relativities, the base household is a married couple with no children (see Banks and Johnson 1993 for a fuller analysis of the effects of using different scales).

Table 4.12   Expenditure by Age (£ per week, 1987 prices)

Age Band	Total Expenditure	Total Nondurable Expenditure	Equivalent Total Expenditure	Equivalent Nondurable Expenditure
< 25	148.16	108.26	149.02	108.16
25–29	174.60	127.55	163.60	118.40
30–34	190.11	139.01	158.45	114.91
35–39	208.87	154.13	158.87	116.27
40–44	229.50	173.48	168.34	126.16
45–49	236.06	180.10	175.82	132.70
50–54	220.12	166.20	178.52	133.05
54–59	190.54	141.54	170.68	125.08
60–64	155.07	113.38	152.34	109.93
65–69	120.85	86.86	127.51	90.58
70–74	101.04	73.32	113.80	81.45
74+	82.99	58.17	100.31	70.27
All	173.01	127.95	151.76	110.73

Source: FES for 1969–90.

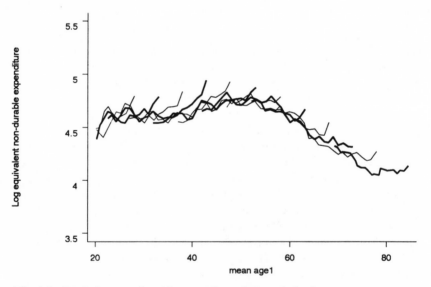

Fig. 4.5   Equivalent nondurable expenditure by age and cohort

inherent in the age plots anyway). Figure 4.6 shows time-series plots of expenditure and income from 1969 to 1990 for a single cohort of our sample that is observed for the entire period (those born between 1930 and 1934). The divergence between income and consumption for this cohort in the FES over recent years is clear.

Apart from the "pure" demographic effects on preferences and needs, how-

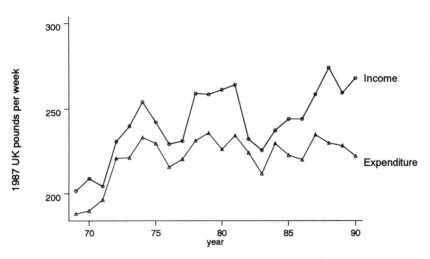

Fig. 4.6   Income and expenditure by year: households with head born in 1930–34

ever, the issue of adjusting for household size is important when comparing any U.K. microdata over the last 20 years, since this period has seen a change in the structure of households. The number of "small" households (with one or two people) has risen from about 50 percent to more than 60 percent of the total number of households in the FES (see Banks and Johnson 1993). This is a significant change and must be borne in mind whenever one compares any long time series of U.K. microdata.

Home Ownership

Unfortunately, little is known about the composition of home-purchase payments themselves in the United Kingdom. The advent of the British Household Panel Survey (the first wave of which should become available toward the end of 1993) might go some way toward rectifying this. What is clear, however, is that home ownership is much more prevalent at a much earlier age in the United Kingdom than in many other countries. Figure 4.7 shows the proportion of households that own their own home (either outright or through mortgage purchase). The two striking features are the high levels of home ownership in general and the marked increases in ownership both through successive cohorts of the data and, within each cohort, over the period of our sample. Unfortunately, very little is known about down payments for mortgages, or indeed about borrowing to obtain such down payments. Typically, down payments will need to be at least 5 percent of the house value to obtain a mortgage in the United Kingdom (although this will depend on the characteristics of the household). Despite this, it was possible in the 1980s to finance a house purchase with, in effect, a 100 percent mortgage by simultaneously borrowing the 5 percent deposit as a secured loan from the mortgage company.

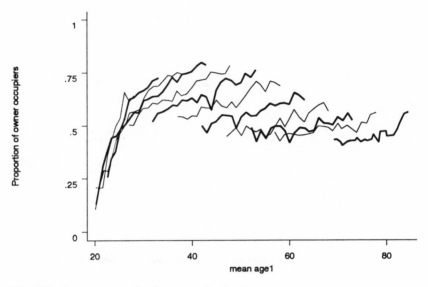

Fig. 4.7   Owner occupation by age and cohort

Health Expenditure

The subject of uninsured health expenditure and precautionary saving is impossible to analyze for the United Kingdom. What little information there is comes from the GHS, which asks a battery of questions regarding the health of the respondents. However, there is no information regarding the expenditure associated with health problems, and in general these expenditures will be small—representing the costs of prescriptions both privately and through the National Health Service (an average expenditure of £1.38 per week in the 1990 FES). And indeed some of these costs will be borne by the benefit system (in particular for children, pensioners, families on Income Support, and individuals with particular health needs).

4.3.3   Saving and Wealth

As mentioned in the introduction, there are very few data that focus on household saving levels in the United Kingdom. Attanasio and Weber (1992) have shown that simply computing residuals from FES income and expenditure codes will be problematic when using recent years, due to unusually high income growth in the FES from 1987 onward. Informal checks (at IFS) on these data have also suggested that this may be due, to a large extent, to a small number of very large self-employment incomes. In the absence of other information, however, the next section considers what we can learn from the FES about household saving profiles, and then we go on to consider issues concerning wealth, and particularly wealth/saving around the time of retirement—an area of the life cycle about which, at present, economists still seem to know comparatively little.

Household Saving: Evidence from the FES

If we can assume that the income growth observed in the last four years of the FES that is not picked up in the U.K. national accounts is mostly attributable to a few large income observations, then looking at the cohort median saving rates should give us at least some idea of the age structure of saving. Indeed it is quite plausible that median saving rates may be a better guide anyway. Figure 4.8 presents these cohort median age-saving profiles for the 22-year sample. Even though we use cohort medians there is still a large amount of noise in the FES data, although an age pattern does emerge—saving appears to be hump-shaped in age until retirement and then begins to rise again. We will investigate this phenomenon in more detail in the sections that follow.

It is interesting to look at these saving profiles alongside the numbers of dependent children in FES households over the same period. Figure 4.9 is taken from Banks and Johnson (1993) and shows extremely well defined cohort effects as well as the expected life-cycle profile. In this figure the cohort number marks the exact average, and profiles are then smoothed by cubic splines.

We can decompose this analysis further by household type and focus more specifically on the impact of children on saving profiles. In table 4.13 we report median saving levels and saving rates (both out of expenditure and out of in-

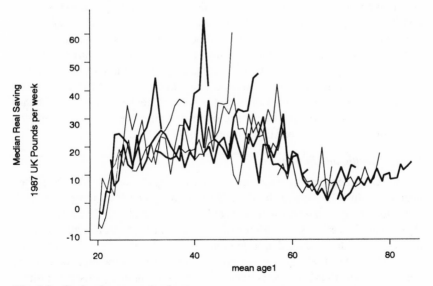

Fig. 4.8   Saving by age and cohort

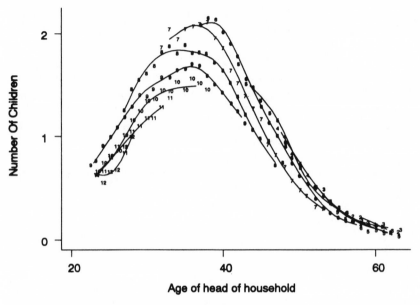

Fig. 4.9   Number of dependent children in household
Source: Banks and Johnson (1993).

come) for households of "child-rearing" age by number of children. These summary statistics are calculated over two adjacent cohorts for all households with one male and one female. Two patterns emerge. Children clearly have an effect on household saving (and households with one child appear to save less than those with more than one). However, as the head of the household gets older, given a certain household composition, saving begins to rise again.

This section has demonstrated just how much cross-sectional variation there is in U.K. savings levels and saving rates from the FES at any particular time. We go on to investigate how wealth levels might be affected by this and, given the variation in saving as measured by the residual between income and consumption, whether looking at consumption growth alone across the sample across time can improve our understanding of household saving behavior.

Saving, Wealth, and Retirement

The Retirement Survey (Bone et al. 1992) provides some evidence on the degree to which households hold wealth as they approach retirement and indeed, to a certain extent, on how wealth and saving change thereafter. The Retirement Survey was a single cross-sectional study of work and earnings histories providing detailed information on over 3,500 individuals between ages 55 and 69 in 1988. The survey provides valuable information, not least in that it allows us to analyze respondents according to their *self-assessed* retirement status rather than by age or by some imposed economic position variable.

Table 4.13   **Median Saving by Age and Number of Children**

Age Band	No Children	One Child	Two Children	Three or More Children	All
		Household Saving			
25–29	64.96	4.06	10.07	7.41	23.63
30–34	77.97	20.86	22.10	18.04	29.37
35–39	60.51	25.46	31.41	26.96	32.96
40–44	36.42	31.42	46.82	46.02	41.10
All	61.45	19.28	27.68	24.78	31.38
		Saving as a Proportion of Total Household Income			
25–29	0.301	0.022	0.065	0.046	0.118
30–34	0.316	0.119	0.123	0.098	0.146
35–39	0.252	0.140	0.150	0.138	0.158
40–44	0.142	0.144	0.185	0.181	0.166
All	0.263	0.101	0.133	0.120	0.147
		Saving as a Proportion of Total Expenditure			
25–29	0.432	0.022	0.070	0.048	0.157
30–34	0.461	0.135	0.140	0.109	0.180
35–39	0.337	0.163	0.176	0.160	0.190
40–44	0.165	0.168	0.227	0.221	0.200
All	0.366	0.116	0.156	0.139	0.182
		Cell Sizes			
25–29	1235	1225	1403	495	4358
30–34	859	1209	2551	1141	5760
35–39	687	973	2586	1270	5516
40–44	715	883	1530	636	3764
All	3496	4290	8070	3542	19398

Source: FES for 1969–90.

Note: Figures for households with one male and one female and head born between 1935 and 1944.

For this exercise, however, we can use the survey to look at the result of asset and wealth accumulation for one large cohort (born between 1919 and 1933) over their working lifetimes.

Table 4.14 shows the total value of nonpension nonhousing savings and investments by age for men and women in the Retirement Survey. At this point we are only trying to look at the wealth rather than the incomes of those in retirement. Income sources after retirement will be considered in more detail in section 4.6 of this paper.

Almost one-quarter of individuals had no assets or savings (excluding pensions and housing) at the time of the interview, and the proportions of people in each value band differed little when split by whether or not they had already retired (Bone et al. 1992). On the other hand, the survey shows a positive correlation between those who had retired early or planned to retire early and the value of their assets and savings. Unsurprisingly, the greatest difference in asset holdings is observed between those who were in employment as they approached retirement and those who were not. The proportion of all men who

Table 4.14   Nonpension Nonhousing Asset Value by Age and Sex (%)

Value	Age 55–57		Age 58–60		Age 61–63		Age 64–66		Age 67–69		All	
	Men	Women	Men	Women	Men	Women	Men	Women	Men	Women	Men	Women
None	26	21	25	26	20	24	23	24	17	22	22	24
<3,000	31	37	32	35	32	36	32	37	32	38	32	36
3,000–6,000	14	10	14	10	7	10	8	10	8	11	10	10
6,000–8,000	3	4	3	4	6	5	5	2	6	8	4	4
8,000–10,000	3	4	4	3	3	4	4	4	5	3	4	4
10,000–20,000	7	8	9	8	10	8	9	8	9	4	9	7
20,000–30,000	4	2	3	4	7	3	4	2	4	1	4	2
30,000+	8	5	5	6	8	5	8	4	12	8	8	6
No answer	4	8	5	5	6	6	6	8	8	5	6	7

Source: Bone et al. (1992).

had no savings or investments, for example, was 22 percent, whereas 46 percent of those who were not working when they retired fell into this category.

The survey also provides information on tenure type and house values (for owner-occupiers; table 4.15). About one-third of the survey participants were living in rented accommodation and would correspondingly have no primary housing wealth. Of owner-occupiers, housing wealth values are concentrated between £25,000 and £100,000, with little difference between retirement status or sex.

The final analysis from the Retirement Survey that we want to present in this section concerns how these stocks of saving and wealth are affected by the individual's retirement. Figure 4.10 shows changes in savings since retirement, for those households that had already retired. Only 32 percent of all individuals in the survey had begun to run down their wealth (37 percent for people whose main life job was nonmanual).

Figure 4.11 seems to suggest that households might adjust their behavior at retirement rather than simply smooth consumption over the anticipated change of retirement status, but this does not take any account of income (from pensions, other assets, or benefits) during retirement. To try to pursue further the issue of dissaving during retirement, we can look at FES consumption and income profiles in detail for old households only. We use consumption and income together rather than saving, given the problems that we have outlined earlier in the paper. Table 4.16 presents means of consumption and income by age for two cohorts that are observed to be around retirement age throughout the 22 years of our sample. The income measure we use is the simple FES aggregate of net weekly household income from all sources at the household level, and we correspondingly use total real expenditure at the household level for comparability. For brevity we report every other mean by age, although we should still stress that these are not two-year banded averages.

Table 4.15   **Tenure Type and Housing Wealth by Retirement Status and Sex (%)**

	Men			Women		
	Retired	Not Retired	All	Retired	Not Retired	All
Tenure Type						
Rented	37	28	33	40	28	36
Owned with mortgage	13	30	21	9	26	14
Owned outright	50	42	46	51	27	50
Housing wealth band (owner-occupiers only)						
<25,000	7	7		8	7	
25,000 to 50,000	29	22		28	23	
50,000 to 100,000	34	39		40	39	
100,000 to 150,000	16	17		13	15	
150,000+	13	13		9	14	

Source: Bone et al. (1992).

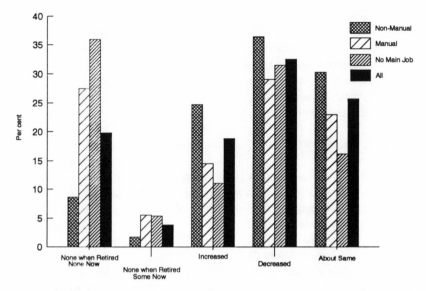

Fig. 4.10 Changes in savings and asset holdings since retirement, by main job type

Source: 1988 Retirement Survey data, see Bone et al. (1992).

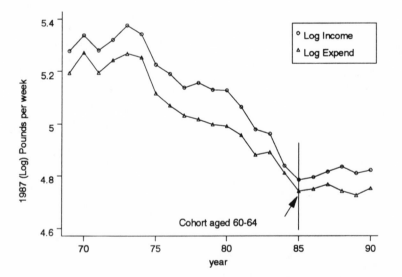

Fig. 4.11 Income and consumption over time: households with head born in 1920–24

Table 4.16 provides strong evidence that consumption tracks income as income falls when households retire. For the breakdown by retirement in the last three rows of the table, we use the FES employment status code to categorize households as either retired or not retired. The drop in both income and expenditure is clearly defined as the retirement proportion jumps upward at the male retirement age. This feature is also apparent in figure 4.11, which presents the time series of the log of income and the log of expenditure for households in a particular cohort. Male heads in the cohort begin to retire in 1985 (females five years earlier), and income and expenditure are very similar around this time. However from then on expenditure falls again and households continue to save. This confirms that the pattern of behavior seen in table 4.1 was not simply a legacy of single cross-sectional data but holds up even when conditioning on the date-of-birth cohort of the household.

The natural extension of this analysis is the more formal consideration of what happens to consumption growth as households retire. Given the nature of this paper we pursue a simple empirical specification without much discussion—more as a way of describing the observed data than a structural model of any significance. Using the time series of pooled cross sections aggregated by date-of-birth cohort, we estimate an exactly aggregated stochastic Euler equation for the log of nondurable consumption growth in which the intertemporal substitution elasticity is made dependent on the demographics of the

Table 4.16   **Income and Total Expenditure by Age and Cohort for Households around Retirement Age**

	Cohort 2				Cohort 3			
Age	Total Income	Total Expenditure	Proportion Retired	Cell Size	Total Income	Total Expenditure	Proportion Retired	Cell Size
55	206.95	199.38	0.00	123	216.82	200.28	0.00	514
57	184.15	179.88	0.02	381	207.40	190.80	0.00	599
59	177.98	164.68	0.01	663	187.69	173.52	0.02	551
61	172.92	165.37	0.10	612	167.85	156.40	0.11	528
63	150.10	139.38	0.14	633	151.27	141.05	0.19	467
65	120.70	116.81	0.63	652	124.85	127.39	0.72	579
67	123.10	114.60	0.67	671	129.29	122.77	0.75	572
69	112.30	105.81	0.71	606	124.44	122.79	0.78	488
71	108.74	107.00	0.75	572	134.14	125.50	0.83	473
73	102.02	90.28	0.80	499	123.23	114.44	0.81	292
75	114.98	100.35	0.86	462	96.69	85.00	0.77	69
All ages 55–75 inclusive:								
Ret=0	162.24	149.40	0.00	6,395	179.28	163.83	0.00	5,861
Ret=1	112.82	109.11	1.00	4,996	122.43	120.84	1.00	4,051
Total	140.11	131.73	0.56	11,391	156.15	146.26	0.59	9,912

Source: FES for 1969–90.

Note: Cohort 2 consists of households with heads born between 1910 and 1914; cohort 3 consists of households with heads born between 1915 and 1920.

household (for a comparison of working age households see Banks, Blundell, and Preston 1994; or Blundell, Browning, and Meghir 1994). Table 4.17 presents our results. The dependent variable is the change in the log of real consumption, and the first group of variables in the table are the changes in the aggregated interactions of demographics and the log of consumption. Other variables are the real interest rate[7] and a dummy to capture the effect of the 1980s.[8] Past consumption growth and its interactions, all lagged two periods (i.e., years), are used as instruments[9] to identify the effect on consumption growth of *anticipated* changes in demographics and in the real interest rate.

The intertemporal elasticity of substitution in this model is simply the parameter on the real interest rate divided by one minus the sum of the parameters on the relevant interactions. Thus for a base household (employed, blue-collar, two or fewer adults, and no children of school age) the elasticity is 0.296. A positive sign on an interaction increases the substitution elasticity from this base number. Predictable changes in retirement status or employment status clearly reduce the level of substitution, whereas households with white-collar heads, multiple adults, or schoolchildren tend to substitute more. This is consistent with our lifetime consumption profiles in section 4.3.1, which were clearly flattened when controlling for household size and numbers of children.

From table 4.17 it could be argued that the retirement variable simply captures an "out of the labor market effect" as the parameter on the interaction of head___retired is very close to that on the interaction with head___unemployed. To try and establish whether this consumption growth effect is due to age or retirement we re-estimate an Euler equation with age and retirement separately affecting the substitution elasticity. The results of this are shown in table 4.18. The retirement effect on intertemporal substitution is still negative (and similar to the unemployed effect), and the age effect is insignificant for households that are both old and retired. Anticipated retirement has much the same effect on consumption growth as an anticipated spell out of the labor market. Therefore the large fall in expenditure at retirement must be partly a consequence of an unanticipated fall in income or some other unanticipated changes in circumstances.

There might be a number of factors that could lead to our observation of less consumption smoothing after retirement. For example, nonzero death probabilities or endogenous attrition within the cohort could well be important when estimating these models. Alternatively, there might be some consumption costs of being employed or an increased focus on health costs as house-

---

7. For the purposes of this exercise, we use household-specific after-tax interest rates—equal to the building society lending rate if the household has a mortgage, or the building society borrowing rate if the household does not—deflated by a cohort-specific inflation measure (equal to the change in the cohort aggregate of the individual specific Stone log price indices).

8. Blundell, Browning, and Meghir (1994) suggest that this is necessary to capture a decrease in the precautionary motive for saving during this period.

9. Extra instruments are just education, age, and a dummy for white-collar head (lagged twice).

Table 4.17   **Consumption Euler Equation**

Variable	Coefficient	t-ratio
dc * child_5_18	0.066	2.120
dc * multiple_ad_household	0.215	2.411
dc * head_retired	−0.189	−2.731
dc * head_white_collar	0.271	2.463
dc * head_unemployed	−0.185	−1.922
real_interest_rate	0.296	2.743
thatcher (1980–89 dummy)	−0.033	−3.985
constant	0.012	1.723

Source: FES for 1969–90.

Table 4.18   **Consumption Euler Equation: Age and Retirement Separate**

Variable	Coefficient	t-ratio
dc * child_5_18	0.056	1.713
dc * multiple_ad_household	0.198	1.789
dc * head_retired	−0.244	−2.557
dc * head_white_collar	0.256	2.176
dc * head_unemployed	−0.194	−2.001
dc * head_is_over_65	0.036	0.820
real_interest_rate	0.264	1.966
thatcher (1980–89 dummy)	−0.023	−2.347
constant	0.012	1.171

Source: FES for 1969–90.

holds get older (although in the United Kingdom, as we have said, there is universal coverage by the state for health costs).

Saving Patterns

In the absence of any microdata on the nature of the composition of savings levels for households, we cannot say very much about patterns of saving by household type or income group. The most recent and relevant study for the United Kingdom is that of Saunders and Webb (1988), which used the FRS data set from 1987–88 designed explicitly to investigate household financial behavior. We have used the results of this study as a valuable source in Banks and Blundell (1994), but for completeness we reproduce their results on the pattern of household saving by household wealth level in table 4.19.

4.4   Retirement Income

In this section we consider the incomes of retired households in the United Kingdom. The composition of these incomes will be a clear indication of the

Table 4.19   **Holdings of Financial Assets by Investor's Wealth**

| | Investor's Level of Wealth | | | | |
| | Top | | | Middle | Bottom |
Percentage of Savings Held in:	1%	2%–5%	6%–25%	26%–75%	25%
Bank and building society accounts	34.2	68.4	76.9	83.8	83.5
Equity	42.0	21.1	13.9	6.4	7.5
Gilts and local authority bonds	16.6	1.2	0.3	0.0	0.0
Tax-free National Savings	3.6	2.7	2.4	1.0	0.8
Other National Savings and savings clubs	3.6	6.7	6.6	8.7	8.2

Source: Saunders and Webb (1988).

financial behavior they have engaged in during their working lifetimes. Initially, we look at the structure of total retirement income by age at the beginning and end of our sample—drawing from the analysis of Johnson (1992). Figure 4.12 shows the breakdown of income into four sources. Earnings for the 50–74 age group as a whole was 57 percent of income in 1989, compared with 70 percent in 1971. The biggest drops in this proportion have occurred for those over age 60.

The figure has a number of other interesting features. First, although income from the state continuously rises with age, since 1971 it has become more important for those under age 70 and less important for those over age 70. On the other hand, all age groups have experienced a rise in the proportion of income coming from investments and private pensions. In 1989, these two sources contributed over 40 percent of total income for those over age 65. Johnson (1992) shows that 1971 and 1989 were not atypical years to analyze and, indeed, that these trends were remarkably smooth over the intervening years. Over the same period, total real incomes grew from £206 to £294 for 50–54-year-olds and £71 to £118 for 70–74-year-olds.

Pension income for the retired could be from any of three components. All pensioners are entitled to the basic state pension (subject to having contributed a minimum level of National Insurance) and may receive some earnings-related element also (see Banks and Blundell 1994 for a brief summary of the state pension regulations). If they have contracted out of SERPS at any time, then they could also be receiving private pension payments (either occupational pensions or even, in the future, personal pensions). The basic state pension currently stands at £54 per week in 1992, or £88.70 for a married couple on the husband's insurance only. Occupational pensions can, in theory, provide up to two-thirds of final salary, although they rarely do. Currently there are no personal pensions in payment to retired households.

In table 4.20 below we show the recipiency patterns of the flat-rate state pension by age and sex. The more even spread of women recipients by age band simply demonstrates the fact that women, in general, retire earlier and live longer than men.

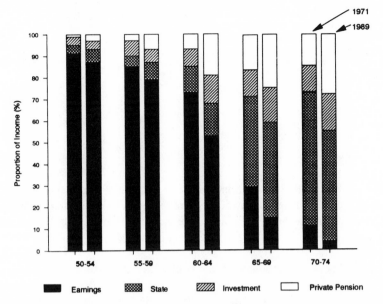

Fig. 4.12   Composition of income by age, 1971 and 1989
Source: Taken from Johnson (1992, table 1.1).

Table 4.20   **Age Recipiency Patterns of State Pension, 1990 (%)**

Age	Men	Women	Men and Women
60–64	–	16.8	10.9
65–69	31.4	22.4	25.6
70–74	29.1	20.1	23.3
75–79	21.2	17.5	18.8
80–84	12.1	12.9	12.6
85–89	4.8	7.2	6.3
90+	1.3	3.2	2.6

Source: DSS (1992).

Replacement rates for the U.K. state pension naturally decline with earnings since the basic state pension is fixed rather than earnings related. Table 4.21 shows the basic state pension as a percentage of gross earnings for different quantiles of the earnings distribution. Earnings data is from the 1992 New Earnings Survey. Male replacement rates vary from 31.7 percent of average gross male earnings at the bottom decile to just under one-tenth of earnings at the top decile point. Rates are higher for women as average earnings are lower, and higher for married couples on the husband's insurance only as the state pension is higher.

A similar analysis for occupational pensions in payment is undertaken in

Table 4.21   State Pension as a Percentage of Gross Earnings, 1992

Percentile of Gross Earnings	Men	Married Couple on Husband's Insurance	Women
10	31.7	48.9	41.8
25	24.6	38.0	33.5
50	18.2	28.1	25.6
75	13.4	20.7	18.2
90	9.9	15.3	13.9
Mean	15.9	24.3	22.1

table 4.22. We use Retirement Survey data as a source of information on payments and again calculate payments as a proportion of gross earnings from the 1992 New Earnings Survey. Replacement rates are significantly higher for men, even at the median rather than the mean payment, and significantly lower for women.

The number of occupational pension holders as a proportion of the working population has been broadly constant for the last 20 or 30 years—standing at just over 50 percent. In the Retirement Survey, 48 percent of all 55–69-year-olds had some retained rights to at least one occupational scheme and 59 percent had joined an occupational scheme at some time. The major change in the structure of pensions in the current population is the dramatic take-up of personal pensions, which does not appear to have been at the expense of the occupational schemes (of which the proportion of holders has remained constant). Within a very short time (between 1988 and 1990) over 4 million people had taken out personal pension plans. Take-up was highest among young males—approaching 50 percent for 22–26-year-olds—and one-half of all optants were below the age 30. The success of the schemes was undoubtedly attributable in part to the large tax privileges associated with saving in this form and also partly to a sustained advertising campaign by the pension fund providers. Disney and Whitehouse (1992) provide a full summary of the issues and implications of this phenomenon. For whatever reason it did take place, however, the advent of private pension income in the future will be the biggest feature of future retirement incomes in the United Kingdom.

4.5 Conclusions

In this paper we have tried to give the reader a broad overview of household saving behavior in the United Kingdom. In general the data available are of sufficient quality for us to establish a number of results. One of the main points of this paper has been to show that there is evidence of strong date-of-birth cohort effects in much of household financial behavior. Indeed, a lot of the hump-shaped profiles that emerge when looking at single cross-section studies are almost entirely attributable to cohort rather than age effects. We have

Table 4.22   Occupational Pensions as a Percentage of Gross Earnings, 1992

	Men		Women	
Percentile of Gross Earnings	(1)	(2)	(1)	(2)
10	55.1	37.5	34.2	25.0
25	43.9	30.0	28.3	20.7
50	33.4	22.8	22.3	16.3
75	25.1	17.2	16.4	12.0
90	18.9	12.9	12.8	9.4
Mean	29.4	20.1	19.6	14.3

Notes: Col. (1) for each sex reports replacement rates for mean occupational pensions in payment to retired households in 1988 retirement survey (up-rated to 1992 prices) as a percentage of gross earnings in 1992. Col. (2) is similar but uses median pension payments.

placed particular stress on the impact of children and retirement and labor market status on consumption and saving decisions. It is clear that anticipated changes in household composition will affect saving profiles, and also that there is a shift in household saving behavior after retirement that is very similar to that caused by an anticipated spell out of the labor market. However, anticipated changes alone cannot explain the fall in consumption that is observed at this time.

Appendix

Table 4A.1, which follows, shows a cross-tabulation of the numbers of households in each annual FES with the head of household's date of birth falling into a particular range. It includes all households except those resident in Northern Ireland and those that record negative total nondurable expenditures. The process of constructing the pseudocohort data set that we use for the figures in this paper involves taking means (or alternatively medians) within each of these cells. It is important to realize that by doing this we do not need to assume that all the households in each cell are, to some extent, the same. Instead all we require is that the *composition* of the cohort is *constant over the time period involved.* Consequently, we exclude cohorts that may contain very young or very old members.

Table 4A.1   FES Pseudocohort Data from a Time Series of Cross Sections: Dates of Birth and Cell Sizes over Time

| | | | | | | Cohort | | | | | | | |
Year	(1)	(2)	(3)	(4)	(5)	(6)	(7)	(8)	(9)	(10)	(11)	(12)	Total
Earliest	n.a.	1910	1915	1920	1925	1930	1935	1940	1945	1950	1955	1960	
Latest	1909	1914	1919	1924	1929	1934	1939	1944	1949	1954	1959	1964	
Example	Queen Mother	Ronald Reagan	Dennis Healey	George Bush	Margaret Thatcher	Norman Tebbit	John Smith	John Major	Bill Clinton	Graham Gooch	Madonna	Frank Bruno	
1969	2,165	648	614	701	647	611	626	530	284	8	0	0	6,834
1970	1,866	603	493	623	558	594	511	547	404	31	0	0	6,230
1971	2,025	684	583	719	616	592	644	607	523	94	0	0	7,087
1972	1,776	610	565	692	621	610	598	671	569	154	1	0	6,867
1973	1,874	641	534	752	566	569	560	591	655	220	9	0	6,971
1974	1,624	589	537	615	535	549	587	597	618	279	19	0	6,549
1975	1,589	690	534	642	582	582	613	649	713	415	49	0	7,058
1976	1,525	665	557	672	567	559	586	605	704	495	115	1	7,051

1977	1,366	649	566	645	564	580	580	613	785	553	148	6	7,055
1978	1,211	613	548	642	613	529	555	604	752	571	226	8	6,872
1979	1,141	594	460	624	504	507	557	581	708	658	288	29	6,651
1980	1,000	617	525	605	554	539	557	641	741	590	396	45	6,810
1981	999	632	570	695	583	578	603	687	832	670	450	96	7,395
1982	855	599	527	656	614	564	584	626	828	676	575	175	7,279
1983	749	551	522	629	514	525	554	609	736	682	528	237	6,836
1984	676	506	530	685	575	535	530	629	675	698	567	281	6,887
1985	616	545	481	637	555	518	545	569	762	660	604	353	6,845
1986	550	492	511	655	507	501	543	612	706	680	660	497	6,914
1987	473	443	523	682	600	483	546	580	742	692	728	578	7,070
1988	465	458	463	637	540	525	532	587	759	683	650	611	6,910
1989	368	405	482	661	599	534	534	577	721	660	685	663	6,889
1990	328	394	424	587	545	506	500	536	648	623	695	683	6,469
Total	25,241	12,628	11,549	14,456	12,559	12,090	12,445	13,248	14,865	10,792	7,393	4,263	151,529

Note: Cells in which members may be over 65 or under 21 years of age are included in the table for completeness but are dropped in some of the profiles reported earlier (i.e., earnings, pension contributions, and children).

References

Atkinson, A., and J. Micklewright. 1983. On the reliability of the income data in the Family Expenditure Survey 1970–1977. *Journal of the Royal Statistical Society,* ser. A, 146:33–61.

Atkinson, A. B., J. Micklewright, and N. H. Stern. 1982. A comparison of the Family Expenditure Survey and the New Earnings Survey: Part II, Hours and earnings. LSE Taxation and Incentives Discussion Paper no. 32. London School of Economics.

Attanasio, O., and M. Browning. 1992. Consumption over the life-cycle and over the business cycle. Stanford University. Mimeograph.

Attanasio, O., and G. Weber. 1989. Intertemporal substitution, risk aversion and the Euler equation for consumption. *Economic Journal Conference Supplement* 99:59–73.

———. 1992. The UK consumption boom of the late 1980's: Aggregate implications of microeconomic evidence. IFS Working Paper no. 92/17. London: Institute of Fiscal Studies.

Auerbach, A. J., J. Cai, and L. J. Kotlikoff. 1990. US demographics and saving: Predictions of three saving models. NBER Working Paper no. 3404. Cambridge, Mass.: National Bureau of Economic Research.

Banks, J. W., and R. W. Blundell. 1994. Taxation and Personal Savings Incentives in the United Kingdom. In *Public Policies and Household Saving,* ed. J. Poterba, 57–80. Chicago: University of Chicago Press.

Banks, J. W., R. W. Blundell, and A. Brugiavini. 1994. Income uncertainty and consumption growth in the UK. IFS Working Paper no. 94/11. London: Institute for Fiscal Studies.

Banks, J. W., R. W. Blundell, and I. P. Preston. 1994. Equivalence scales and the life-cycle costs of children. *European Economic Review,* in press.

Banks, J. W., and P. Johnson. 1993. *Children and household living standards.* London: Institute for Fiscal Studies.

Blundell, R. W., M. J. Browning, and C. Meghir. 1994. Consumer demand and the life-cycle allocation of household expenditures. *Review of Economic Studies* 61(1), no. 206: 57–81.

Blundell, R. W., and I. P. Preston. 1991. The distinction between income and consumption in the measurement of household welfare. IFS Working Paper no. 91/1. London: Institute of Fiscal Studies.

Bone, M., J. Gregory, B. Gill, and D. Lader. 1992. *Retirement and retirement plans.* London: HMSO.

Browning, M. J., A. Deaton, and M. Irish. 1985. A profitable approach to labour supply and commodity demands over the life-cycle. *Econometrica* 53:503–43.

Carroll, C. D., and L. H. Summers. 1991. Consumption growth parallels income growth: Some new evidence. In *National saving and economic performance,* ed. B. D. Bernheim and J. B. Shoven. Chicago: University of Chicago Press.

Department of Social Security (DSS). 1992. *Households below average income: A statistical analysis 1979–1988/89.* London: HMSO.

Dilnot, A., and P. Johnson. 1993. *The taxation of private pensions.* London: Institute for Fiscal Studies.

Disney, R., and E. Whitehouse. 1992. *The personal pensions stampede.* London: Institute for Fiscal Studies.

———. 1993. What are occupational pension entitlements in Britain worth? London: Institute for Fiscal Studies. Mimeograph.

Giles, C., and S. Webb. 1993. Poverty statistics: A guide for the perplexed. IFS Commentary Series, 34. London: Institute for Fiscal Studies.

Hall, R. E. 1978. Stochastic implications of the life-cycle permanent income hypothesis: Theory and evidence. *Journal of Political Economy* 86:971–88.

Johnson, P., 1992. *Pensions, earnings and savings in the third age.* Fife: Carnegie UK Trust.

Kemsley, W., R. Redpath, and M. Holmes. 1980. *Family Expenditure Survey handbook.* London: HMSO.

McClements, L. 1977. Equivalence scales for children. *Journal of Public Economics* 8 (2):191–210.

Office of Population Censuses and Surveys (OPCS). 1992. *The General Household Survey 1990.* London: HMSO.

Pissarides, C. A., and G. Weber. 1989. An expenditure-based estimate of Britain's black economy. *Journal of Public Economics* 39:17–32.

Saunders, M., and S. Webb. 1988. Fiscal privilege and financial assets: Some distributive effects. *Fiscal Studies* 9(4):51–69.

Skinner, J. 1988. Risky income, life-cycle consumption and precautionary savings. *Journal of Monetary Economics* 22:237–55.

———. 1992. Precautionary saving, wealth accumulation and the saving downturn of the 1980's. *National Tax Journal 43:247–57.*

5 Savings in Germany—Part 2: Behavior

Axel Börsch-Supan

5.1 Introduction

This paper is the second of two papers that report on household saving behavior in Germany. While the first paper concentrated on incentives for saving (Börsch-Supan 1994), this paper provides descriptive statistics on household saving behavior and the factors that influence it. I construct age-saving profiles, describe portfolio composition with a particular emphasis on housing wealth, and try to give an indication of how robust these findings are in the presence of cohort effects.

German saving behavior exhibits rather dramatic differences from the American pattern. Germany features a very high household saving rate. In 1975, the aggregate household saving rate peaked at 16.2 percent. In the following 10 years, the saving rate declined to 13.0 percent in 1985, then increased again to 14.8 percent in 1990.[1] Moreover, we will see that there is no evidence that German age-saving profiles exhibit dissaving in old age. Rather, saving rates peak in old age after a small decline in the first five to ten years after retirement. As in the United States, household wealth in Germany is dominated by housing wealth, which accounts for about two-thirds of total household wealth for all except the very rich. However, the German portfolio of financial assets is different from the American one and includes mainly pass-

Axel Börsch-Supan is professor of economics at the University of Mannheim and a research associate of the National Bureau of Economic Research.

The author is indebted to Oliver Lang for very able research assistance and valuable comments. The author also appreciates comments by Angus Deaton, Martin Feldstein, Larry Kotlikoff, Jonathan Skinner, and David Wise.

1. Net savings divided by net income as reported by the Deutsche Bundesbank, *Monatsberichte der Deutsche Bundesbank* (Frankfurt am Main: various issues). The Bundesbank definition of households includes nonprofit organizations and therefore overestimates household savings as defined in section 5.3.

book savings and life insurance. Among younger households, building society savings are a third important asset choice.

This paper has three parts. Part I parallels the other chapters in this volume. Section 5.2 describes data sources and discusses the reliability of the data. Section 5.3 presents summary statistics on saving and wealth based on the latest available cross section. Part II provides additional data on saving drawn from earlier cross sections and longitudinal data. Section 5.4 investigates how cohort effects might distort age-saving profiles, while section 5.5 is devoted to an analysis of portfolio composition in Germany. Part III furnishes background information in order to guide the interpretation of the numbers provided in the first two parts. To this end, section 5.6 is concerned with household income in Germany, section 5.7 describes consumption patterns, and section 5.8 briefly discusses other household characteristics. Section 5.9 summarizes and draws conclusions.

PART I: SUMMARY STATISTICS ON SAVINGS AND WEALTH

5.2 Data Sources

The paper is based on two microdata sets—the German Income and Expenditure Survey and the Socio-Economic Panel—and aggregate data provided by the Deutsche Bundesbank.

Main data sources are the German Income and Expenditure Surveys (Einkommens- und Verbrauchsstichproben [EVS]). These surveys are collected every five years by the German Bureau of the Census. In design they roughly correspond to the U.S. Consumer Expenditure surveys. The surveys include a very detailed account of income by source, consumption by type, and savings flows and asset stocks by portfolio category. The official surveys are not accessible to researchers. However, extensive descriptive analyses have been carried out by members of the German Bureau of the Census (Euler, various years). The surveys of 1978 and 1983 are available in public-use form, although at high cost and under tight confidentiality restrictions. All regional identifiers have been removed, and age and several other variables are coded in categories only. These public-use files have been analyzed with respect to household savings by Börsch-Supan and Stahl (1991a, 1991b) and Börsch-Supan (1992c). Unfortunately, the 1988 wave has still not been released, although interviews for the 1993 wave have already started.

The EVS are representative cross sections of all West German households with annual gross incomes below DM 300,000. They included about 46,000 households in 1978 and about 43,000 households in 1983. These large sample sizes provide for sufficiently large cell sizes in each age category, even for old ages. The EVS therefore allow for a separate analysis of consumption and saving patterns among the very old, unlike many American data sets which have been previously used for investigations of the saving behavior of the elderly.[2]

The data exclude very wealthy households and the institutionalized population. The former represent about 2 percent of households, who have annual gross incomes in excess of DM 300,000 (Euler 1985b). For this reason, the data cannot be expected to add up to national accounting figures, in particular not the wealth data. Due to the rather skewed wealth distribution, omission of the upper 2 percent tail of the income distribution results in a substantial underestimation of total household wealth in Germany. For the same reason, the saving rate aggregated from the EVS is lower than the aggregate household saving rate reported by the Bundesbank.[3] All statistics drawn from the EVS are only representative for the first 98 percent of the income distribution.

Omission of the institutionalized is only serious among the very old. Although less than 1 percent of all persons aged 50 and over in Germany are institutionalized, this percentage increases rapidly with age and is estimated to be about 9.3 percent of all persons aged 80 and over.[4] The institutionalized elderly are more likely to have few assets and no savings.

The EVS are stratified quota samples on a voluntary basis. The German Bureau of the Census establishes a target number of households for each stratum defined by household size, income, and employment status. To meet these targets, a large number of households are contacted by various mechanisms; e.g., former participants in previous waves of the EVS or other surveys are asked by mail whether they would volunteer for another survey. The ratio of final acceptances to target size is published and was in excess of 120 percent in 1983. However, this ratio varied between 20 and 150 percent across strata (see Braun 1978; Pöschl 1993). Moreover, response rates with respect to initial inquiries are not available and are only vaguely alluded to as rather small.[5] Acceptance rates are lowest in the strata of low-income households, one-person households, and blue-collar workers and the self-employed.

In addition to basic socioeconomic household characteristics such as household composition, age, gender, and employment status of the household head, the data contain a detailed account of income by sources, wealth by asset categories, and household expenditures. Unfortunately, there is no information on health status nor on the number of children outside the household or other potential heirs. While response rates to questions about household characteristics and labor income are virtually 100 percent, questions about nonlabor in-

2. Such as the Longitudinal Retirement History Survey (LRHS), the National Longitudinal Survey (NLS), and the Panel Study of Income Dynamics (PSID).

3. Adding up the 1983 EVS savings yields a net saving rate of 9.5 percent, while the "official" Bundesbank figure is 13.2 percent. This divergence is due to two differences in the base: the EVS omit the upper 2 percent of the income distribution, while the Bundesbank also includes nonprofit organizations.

4. Special tabulations from the 1987 German Mikrozensus, Zuma, Mannheim.

5. Braun (1978, 411) mentions "12 out of 100 households." However, it is not clear how pressing these first inquiries really are.

come and wealth have substantially lower response rates, particularly among the elderly.[6]

The flows—income, consumption, and saving—are measured rather precisely because they are aggregated from weekly diaries and carefully cross-checked against yearly records such as salary slips. Most types of income add precisely to the national accounting totals, with the qualification that the data cover only the first 98 percent of the income distribution. Schüler (1988) reports coverage rates of 99 percent for wages, salary, and retirement income. Major exceptions to the high coverage rates are business and asset income, covered only at a rate of 61.5 percent. These income sources dominate among those 2 percent of German households which have incomes exceeding DM 300,000 and which are thus not sampled in the EVS.

Net savings will be computed as the sum of purchases of assets minus sales of assets. Changes in financial assets reported in the EVS are deposits to and withdrawals from the various kinds of savings accounts, purchases and sales of stocks and bonds, deposits to and withdrawals from dedicated savings accounts at building societies (*Bausparkassen*), which are an important savings component in Germany (see Börsch-Supan and Stahl 1991a), and contributions to life insurance and private pension plans minus payments received. New loans are subtracted, and repayments are added to net savings. Not reported are changes in cash and checking accounts. Changes in real assets reported in the EVS are purchases and sales of real estate and business partnerships.[7] Not reliably reported are changes in durables (other than real estate). Unrealized capital gains remain unreported.

Asset stocks are less precisely measured at the end of each survey year. Because their coverage rates are substantially less than for the corresponding flows, I will concentrate on flows in this paper and base the analysis of portfolio choices on aggregate data provided by the Deutsche Bundesbank.

Because the microdata for 1988 have not yet been released, this paper is mainly based on the 1983 cross section of the EVS. In addition, I will employ the 1978 cross section in order to investigate changes in saving behavior and to disentangle cohort effects. The households in the EVS cross sections are not necessarily the same and cannot be matched. It is therefore impossible to construct a true panel of individuals, although this would be most desirable for the estimation of true age profiles. By aggregating into age categories, however, I will construct a panel of synthetic cohorts and compare a representative household headed, say, by a 60-year-old in 1978 with a household of the same age category five years later. The large sample sizes are of considerable help in the synthetic cohort approach because aggregation units can be defined sufficiently narrowly to assure homogeneity without loss of statistical precision.

---

6. Many questions allow for a choice between categorical answers and answers on a continuous scale. The nonresponse rate for the former is 10–15 percent, higher for the latter.

7. The latter only in 1978.

The second source of microdata is the Socio-Economic Panel (SOEP). It is an annual panel study of some 6,000 households and some 15,000 individuals. Its design closely corresponds to that of the U.S. Panel Study of Income Dynamics (PSID). The panel started in 1984; seven waves through 1990 are currently available. Response rates and panel mortality are comparable to those of the PSID. The data are used extensively in Germany, and increasing interest in the United States prompted the construction of an English-language user file available from Richard Burkhauser and his associates at Syracuse University.[8]

The SOEP data provide a detailed account of income and employment status. Moreover, they furnish information on insurance such as private health insurance, life insurance, and employer-provided pension plans. In a special module, the 1988 wave includes information on savings and assets. However, response rates to those questions were very low, and it is difficult to construct statistically reliable age-saving and age-asset profiles from these data. I will employ the SOEP mainly for income statistics and exploit its panel property for a decomposition of age and cohort effects.

Because at this point no reliable data on East German savings and assets are available, this paper describes West German saving behavior only.

5.3 Summary Savings Measures: Cross-Sectional Evidence

Measures of household saving can be constructed in two ways from data in the EVS. The first measure consists of summing up all purchases minus sales of different asset types that are reported in the EVS. New loans are subtracted, and net repayments of loans are added. The second measure is computed by subtracting consumption expenditures from net household income. Although the second method is likely to overestimate saving (due to unreported consumption expenditures) and the first one to underestimate saving (due to unreported investments), the actual difference between the two measures is very small in the EVS.

Neither of the two methods takes account of unrealized capital gains or of the windfall effects of inflation. A third method—subtracting beginning-of-year assets from those at the end of the year—is unreliable for the EVS data because it determines saving as the (typically small) difference between two large numbers contaminated by reporting errors similar in magnitude to the difference to be computed. Moreover, the EVS report only end-of-year assets. Hence, differences can only be computed for five-year intervals, which amplifies reporting errors.

5.3.1 Saving Rates

Table 5.1 presents household saving rates by age as reported in the 1983 EVS cross section, based on the first measure of savings. While the left three

---

8. Burkhauser (1991) reports on the usefulness of the German panel data and provides English-language code books as well as an internationally accessible version of the SOEP.

columns display medians of individual saving rates, the right three columns are computed as means of individual saving rates. Also distinguished are financial and real savings, the latter mainly savings for owner-occupied housing. The irregular age categories between ages 60 and 70 reflect the peculiarities of the German retirement system.[9]

Household saving rates in Germany are high compared to most other countries. In 1983, median saving rates varied between 4 and almost 10 percent, mean saving rates between 9.2 and 12.5 percent of net household income. Current saving rates are even higher. The aggregate household saving rate reported by the Deutsche Bundesbank was 13.0 percent in 1983, 14.8 percent in 1990, and 14.2 percent in 1992.[10]

However, the distribution of saving rates is rather skewed. This is visible in the difference between median and mean saving rates. Median saving rates are lower for all age categories. This difference is particularly dramatic for real savings. While average real saving rates exceed 6 percent before retirement, their median is positive only in the main home-purchasing ages. At these ages, mean financial saving rates are actually lower than the respective medians, as discussed later.

Both median and mean saving rates for all assets exhibit an age pattern with two peaks. Median savings increase to an early peak of almost 10 percent around ages 35–39, and then decline slowly until they reach a minimum of 4 percent around ages 70–74. At very old ages, saving rates increase again to a new peak of 7.1 percent for households headed by a person aged 80 or over.

Mean saving rates have the same up-down-up pattern. However, the first peak is not achieved until retirement. Mean saving rates decline during the first five to ten years after retirement, and then feature a similar strong increase as median saving rates, until the highest mean saving rates over the life course are achieved in very old age.

Table 5.1 exhibits a dramatic change in the portfolio composition of new savings. Mean financial saving rates are very low until age 55, never exceeding 2.5 percent. After age 55, they increase and surpass 10 percent at old age. In turn, mean and median real saving rates peak at ages 35–44, which is the prime first-home purchasing age range in Germany, substantially later than in the United States. Because few of the elderly purchase real estate, real saving rates then decline and are dominated by financial saving rates after retirement. Mean financial saving rates are actually lower than their respective medians during prime first-home purchasing ages. This is due to financial dissaving by the home buyers, who shift financial savings into real savings.

5.3.2   Saving/Expenditure Ratios

The life-cycle pattern which was visible in the saving rates with respect to net income (table 5.1) is even more pronounced in the ratio of net saving to

9. Exact ages had been removed from the public-use files; see section 5.2.
10. This includes nonprofit organizations with relatively high saving rates.

Table 5.1   **Saving Rates (%)**

Age	Median			Mean		
	All Assets	Financial Assets	Real Assets	All Assets	Financial Assets	Real Assets
25–29	6.1	4.1	0.0	9.8	1.9	7.9
30–34	9.4	4.4	0.0	9.8	1.3	8.5
35–39	9.9	3.5	0.7	10.6	0.2	10.5
40–44	9.4	3.1	1.8	10.2	1.1	9.1
45–49	8.8	3.8	1.2	10.2	2.5	7.7
50–54	7.9	3.4	0.3	10.4	1.9	8.5
55–59	8.2	3.9	0.0	11.0	4.4	6.6
60–62	6.5	3.4	0.0	11.7	5.4	6.4
63–65	5.8	2.2	0.0	12.5	6.6	5.9
66–69	5.4	3.0	0.0	9.2	3.8	5.4
70–74	4.0	2.3	0.0	9.7	5.9	3.8
75–79	4.2	2.8	0.0	10.2	7.2	3.1
80–99	7.1	4.9	0.0	13.7	10.5	3.2

Source: EVS for 1983.

Note: Financial and real saving as percentage of net household income.

consumption expenditures, (table 5.2). This is an obvious implication of declining consumption expenditures when saving increases—even though saving and consumption expenditures do not exactly add up to net income because of transfer payments. The difference between the mean and median ratios becomes more pronounced with age, an indication of a growing dispersion in the distribution of savings.

5.3.3   Absolute Household Saving

Similar life-cycle patterns also appear in table 5.3, which depicts the mean and median annual net financial saving in absolute terms. Moreover, the proportion of households with positive (and with negative) net financial saving also echoes these life-cycle patterns. Median financial saving is larger than mean financial saving until age 55. After age 55, the relation is reversed. This can be explained by large negative saving for a small group of young households, mostly for the purpose of purchasing a house. Unlike in the United States, in Germany only about a third of all households purchase a house. Even though slightly more than 50 percent of German households will eventually be home owners, about 28 percent of them inherit their house and will not incur the high costs of home purchase. After age 55, the mean exceeds the median as the income distribution becomes more skewed and absolute saving strongly increases with income.

It is impressive to see the increase in savings among the very old reflected in all of the various statistics. It is not a phenomenon of a few rich elderly who cannot consume their wealth and have a leveraged influence on mean saving rates. This can be seen by the increase in the median annual saving. Moreover,

Table 5.2   Saving/Expenditure Ratios (%)

Age	Median	Mean
25–29	6.4	10.4
30–34	10.9	11.3
35–39	11.2	12.0
40–44	10.6	11.4
45–49	10.2	11.7
50–54	9.3	12.1
55–59	9.6	12.7
60–62	7.6	13.2
63–65	6.6	13.8
66–69	6.2	10.4
70–74	4.7	11.1
75–79	4.8	12.2
80–99	8.8	17.3

Source: EVS for 1983.
Note: Financial and real saving as percentage of total consumption expenditures.

Table 5.3   Financial Saving and Dissaving

Age	Net Annual Household Saving (DM)		Proportion (%) of Households With	
	Mean	Median	Positive Saving	Negative Saving
21–24	323	500	55.0	39.8
25–29	647	1,000	59.8	36.6
30–34	563	1,600	62.8	34.6
35–39	93	1,500	62.0	35.9
40–44	623	1,300	60.8	37.3
45–49	1,388	1,600	62.8	35.0
50–54	975	1,300	62.3	35.6
55–59	2,003	1,300	63.5	33.6
60–62	2,157	900	62.1	33.3
63–65	2,431	600	57.5	36.4
66–69	1,266	700	60.9	32.3
70–74	1,618	500	59.1	31.2
75–79	1,800	600	62.6	28.2
80–99	2,574	900	69.0	20.2

Source: EVS for 1983.
Note: Includes saving in form of financial assets only. DM 1,000 in 1983 corresponds to a purchasing power of U.S. $650 in 1993.

the proportion of households with positive saving is large (about 60 percent) and increasing with old age, while the proportion of households who deplete their assets becomes smaller with old age, rather than larger as a naive version of the life-cycle hypothesis would imply.

Of course, the sample selectivity issues of the EVS should be kept in mind. While including the very wealthy probably strengthens the conclusion about increasing saving rates in old age—the very wealthy are the least likely to decumulate their assets—the omission of the institutionalized may bias this profile upward because the sample omits those who are most likely to deplete their assets. However, taking into account this selectivity problem cannot reverse the age-saving profiles in old age because the share of the institutionalized among persons aged 80 and over is only 9.3 percent. Even if all of these households were to deplete their assets completely, their inclusion in the survey could not offset the 16.2 percent decrease in the number of households who have negative saving.

5.3.4 Financial Assets

Asset levels are less reliably reported in the EVS than are saving flows. Adding up the financial assets reported in the 1983 EVS yields only 29 percent of what the Deutsche Bundesbank accounts describe as "financial assets held by private households." There are several reasons for this underreporting. The first and most important reason is that the data only represent the first 98 percent of the income distribution. The remaining 2 percent hold a share of total wealth which is substantially larger than proportional to income. The second reason is that the data do not report the end-of-year stocks of cash and checking accounts, nor the current value of life insurance and private pension claims. According to the 1983 Finanzierungs- und Geldvermögensrechnung of the Deutsche Bundesbank, these unreported assets represent 33 percent of all financial assets held by private households (7.7 percent in cash and checking accounts, 18.2 percent in life insurance, and 7.5 percent in private pension wealth).[11] The third reason is the common problem of underreporting in survey questions about wealth.

Table 5.4 shows that coverage rates with respect to national accounting totals vary considerably by asset category, ranging from low rates for time deposits and investment funds to almost complete coverage of building society wealth. Most of these biases can be traced to the omission of the upper 2 percent of the income distribution, the richest households who hold a considerable proportion of time deposits and investment funds. We will present some evidence on the portfolio composition of the rich in section 5.5.

The following age-wealth profiles thus represent only the 98 percent of households covered by the EVS, excluding the very rich. Also implicit is the assumption that there are no further reporting biases with respect to age. If at all, assets are more likely to be underreported by the elderly, which will strengthen the conclusions that follow.

---

11. This figure is somewhat overestimated because it includes cash and checking accounts of nonprofit organizations, which are included as private households in the national accounting definition of the Bundesbank. This also implies that the 29 percent coverage rate is a lower bound and that the actual coverage rate more favorable.

Table 5.4   **Coverage of Private Financial Wealth by the 1983 EVS (as % of 1983 FuGVR)**

Financial Asset	Deutsche Bundersbank 1983 FuGVR		1983 EVS		
	Amount (billion DM)	Percentage of Total	Amount (billion DM)	Percentage of Total	Percentage of FuGVR Total
Cash, checking accounts	143.4	7.7	n.a.	n.a.	0.0
Life insurance	338.8	18.2	n.a.	n.a.	0.0
Private pensions	139.9	7.5	n.a.	n.a.	0.0
Savings accounts	545.8	29.3	229.9	42.6	42.1
Savings certificates	128.5	6.9	47.4	8.8	36.9
Building societies	120.8	6.5	112.0	20.7	92.7
Time deposits	125.5	6.7	34.1	6.3	27.2
Bonds	218.5	11.7	75.8	14.0	34.7
Stocks	70.3	3.8	32.4	6.0	46.0
Investment funds	31.8	1.7	8.4	1.6	26.3
Total	1,863.3	100.0	539.9	100.0	29.0

Source: Adapted from Lang (1993b). The first column is based on the 1983 Finanzierungs- und Geldver-mögensrechnung (FuGVR) by the Deutsche Bundesbank.

Table 5.5 displays the age profile of average gross financial assets and its three quartiles. Since consumer loans are very small in Germany, net financial assets (excluding mortgages) are only about 1 percent lower. The mean profile shows the familiar accumulation over the working life with a peak around age 60, about the average retirement age in Germany. At this peak, average financial assets are 72 percent of net annual income. Median assets are a little less than half of mean assets and about 40 percent of median income.

After retirement, the asset profiles are complex. Although there is dissaving after retirement, the speed is slow and all except the median profile show a renewed increase in assets at very old ages. The mean asset level of households aged 80 and over is 88 percent of the peak level. Apparent dissaving in the five to ten years after retirement is a little faster among the poorer households—the median asset level among those aged 80 and over is 65 percent of the peak level—but even among those households there is little sign of running down all financial assets. As a matter of fact, financial assets among the first-quartile households increase in old age, as do those of the third-quartile households.

The wealth distribution is very skewed and displays a large coefficient of variation. It is interesting to observe that the coefficient of variation as well as the ratio of mean to median wealth increases with age. This indicates increasing inequality of the wealth distribution as households age.[12]

---

12. Or—because all numbers are drawn from the 1983 cross section—it implies increasing inequality as we consider older birth cohorts.

Table 5.5   **Gross Financial Assets**

Age	Mean (DM)	Coefficient of Variation	First Quartile (DM)	Median (DM)	Third Quartile (DM)
21–24	8,500	1.9	1,000	4,000	10,000
25–29	15,800	1.4	3,000	9,000	20,000
30–34	19,700	1.4	4,000	11,000	25,000
35–39	22,500	1.5	5,000	12,000	27,000
40–44	24,300	1.6	6,000	14,000	30,000
45–49	25,000	1.4	6,000	14,000	31,000
50–54	26,400	1.7	5,000	14,000	32,000
55–59	26,100	1.6	5,000	13,000	30,000
60–62	28,900	1.8	4,000	14,000	34,000
63–65	27,800	1.9	4,000	12,000	29,000
66–69	25,100	1.9	3,000	11,000	29,000
70–74	23,100	2.2	2,000	9,000	24,000
75–79	23,000	1.9	2,000	9,000	23,000
80–99	25,400	2.3	3,000	9.000	27,000

Source: EVS for 1983.

Note: Excludes cash, checking accounts, and life insurance. See discussion of coverage rates in section 5.3.4. DM 1,000 in 1983 corresponds to a purchasing power of U.S. $650 in 1993.

5.3.5   Net Worth

The determination of total household net worth in Germany is also complicated by sample selection and data limitations of the EVS. On the one hand,
the coverage of housing wealth and its associated mortgage debt is close to
perfect (Euler 1985b, 409). This is mainly because real estate wealth, mostly
owner-occupied housing, is far more equally distributed than financial wealth.
On the other hand, business partnerships and related real wealth, mainly held
by the upper 2 percent of the income distribution, are not reliably covered by
the 1978 EVS and not at all by the 1983 EVS.[13]

The net worth of the EVS households is dominated by housing wealth (see
table 5.6). Although the home ownership rate is relatively low in Germany, the
high land and housing prices mean that housing makes up a large proportion
of aggregate wealth. Table 5.6 indicates two effects: Housing wealth is higher
for middle-aged than for young households. This is due to the higher proportion of home ownership among 35–62-year-olds. In turn, housing wealth is
lower for the elderly than for households aged 35–62. This is a cohort effect
due to the lower quality of homes purchased in the 1950s and 1960s by this
generation and to their low mobility after the acquisition of their home.[14] The
apparent change in portfolio composition between financial and real assets as

13. This the case mainly because of valuation problems: assessment ratios vary immensely
across different types of real capital.
14. These cohort effects are analyzed in Börsch-Supan (1992c).

Table 5.6   **Net Worth**

| | Gross Wealth | | | Debt | | |
Age	Financial	Housing	Total	Mortgages	Consumer Credit	Net Worth
16–34	16,170	22,238	38,408	23,362	2,991	12,022
	(42.1)	(57.9)	(100.0)	(60.9)	(7.8)	(31.3)
35–62	25,113	54,610	79,723	31,596	2,099	46,080
	(31.5)	(68.5)	(100.0)	(39.6)	(2.6)	(57.8)
63–99	24,127	26,454	50,581	3,448	398	46,737
	(47.7)	(52.3)	(100.0)	(6.8)	(0.8)	(92.4)

Source: EVS for 1983.

Note: Excludes business partnerships, cash, checking accounts, life insurance, and private pension wealth. Wealth amounts are in deutschemarks (DM 10,000 in 1983 corresponds to a purchasing power of U.S. $6,500 in 1993). Numbers in parentheses represent share in gross wealth. See discussion of coverage rates in section 5.3.4.

households pass retirement age is therefore mainly caused by this cohort effect and not by a depletion of financial assets.

Table 5.6 also depicts debt. Net worth increases with age because debt decreases and financial wealth remains rather flat. In turn, the large mortgages among young households make net wealth a small proportion of their gross wealth. Consumer credit is small. This is a typical feature of German saving behavior, quite different from American households. Credit cards are still not popular, and neither is purchasing consumption goods using other types of consumer credit. The lack of popularity of consumer credit is one reason for the high saving rates in Germany.

As already stressed, these figures refer to the first 98 percent of the income distribution. Housing wealth and mortgage debt represent a substantially smaller share of gross wealth among the very rich as is shown in section 5.5.

5.3.6   Household Saving by Income Class

The difference between mean and median saving in table 5.3 is an indication of a skewed distribution of savings. This skewness has two causes. First, saving inherits the skewness of the income distribution, which will be discussed in section 5.4. Second, this is amplified by higher saving rates among the rich. This is shown in table 5.7, which depicts the average saving rate in each income quintile.

While the saving rate in the lowest income quintile is slightly negative, it increases quickly with income to reach 17.4 percent of net income at the highest quintile. The rich not only save more in absolute terms, but also more than in proportion to their incomes.

5.3.7   Age-Savings Profiles by Income Class

Table 5.8 extends table 5.7 by displaying the interaction between age and income for financial saving rates. Due to the large sample size of the EVS, the

Table 5.7   **Saving Rates by Income Quintile**

Quintile	Mean Net Household Income (DM)	Mean Saving Rate (%)
1	14,181	−0.88
2	24,614	4.87
3	34,642	7.50
4	46,364	10.59
5	72,801	17.35

Source: EVS for 1983.

Note: Financial and real saving as percentage of net household income. DM 10,000 in 1983 corresponds to a purchasing power of about U.S. $6,500 in 1993.

Table 5.8   **Financial Saving Rates by Age and Income (%)**

	Monthly Net Household Income$			
Age	Less than DM 2,000	DM 2,000–3,000	DM 3,000–5,000	DM 5,000 and Above
21–24	−1.2	2.5	5.5	n.a.
25–29	−2.7	2.1	2.9	3.4
30–34	−4.8	−0.4	2.1	2.2
35–39	−0.9	0.8	−0.3	0.6
40–44	−3.5	−0.6	0.0	2.5
45–49	1.4	1.7	1.7	3.3
50–54	−1.8	−1.5	0.2	4.3
55–59	−2.1	−1.2	3.1	9.0
60–62	−1.4	3.1	6.4	8.3
63–65	−1.5	4.2	5.3	14.4
66–69	−1.3	0.8	3.8	11.7
70–74	2.3	4.1	5.8	16.5
75–79	0.2	9.1	11.3	15.7
80–99	5.6	9.8	14.6	20.9

Source: EVS for 1983.

Note: Includes financial saving without cash, checking accounts, and life insurance. DM 3,000 in 1983 corresponds to a purchasing power of about U.S. $2,000 in 1993. Standard errors are below 1 percent, except for the lower right cell.

cell sizes in table 5.8 are large. In the poorest income class, they range from 157 (ages 45–49) to 937; they are considerably larger for the middle income classes, and they range from 56 and 111 (ages 80+ and ages 75–79) to over 2,000 (ages 40–49). Hence, only the value in the lower right corner is subject to a sampling error of more than 1 percentage point.

Table 5.8 shows that the inverted profile of financial savings holds for all income groups. At young ages, there is mainly dissaving, while saving rates become positive at older ages. The switch from dissaving to saving comes earlier, the more income the household has. Note, however, that saving rates are highest and positive for the oldest old even among the poor households.

PART II: LONGITUDINAL STATISTICS ON SAVINGS AND WEALTH

This second part of the paper augments the cross-sectional evidence on saving behavior with data drawn from earlier cross sections and longitudinal data. Section 5.4 investigates possible cohort effects, and section 5.5 describes the portfolio composition of the EVS households and the very rich, as well as changes in the portfolio composition during the last two decades.

5.4   Cohort Effects

5.4.1   Cohort Effects in Savings

All age-saving profiles considered so far were based on the 1983 cross section of the EVS and are thus subject to the confounding effects of cohort differences and calendar year effects. In this section, I employ a synthetic cohort approach with the 1978 and 1983 cross sections of the EVS for a first-order separation of cohort, year, and age effects. As table 5.9 shows, the main results achieved in the preceding sections stand up to this separation.

Table 5.9 shows that the saving rates of the younger cohorts went down before and immediately after retirement age. However, this decline is reversed after age 70. Saving rates of the older cohorts actually increased as these cohorts aged from 1978 to 1983. In other words, representative households headed by persons aged 65 and over in 1978 saved more in 1983 when they were five years older. Börsch-Supan (1992b) examines this increase and rules out the possibility that it was generated by selection effects due to income-related mortality differences, omission of the institutionalized, and others.

Table 5.9   **Saving Rates by Cohort, Year, and Age**

	Cohort					
	1924–28	1919–23	1913–18	1909–12	1904–08	1879–03
Year	1978	1978	1978	1978	1978	1978
	1983	1983	1983	1983	1983	1983
Age	50–54	55–59	60–65	66–69	70–74	75+
	55–59	60–64	65–70	71–74	75–79	80+
Saving rate (%)	7.3	7.0	3.8	3.9	4.8	8.8
	5.3	3.5	2.4	4.1	5.8	9.7

Source: Adapted from Börsch-Supan (1992b), based on EVS for 1978 and 1983.

Note: The saving rates in this table are based on net income and saving definitions slightly different from those in table 5.1.

5.4.2   Cohort Effects in Financial Wealth

Applying the same methodology as in the preceding subsection, Börsch-Supan (1992b) reports a positive cohort effect in financial wealth: later cohorts of the same age have higher financial wealth levels. This is not surprising in the light of similar cohort effects in earnings (see section 5.6). However, this cohort effect does not account for the reversal of the financial asset profiles at very old ages, as is visible in table 5.10. The representative households in the synthetic cohorts actually increased their financial assets from 1978 to 1983, except for the elderly immediately past retirement age, whose financial assets remained constant.

These results strengthen the finding that saving rates in Germany do not conform to a naive version of the life-cycle hypothesis. Of course, the separation of age and cohort effects rests on only two cross sections and does not account for the many selectivity and data quality problems mentioned in this paper. More research using additional cross sections is needed to support these findings.

5.4.3   Cohort Effects in Housing Wealth

Finally, it is important to point out that real wealth, mainly owner-occupied housing, features very little change after age 50. Because mobility rates of German households aged 50 and over and particularly of home owners are extremely low, housing wealth remains essentially unchanged except for occasional modernizations and additions. Housing depreciation in Germany is also very low. Thus, longitudinal age–housing wealth profiles are more or less flat, and cross-sectional profiles are dominated by cohort effects. The main cause for cohort effects is the low quality of homes purchased in the 1950s and 1960s by the generation who acquired homes at this time. These issues are studied in more depth by Börsch-Supan (1992c).

5.5   Portfolio Composition of Financial Assets

Portfolio composition varies greatly with income and has changed considerably during the past two decades. This section provides summary statistics on

Table 5.10   **Change in Financial Wealth among the Elderly by Cohort, 1978–83**

	Cohort					
	1928–24	1923–19	1918–13	1912–09	1908–04	1903–
Age in 1978	50–54	55–59	60–65	66–69	70–74	75+
Age in 1983	55–59	60–64	65–70	71–74	75–79	80+
Change in financial assets (%)	+ 2.2	+ 2.1	± 0.0	+11.2	+ 9.1	+ 5.3

Source: Adapted from Börsch-Supan (1992b), based on EVS for 1978 and 1983.

financial portfolios based on several data sets. First, I consult the EVS for the portfolio composition of the first 98 percent of the income distribution. Second, and in order to complement the EVS data, I employ property tax returns which shed light on the portfolio composition of the very rich. The third subsection uses aggregate data provided by the Deutsche Bundesbank to report on changes in the portfolio composition during the past two decades.

5.5.1   Portfolio Composition in the EVS

We first consider the EVS households in the first 98 percent of the income distribution. Table 5.11 displays how their financial portfolio composition changes with age. We observe large changes, the most dramatic one in dedicated savings. Since these savings have to be related to future home purchases, they dominate the portfolio of the young and almost vanish among the elderly.

This is a typical German phenomenon.[15] Until recently, the "golden rule" of German home financing was a 40 percent down payment together with a 30 percent building society loan, topped by a 30 percent bank mortgage. The down payment consisted mainly of dedicated savings in building societies, because a building society loan requires a matching savings account at that building society. This scheme was supported by the government which subsidized savings at building societies.[16] The financing scheme explains the large share of financial wealth held in building societies, among the younger households in 1983.

Since 1990, home ownership financial deviates increasingly from the old golden rule for two reasons. First, the government has essentially stopped the favorable treatment of building society savings. Second, land and house prices have increased very quickly, making the large down payment unaffordable to all but very wealthy households and thereby prompting higher shares of commercial mortgages.

Passbook savings is the other popular form of savings among the EVS households in table 5.11. Eighty-five percent of households have a savings account, and almost 50 percent of all financial wealth reported in the EVS is held as passbook savings among the elderly. Less popular are savings certificates and bonds.

5.5.2   Portfolio Composition of the Very Rich

The portfolios of the very rich look rather different. Table 5.12, compiled by Baron (1988) from 1980 property tax returns, shows how much of total wealth is held by the top 0.5, top 1, and top 1.5 percent of the wealth distribution. Property tax returns cover the wealth of the rich but not of the poor and the

---

15. The only other country with a similarly important role for building society savings is Austria.
16. See the first paper of this sequence, Börsch-Supan (1994).

Table 5.11   **Portfolio Composition of Financial Wealth (%)**

Age	Passbook Savings	Savings Certificates	Dedicated Savings	Public Bonds	Private Bonds	Stocks	Investment Funds	Other
16–34	36.1	4.8	42.3	3.3	3.8	3.0	0.6	6.1
	(81.0)	(8.6)	(53.1)	(5.4)	(5.9)	(6.9)	(1.3)	(7.1)
35–62	40.7	8.5	24.1	4.5	6.4	5.7	1.4	8.7
	(87.3)	(15.7)	(50.0)	(6.6)	(8.7)	(10.4)	(2.8)	(8.9)
63–99	48.6	11.0	5.6	6.4	10.8	7.7	2.3	7.6
	(85.0)	(14.2)	(40.9)	(6.5)	(9.3)	(8.6)	(2.8)	(7.1)
All	42.6	8.8	20.7	5.0	7.4	6.0	1.6	8.0
	(85.3)	(13.8)	(40.0)	(6.4)	(8.3)	(9.1)	(2.5)	(8.0)

Source: EVS for 1983.
Note: Figures represent the share of the respective financial asset in total financial assets. Excluded are cash, checking accounts, life insurance, and pension wealth. Numbers in parentheses are the proportions of households holding the respective financial assets.

Table 5.12   **Distribution and Compositon of Household Wealth among the Very Rich**

	Average Household Wealth of Top x Percent (thousand DM) and Percentage of Total Wealth Held by Top x Percent							
x	Agricultural Property	Real Estate	Business Partnerships	Stocks and Bonds	Other	Gross Wealth	Debt	Net Wealth
0.5	12	1,240	1,522	441	537	3,754	379	3,374
	3.6	13.2	61.8	50.7	6.1	17.2	12.0	8.1
1.0	9	894	877	251	355	2,389	243	2,146
	5.2	19.1	71.3	57.9	8.1	21.9	15.5	23.0
1.5	7	721	624	179	278	1,811	184	1,627
	6.4	23.1	76.2	61.8	9.5	24.9	17.6	26.1

Source: Baron (1988, 188), based on 1980 property tax returns.
Note: Excludes households with wealth below property tax exclusion.

middle class, because households below the exclusion limits do not have to file property tax returns and the exclusion limits are rather generous.[17]

Of the financial wealth reported in the 1980 property tax returns, more than 50 percent was held by the top 1.5 percent of the wealth distribution. These households are likely to be in the top 2 percent income range and are thus not sampled in the EVS. Particularly noticeable is the concentration of business partnerships among the very rich: More than three-quarters are held by the top 1.5 percent in the wealth distribution. Also highly concentrated are stocks and bonds, of which almost 62 percent are held by the top 1.5 percent in the wealth distribution.

17. The exclusion is approximately U.S. $44,000 per household member (see Börsch-Supan 1994). Housing wealth is counted only as assessed value, which is less than a sixth of sales value.

In turn, real estate is much less concentrated. Therefore, as opposed to the portfolio composition of the EVS households in table 5.11, housing wealth plays a less dominant role in the wealth of the rich. Similarly, the ratio of debt to gross wealth is smaller among the rich than among the EVS households.

5.5.3   Changes in Portfolio Composition

To conclude the summary statistics on savings and wealth, this subsection deals with changes in portfolio composition. Table 5.13 is compiled from aggregate data provided by the Deutsche Bundesbank and covers assets held by German banks, building societies, and insurance. The figures include households across all income ranges but also nonprofit organizations. The upper half reports on short-term assets (maturity less than four years), the lower one on long-term assets (maturity four years or more).

Household portfolio composition has changed considerably during the last two decades. The table clearly shows the decline of passbook savings. While short- and long-term savings accounts made up almost 40 percent of all financial assets in 1970, their share shrank to about 23 percent 20 years later. In turn, fixed-interest bonds and life insurance rose from a share of about 21 percent to almost 36 percent. This trend has continued since 1990. At the beginning of this year, the Bundesbank announced that the share of life insurance in financial wealth had surpassed that of savings accounts.

At the same time, the portfolio changed in favor of longer-term assets. While less than 63 percent of all financial assets had a maturity of four or more years in 1970, this share increased to 67.6 percent in 1990.

Not accounted for in table 5.13 are assets held abroad. The introduction of a tax on interest income at the source is said to have prompted many house-

Table 5.13   **Changes in Portfolio Composition, Aggregate Data 1970–90 (%)**

Financial Asset	1970	1975	1980	1985	1990
Cash, checking accounts	10.7	9.5	8.7	7.1	7.8
Short-term savings accounts	23.4	22.9	20.7	18.3	15.2
Time deposits	1.5	1.7	4.2	4.4	6.0
Money market funds	1.6	2.0	2.4	2.5	3.4
Short-term assets	37.2	36.2	35.9	32.3	32.4
Long-term savings accounts	16.2	17.5	12.7	9.6	7.7
Savings certificates	1.2	3.3	6.6	7.1	7.1
Building societies	7.6	7.8	7.3	5.6	4.2
Life insurance	13.5	13.3	14.6	16.5	18.9
Bonds	7.8	9.2	11.5	15.2	16.6
Stocks	10.1	6.5	4.2	6.3	5.5
Private pensions	6.3	6.3	7.2	7.5	7.7
Long-term assets	62.8	63.8	64.1	67.7	67.6

Source: Ergebnisse der gesamtwirtschaftlichen Finanzierungsrechnung 1981–90 (Frankfurt: Deutsche Bundesbank, 1991).

holds to move their financial assets to Luxembourg. However, little is known about the actual magnitudes involved.[18]

PART III: BACKGROUND

This third part of the paper augments the descriptive statistics on saving behavior by a description of related variables such as income, consumption, and demographic household characteristics in order to guide the interpretation of the numbers provided in parts I and II. I begin with household income.

5.6 Household Income

5.6.1 The Level of Household Income

Per capita GDP in West Germany in 1989, the last year before unification, was lower than in the United States (see table 5.14). Due to different household sizes and tax structures, the income differential is a little smaller with respect to household disposable income. Most of the 25 percent lower income can be accounted for by the 20 percent fewer work hours in Germany.[19] Therefore, the lower per capita income in Germany reflects a high level of leisure consumption unaccounted for in national accounting data, and not so much a lower level of social welfare.

Since 1990, the unification of Germany has increased the income differential. In the second half of 1990, GDP per worker in the former GDR was about a fourth of the West German equivalent, and GDP per capita was less than a third. Because East Germans make up 20 percent of the total German population, unification in 1990 has resulted in a (statistical) 14 percent reduction of per capita GDP.[20]

Therefore, the convex relation between saving and income—saving increases more than proportionately with income—which tends to hold in national cross sections such as the one depicted in table 5.7, does not carry over to cross-national comparisons: the United States has lower saving rates in spite of higher per capita GDP.

In turn, the decrease of German per capita income is reflected in the decline of the German household saving rate since 1990.

5.6.2 The Distribution of Household Income

An important difference between the United States and Germany which may contribute to the different saving rates is the income distribution. In compari-

---

18. See Nöhrbaß and Raab (1990) for an estimate during the first and unsuccessful attempt to establish taxation of interest income at the source.

19. In 1990, German workers worked 1,506 hours, American workers 1,847 hours (Institut der Deutschen Wirtschaft 1991).

20. I.e., if we compare the former West Germany with the new unified Germany.

Table 5.14   **Household Income**

	GDP per Capita 1989 (U.S. $)	Net Household Income 1987 (U.S. $)	Income Distribution (%)					
			Bottom 20%	Second 20%	Third 20%	Fourth 20%	Ninth 10%	Top 10%
United States	18,910	24,875	4.7	11.0	17.4	25.0	16.9	25.0
West Germany	13,746	19,401	6.8	12.7	17.8	24.1	15.3	23.4

Sources: U.S. Bureau of the Census (1985); Eurostat; World Bank, *World Development Record,* table 30.

Note: The income distribution figures represent the share of total income in the respective percentile in 1984 (West Germany) and 1985 (United States).

son to the United States, the German income distribution features relatively small tails and a large middle class. While the lowest 20 percent in the income distribution have 6.8 percent of total income in Germany, they have only 4.7 percent in the United States. Conversely, the richest decile in the United States earns a quarter of total income, but only 23.4 percent in Germany. Hence, median income in Germany is closer to mean income than in the United States, and the cross-national income differential with respect to median income is substantially smaller than that with respect to mean income.[21] As we saw in the previous section, the German middle class not only has high saving rates but also constitutes a large proportion of German households.

5.6.3 Age-Income Profiles

Another important ingredient to an explanation of the German saving pattern is the relation to German life-cycle income patterns. Table 5.15 depicts the age-income profile observed in the 1983 cross section of the EVS. The profile exhibits an inverted U-shape with a peak between ages 45 and 49. However, this shape results from a combination of age and cohort effects. I therefore use the seven waves of the SOEP to disentangle age and cohort effects by regressing labor income and age and birth cohort. The results are displayed in table 5.16. After correcting for cohort (and, potentially, time) effects, the individual earnings peak moves from 46.4 to 71.7 years. Hence, the U-shaped age profile is entirely an artifact of cohort and time effects, and individual labor income increases steadily until retirement.[22]

21. In 1989, German median net household income was 91 percent of German mean net household income (SOEP for 1990) while the median money income of U.S. households was only 79.4 percent of the mean money income of U.S. households (U.S. Bureau of the Census 1991, 450–51). However, this comparison ignores the effect of progressive income taxes, which were subtracted in the German but not in the American figures. Based on large samples of the 1978 American Housing Survey and its German counterpart, the 1978 1%-Wohnungsstichprobe, median net household income in 1978 was about equal in the United States and Germany.

22. As a byproduct, the regression also produces an estimate of the large male-female income differential, about DM 1,450 per month (U.S. $8,500 per annum). It should be noted, however, that the age, cohort, and gender gap estimates in table 5.16 do not hold job and schooling differences constant.

Table 5.15   **Age-Income Profile, 1983 EVS**

Age	Gross Annual Household Income (DM)	Net Annual Household Income	
		Amount (DM)	Percentage of Gross
21–24	28,223	21,421	75.9
25–29	42,326	31,532	74.5
30–34	52,904	39,836	75.3
35–39	60,943	46,194	75.8
40–44	65,725	49,951	76.0
45–49	67,630	51,060	75.5
50–54	64,736	49,134	75.9
55–59	55,973	43,379	77.5
60–62	45,330	38,303	84.5
63–65	39,644	35,402	89.3
66–69	34,904	32,356	92.7
70–74	28,101	26,667	94.9
75–79	26,050	24,643	94.6
80–99	25,092	23,862	95.1

Source: Lang (1993a).
Note: DM 10,000 in 1983 corresponds to a purchasing power of U.S. $6,500 in 1993.

Table 5.16   **Age and Cohort Effects in Labor Income—Dependent Variable: Labor Income**

Variable	(1)	(2)	(3)	(4)	(5)
Age	246.1	230.2	140.3	317.8	289.9
	(35.9)	(36.0)	(24.2)	(38.7)	(14.7)
Age*Age	−2.604	−2.481		−2.383	−2.02
	(30.6)	(31.3)		(30.1)	(8.4)
Cohort			109.6	96.92	1,566.9
			(18.8)	(16.1)	(1.7)
Cohort*Cohort					−0.377
					(1.6)
Female		−1,438	−1,460.7	−1,442.4	−1,442.3
		(61.3)	(61.5)	(61.8)	(61.8)
R^2	8.7	20.7	18.8	21.6	21.6
Age at peak	47.3	46.4	n.a.	66.7	71.7

Source: Pooled SOEP for 1984–90; 24,883 observations.
Note: Numbers in parentheses are *t*-statistics.

It is therefore important to note that *holding cohort fixed* the apparent decline in income after age 50 vanishes. Moreover, net income has a less pronounced U-shape which is largely due to the tax exemption of most pension income—visible in the effective tax rates (including social security taxes) implied by the leftmost column of table 5.15. A look at the composition of household income complements these facts.

5.6.4 Composition of Household Income

Table 5.17 gives a detailed account of the various household income sources by age of household head. As mentioned before, labor and retirement income aggregates up to national accounting figures, while only about two-thirds of asset income is reported. For households in the upper 2 percent of the income distribution, the share of asset income is likely to be much higher than that reported in table 5.17.

Transfer income in table 5.17 distinguishes public and private transfers. Public transfers include welfare (*Sozialhilfe*), housing allowances (*Wohngeld*), unemployment compensation and unemployment aid (*Arbeitslosengeld und Arbeitslosenhilfe*), child support (*Kindergeld*), and educational grants (BAFöG). The increase at old ages reflects pockets of poverty among widows who are not covered by the public pension system and receive welfare. The relatively large transfer rates among very young households are due to educational grants. Private transfers include regular transfers (e.g., monthly checks from parents) as well as one-time transfers (such as inheritances). The numbers in table 5.17 are dominated by intergenerational transfers from parents to children (ages below 30) and from adult children to elderly parents (ages above 70).

Labor income is the major component of income up to age 62. After age 62, public pension income is the main income source. The change from labor to pension income is very sharp. This reflects both the sharp change in labor force participation rates after age 57, and the rare occurrence of part-time jobs after official retirement (table 5.18). Statutory retirement age in Germany is 65. However, the actuarially unfair design of the public pension system makes it desirable to retire at the earliest possible date, resulting in an average retirement age of 58.5 years in 1987.[23]

More than 99 percent of households aged 65 and over receive public retirement income. In addition to the coverage, the replacement rate is also generous: on average, the net replacement rate is 71 percent. Because public pensions in Germany are designed to support the standard of living achieved during working life and not to be a subsistence income after retirement (as is the case in many other countries), public pensions are roughly proportional to labor income averaged over the life course and have only a slight redistributive character, much less than in the United States.[24] For this reason, the German pension system calls itself "retirement insurance" rather than "social security" as in the United States.

About a third of households aged 65 and over receive supplemental pension income, mostly firm pensions. However, these pensions amount to only 6 per-

---

23. The official retirement window extends from age 60 to age 65, but efforts to reduce statistical unemployment permitted retirement as early as age 57 in the mid-1980s. For details, see Börsch-Supan (1992a).

24. For details, see the first paper on saving incentives (Börsch-Supan 1994).

Table 5.17   **Sources of Income by Age, 1983 EVS (%)**

Age	Labor Income	Pensions		Transfers		Asset Income	
		Public	Private	Public	Private	Financial	Housing
21–24	85.5	0.8	0.0	5.8	6.2	1.4	0.4
25–29	90.4	0.4	0.0	4.5	2.4	1.8	0.6
30–34	91.2	0.7	0.0	4.0	1.2	1.7	1.2
35–39	90.8	1.0	0.0	3.8	0.7	1.8	1.8
40–44	88.5	1.5	0.1	3.9	0.8	1.9	3.3
45–49	87.7	2.3	0.1	3.2	0.4	2.0	4.3
50–54	84.9	3.9	0.3	2.5	0.4	2.2	5.7
55–59	77.7	9.9	1.0	1.9	0.4	2.9	6.3
60–62	51.9	30.3	3.9	1.3	0.7	3.6	8.3
63–65	30.8	48.4	6.1	1.0	0.7	4.1	8.9
66–69	14.7	63.5	6.7	1.1	0.8	4.6	8.7
70–74	6.7	69.8	6.0	1.5	1.6	5.4	9.2
75–79	4.7	71.4	5.0	1.9	2.6	6.1	8.3
80–99	4.6	71.1	4.3	2.7	2.7	6.9	7.7

Source: Lang (1993a).

Table 5.18   **Male Labor Force Participation Rates (%)**

Age	West Germany			United States		
	Full Time	Part Time	Retired	Full Time	Part Time	Retired
50–54	91.5	0.6	7.8	76.6	11.0	12.4
55–59	79.1	1.5	19.4	65.9	17.4	16.7
60–64	37.7	1.6	60.8	38.8	16.9	44.3
65–69	4.1	7.5	88.4	12.2	22.3	65.4
70–74	1.7	3.2	95.3	7.2	13.7	79.1
75–79	2.5	1.7	95.7	2.5	12.7	84.8
80+	1.2	0.0	98.8	1.6	4.8	93.5

Source: Börsch-Supan (1991), computed from PSID for 1984, SOEP for 1984, male heads of household only.

Notes: Full time: more than 35 hours weekly; part time: between 15 and 35 hours weekly; retired: less than 15 hours weekly.

cent of total retirement income and are much less important in Germany than in the United States. The prevalence of firm pensions increased in the 1980s but has recently stabilized at a level substantially lower than in the United States. Private pension wealth is estimated at 7.5 percent of total financial wealth (see table 5.4) and is much smaller than in the United States.

Pension income also includes occupational pensions and survivor pensions (for orphans, widows, and widowers). Occupational pensions make up most of the pension income below age 60.

The effective continuation of labor income after retirement explains the small role of other income sources among the elderly. Annuitized retirement income amounts to 70 percent (see table 5.17). The high level of annuitized retirement income and the rising labor income profile until retirement is a puzzle in terms of savings: Why save so much before retirement when labor income increases and retirement income is annuitized at such generous levels? The study of consumption patterns below will resolve this apparent contradiction.

5.7   Consumption Patterns

5.7.1   Age-Consumption Profiles

The share of consumption expenditures in net income is higher among the very young and lower among the very old (see table 5.19). This reflects the increase in saving rates with age which was depicted (table 5.1) only partially. The saving rates in table 5.1 and the consumption rates in table 5.19 do not add up because consumption and net income in these tables exclude intrafamily transfers. For the young, transfers received dominate transfers given; in old age, the relation reverses.

The decline in age-specific consumption rates is not monotonic. It is interrupted by a small but significant increase in consumption during the years following retirement. The decline in per capita consumption is less pronounced than that in household consumption. Both effects can be explained by a decrease in those variable consumption expenditures which are most affected by declining health in old age. An inspection of the composition of consumption expenditures clarifies this.

5.7.2   Composition of Consumption Expenditures by Age

To this end, table 5.20 gives a detailed account of the composition of household consumption expenditures stratified by age. The seven consumption categories are defined as follows: "RentHous" includes rent and other housing expenditures including maintenance, utilities, and energy. For renters, the figure includes actual rent, while it includes imputed rent rather than actual mortgage payments for home owners. Major modernizations are not included as consumption but are counted as real saving. The "Food" and "Clothing" categories are defined as one would expect, with the exception that jewelry counts as clothing. "Health" includes private insurance payments, out-of-pocket medical expenditures, hygiene, home care, and nursing home stays not covered by health insurance. It does not include payments to public health insurance, which are treated as payroll taxes, averaging about 12 percent of gross income. The category "TranTrav" encompasses transportation and travel expenses such as commuting, family visits and holiday travel, and all car expenses including the purchase of a car. Finally, two catch-all categories comprise all leisure-related consumption, including education, phone, TV, movies, newspapers,

Table 5.19   **Age-Consumption Profile, 1983 EVS**

Age	Annual Consumption per Household (DM)	Annual Consumption per Capita (DM)	Share of Consumption in Net Income (%)
25–29	30,159	16,123	94.6
30–34	36,951	15,628	86.6
35–39	42,343	15,331	88.7
40–44	45,214	15,172	89.4
45–49	45,136	15,330	87.0
50–54	41,998	15,942	86.0
55–59	36,768	16,889	86.4
60–62	32,993	17,565	88.6
63–65	31,415	17,571	90.5
66–69	28,220	16,770	88.5
70–74	22,827	15,450	87.5
75–79	20,454	14,704	83.5
80–99	18,329	13,621	79.3

Source: Lang (1993a).
Note: DM 10,000 in 1983 corresponds to a purchasing power of U.S. $6,500 in 1993.

Table 5.20   **Household Consumption Expenditures by Age, 1983 EVS (%)**

Age	RentHous	Food	Health	TranTrav	Leisure	Clothing	Durables
21–24	21.8	21.3	7.5	22.3	10.3	8.4	8.5
25–29	21.7	21.2	9.0	21.4	9.7	8.1	9.0
30–34	22.5	21.2	10.8	20.1	8.8	8.2	8.5
35–39	22.1	21.5	11.4	18.8	8.8	8.6	8.9
40–44	21.6	21.8	10.9	19.2	8.5	9.2	8.8
45–49	21.2	22.3	10.7	19.7	7.9	9.3	8.8
50–54	21.4	22.5	10.5	20.3	7.2	9.0	9.0
55–59	22.6	22.0	11.1	18.9	7.2	9.0	9.3
60–62	23.5	21.8	10.8	18.3	7.0	9.0	9.6
63–65	23.9	21.6	10.4	18.6	7.0	9.3	9.2
66–69	25.2	22.0	10.0	17.3	7.2	9.4	9.0
70–74	28.2	23.1	9.1	15.5	6.9	9.2	8.1
75–79	29.0	23.7	10.1	13.3	6.7	8.3	8.9
80–99	31.7	24.2	10.6	10.5	6.7	7.4	8.8

Source: Börsch-Supan (1992b) and Lang (1993a).

pets, garden, smoking, etc. ("Leisure"), and all durables except clothing and jewelry ("Durables"), mainly household appliances and furniture.

Changes in consumption shares are only marginal until age 50, but consumption expenditure patterns clearly change for older households. A dramatic change occurs in the travel and transportation categories. The transportation share decreases sharply from about 20 percent of all expenditures among those aged 20–50 to about 10 percent among the over 80-year-old households. Education and other leisure-related expenditures also decrease significantly as households age.

Among the consumption categories in table 5.20, durables are included in "Clothing" and "Durables," but also in the "Leisure" and "TranTrav" categories. Taken together, durables account for about 26 percent of the consumption expenditures of an average German household.[25] For the elderly, the share of all durables declines to 18 percent after a hump in the years immediately after retirement. The decline is even more pronounced on a per capita basis.

5.7.3   The Role of Housing Consumption

Housing-related expenditures are about 22 percent, of which 9 percent are energy costs. There are striking differences in housing consumption between Germany and the United States. Most notable are the differences in tenure choice and dwelling size. Home ownership is less common in Germany and peaked at 40.2 percent in 1987, compared to 64.4 percent in the United States. Americans also have larger dwellings. Newly constructed houses have on average 149 square meters in the United States, while German houses have on average 86 square meters.[26]

However, in assessing the role of housing in savings and wealth, it should be stressed that German land and housing prices are substantially higher than American. On a per square meter basis, new homes are about 2.3 times more expensive in Germany than in the United States. This difference is due to about 80 percent higher structure costs (quality constant) and about 4.5 times higher land prices. These higher prices result in larger housing consumption expenditures in spite of lower consumption: Comparable expenditure shares are 22 percent in Germany and only 19 percent in the United States. On a different scale, the cost of a new home amounts to 4.6 times the average German household income, while it is only 3.4 times that of an American household. Hence, while fewer households hold housing wealth in Germany, German housing wealth is on average higher for those who are home owners. Moreover, houses are financed by large down payments averaging about 40 percent of the sales price, as was described above, generating the large saving rates among the young depicted in table 5.11.

5.7.4   The Role of Health Consumption

Also the pattern of health expenditures has important implications for saving behavior in Germany. The share of health expenditures remains essentially constant over the life cycle and is about 10 percent of net income. This percentage is considerably lower than in the United States (15.5 percent). The constancy of health expenditures during the life cycle is mainly due to the design

---

25. EVS for 1983 (Fachserie 15, Heft 2, 245).
26. Statistical Abstract of the United States (U.S. Bureau of the Census, various years); Statistical Yearbook of Germany (Statistisches Bundesamt, various years).

of the German health insurance system, which is mandatory (with only a few exceptions) and covers most health expenses. All households are covered by health insurance, 92.2 percent are covered by one of the public health insurance schemes, and the remainder by a private health plan. The coinsurance rate in the public health system is 50 percent for medication, 8 percent for ambulatory care, and 2 percent for hospital care. Most private plans have no coinsurance, and many households have private supplemental insurance covering the coinsurance payment of the public system. The mandatory health insurance system generates large intergenerational transfers which flatten the age–health expenditure profiles.

Two caveats in interpreting the health expenditure profiles in table 5.20 should be mentioned. First, younger cohorts rely more on private insurance and thus have higher health expenditures, while older cohorts rely more on the social insurance system covered by payroll taxes not included in the health expenditure figures in table 5.20. Second, table 5.20 omits the elderly who live in costly institutions such as private old-age homes and attributes health expenses for the elderly who live in a child's household to the younger generation. Both effects may conceal an increase in health expenses with age, although their quantitative impact is probably quite small. The generous mandatory health insurance adds another puzzle to the task of understanding the high German saving rates: To a large extent, the health insurance system makes savings as a precaution against major health expenditures unnecessary.

5.8   Other Household Characteristics

Other household characteristics which might influence saving behavior include employment status and household size. The unemployed have substantially lower, while those not in the labor force have significantly higher saving rates (Lang 1983b). The first is rather obviously related to income, while the second effect is caused by the increase in saving rates among the elderly. Both effects have been described earlier.

An interesting observation is the absence of a clear relation between household size and saving. More specifically, the number of children in a household has little influence on saving behavior. This is visible in table 5.21 which relates financial and real saving to the number of children in a household. An analysis of these figures reveals two effects. First, saving rates do increase faster with age for households with two or more children than for those with no or one child. Second, households with children have about 1 percent higher real saving rates, while households without children have about 1 percent higher financial saving rates. Both effects are statistically significant, although at low confidence levels.

The EVS report children present in a household, but not children ever born. The data are therefore not really suited to a test of a bequest motive. In Börsch-Supan (1991), I regress wealth levels reported in the 1988 SOEP on the number

Table 5.21   Saving Rates by Number of Children, 1983 EVS (%)

Age	No Children	One Child	Two Children	Three or More Children
30–34	10.6	9.5	9.5	7.9
35–39	10.4	10.8	9.9	12.9
40–44	10.4	10.4	9.7	10.8
45–49	10.9	9.4	9.7	10.9
50–54	10.2	11.2	8.5	11.3
55–59	11.1	10.3	11.6	12.9

Source: EVS for 1983.
Note: Standard errors are below 1 percent, except for the lower right cell.

of children ever born. This comes closer to a test of an operating bequest motive. The regressions do not produce significant positive effects once income is held constant. If it exists at all, the correlation between assets and children is negative. One interpretation of such a negative correlation is that an operating bequest motive is offset or even overcompensated by higher expenditures of families with children. Because both effects occur together, there is no way to detect a bequest motive in such data.

5.9   Conclusions

German saving rates are high by international standards. Average net household saving amounted to some 13 percent of net income in 1983. Saving rates have increased since and reached almost 15 percent in 1990, when they surpassed even the Japanese household saving rate. Since then, saving rates have slowly declined to about 14 percent, while consumption remained unchanged and per capita disposable income fell in the wake of German unification.

Housing wealth dominates the wealth of households belonging to the first 98 percent of the income distribution. This may appear to be a contradiction to the German home ownership rate, which is among the lowest in the industrialized countries. However, the high level of land and housing prices offsets the low home ownership rate.

Among financial assets, passbook savings and life insurance policies are the two most popular savings instruments. Traditionally, passbook savings constituted the lion's share of financial wealth, but they were recently surpassed by life insurance. For younger households, savings contracts dedicated to the down payment for a future home purchase are a third important asset choice. These dedicated savings are traditionally popular and are specific to Germany.

The age pattern of saving does not conform to naive versions of the life-cycle hypothesis. While saving rates increase monotonically with age among younger households to reach a local maximum at retirement, saving rates do not decrease monotonically thereafter. In the five to ten years following retirement, consumption increases despite a decrease in income, and saving rates decrease. During these years, however, there is little evidence of a depletion of assets, only a retardation of saving. Moreover, saving rates rebound after this consumption peak and even reach their absolute maximum over the life course at ages past 70 years.

This paper is not the place to speculate at length about the causes of the type of saving behavior observed in Germany. High aggregate saving rates may be caused by the rather balanced income distribution with a dominating middle class, by the need to finance the high land and house prices in Germany, or by a tradition still influenced by the experiences of World War II and an austere period after the war.

The German age-saving pattern characterized by an increase in saving at old age was analyzed by Börsch-Supan and Stahl (1991c). They show that even under perfect foresight declining consumption in connection with a high level of annuity income creates "forced" saving in old age, once the annuity income cannot be borrowed against—as is the case in the German public pension system.

References

Baron, Dietmar. 1988. *Die personelle Vermögensverteilung in der Bundesrepublik Deutschland und ihre Bestimmungsgründe.* Frankfurt am Main: Lang.
Börsch-Supan, Axel. 1991. Implications of an aging population: Problems and policy options in West Germany and the United States. *Economic Policy* 12: 103–40.
———. 1992a. Population aging, social security design, and early retirement. *Journal of Institutional and Theoretical Economics* 148: 533–57.
———. 1992b. Saving and consumption patterns among the elderly: The German case. *Journal of Population Economics* 5: 289–303.
———. 1992c. Wohnungsnachfrage älterer Mitbürger. In *Herausforderung an den Wohlfahrtsstaat im strukturellen Wandel,* ed. R. Hujer, H. Schneider, and W. Zapf. Frankfurt: Campus.
———. 1994. Savings in Germany—Part I: Incentives. In *Public policies and household saving,* ed. J. M. Poterba, 81–104. Chicago: University of Chicago Press.
Börsch-Supan, Axel, and Konrad Stahl. 1991a. Do dedicated savings programs increase aggregate savings and housing demand? *Journal of Public Economics* 44: 265–97.
———. 1991b. Life cycle savings and consumption constraints. *Journal of Population Economics* 4: 433–55.
Braun, Hans-Ulrich. 1978. Werbung der Haushalte für die Einkommens- und Verbrauchsstichprobe 1978. *Wirtschaft und Statistik* 7: 410–12.
Burkhauser, Richard. 1991. An introduction to the German Socio-Economic Panel for English speaking researchers. Syracuse University. Mimeograph.
Euler, Manfred. 1981a. Ausgewählte Vermögensbestände und Schulden privater Haushalte am Jahresende 1978. In *Einkommens- und Verbrauchsstichprobe 1978,* Fachserie 15, Heft 2, 7–29. Wiesbaden: Statistisches Bundesamt.
———. 1981b. Probleme der Erfassung von Vermögensbeständen privater Haushalte in Einkommens- und Verbrauchsstichproben. *Wirtschaft und Statistik* 4: 252.

————. 1982. Einkommens- und Verbrauchsstichprobe 1983. *Wirtschaft und Statistik* 6: 499–507.

————. 1985a. Ausgewählte Vermögensbestände und Schulden privater Haushalte am Jahresende 1983. In *Einkommens- und Verbrauchsstichprobe 1983*, Fachserie 15, Heft 2, 7–60. Wiesbaden: Statistisches Bundesamt.

————. 1985b. Geldvermögen privater Haushalte 1983. *Wirtschaft und Statistik* 5: 408–18.

————. 1987. Einkommens- und Verbrauchsstichprobe 1988. *Wirtschaft und Statistik* 11: 798–808.

————. 1991. Ausgewählte Vermögensbestände und Schulden privater Haushalte am Jahresende 1988. In *Einkommens- und Verbrauchsstichprobe 1988*, Fachserie 15, Heft 2, 11–45. Wiesbaden: Statistisches Bundesamt.

Institut der Deutschen Wirtschaft. 1991. Zahlen zur wirtschaftlichen Entwicklung. Köln: Deutscher Instituts-Verlag.

Lang, Oliver. 1993a. Die Einkommenssituation der Haushalte. Mannheim: Zentrum für Europäische Wirtschaftsforschung. Mimeograph.

————. 1993b. Die Qualität der Vermögensdaten in der Einkommens- und Verbrauchsstichprobe 1983: Ein Abgleich mit aggregierten Statistiken. Mannheim: Zentrum für Europäische Wirtschaftsforschung. Mimeograph.

Nöhrbaß, Karl-Heinz, and Martin Raab. 1990. Quellensteuer und Kapitalmarkt, *Finanzarchiv* 48: 179–93.

Pöschl, Hannelore. 1993. Werbung und Beteiligung der Haushalte an der Einkommens- und Verbrauchsstichprobe 1993. *Wirtschaft und Statistik* 6: 385–90.

Schüler, Klaus. 1988. Einkommensverteilung nach Haushaltsgruppen: Ausgangsstatistiken und ihre Zusammenfassung. In *Aufgaben und Probleme der* Einkommensstatistik - *Erstellung, Nutzung, Interpretation,* Sonderheft zum Allgemeinen Statistischen Archiv 26/88, ed. U. P. Reich, 37–66.

Statistisches Bundesamt. Various years. *Statistisches Jahrbuch für die Bundesrepublik Deutschland.* Stuttgart: Kohlhammer.

U.S. Bureau of the Census. Various years. *Statistical Abstract of the United States.* Washington, D.C.: Government Printing Office.

6 Personal Saving in Italy

Tullio Jappelli and Marco Pagano

6.1 Introduction

It is increasingly recognized that detailed analysis of microeconomic data can shed light on households' motivation for saving, discriminating between life-cycle motives, concern for future generations, the need to insure against income, health, and mortality risks, and the desire to acquire a house. Studies of household behavior have begun to develop along these lines in Italy, in particular drawing on the Survey of Household Income and Wealth conducted by the Bank of Italy. This paper offers an overview of the life-cycle pattern of Italian households' consumption, income, saving, and wealth and provides other background information on the determinants of their saving behavior, based on several waves of this survey.

Section 6.2 presents the main characteristics of the data and compares the implied aggregate measures of income, consumption, and wealth with the corresponding national and financial account aggregates. In section 6.3 we report the cross-sectional age profiles of income, consumption, saving, and wealth in the 1987 Survey of Household Income and Wealth. Section 6.4 compares these profiles with cohort-adjusted profiles estimated on pooled data from the 1984, 1986, 1987, and 1989 surveys and relates the saving behavior of Italian households to demographic and economic variables by regression analysis.

The availability of housing finance, the public provision of health care, and the rules of the social security system can be presumed to influence saving

Tullio Jappelli is associate professor at Istituto Universitario Navale, Naples, and a research fellow of the Centre for Economic Policy Research. Marco Pagano is associate professor at Università Bocconi, Milan, and a research fellow of the Centre for Economic Policy Research.

The authors thank the discussant, Jonathan Skinner, for helpful comments and the Research Department of the Bank of Italy, and particularly Giovanni D'Alessio, for providing the data from the 1987 and 1989 Surveys of Household Income and Wealth.

decisions significantly. In section 6.5 we evaluate the potential impact of these institutional arrangements on saving by Italian households. The timing and the financing of home acquisition shed light on the role of housing purchases in asset accumulation. The incidence of private health expenditure helps indicate the importance of uninsured health risk as a motive for saving. Finally, we use survey data on ex post and ex ante replacement rates to evaluate the role of social security in saving choices.

6.2   The Data

The Survey of Household Income and Wealth (SHIW) is the best source on the saving behavior of Italian households. It provides reliable data on income, consumption, and wealth from a sample that is representative of the population. Appendix A describes the main features of this survey, its sample design, interviewing procedure, and response rate; it also evaluates the survey's relative strengths and weaknesses with respect to the two other Italian databases on households, namely, the National Institute of Statistics (ISTAT) and Banca Nazionale del Lavoro (BNL) surveys.

Table 6.1, which refers to all the individuals covered by the SHIW (including those who are not income recipients), shows a close correspondence between the sample means for selected demographic characteristics and the general

Table 6.1   **Population and Sample Means of Selected Demographic Characteristics of Individuals Covered by the 1989 SHIW**

Variable	Population	1989 SHIW
Gender		
Male	48.6	48.7
Female	51.4	51.3
Age		
<24	32.7	32.9
25–44	28.6	28.8
45–64	24.1	26.1
>65	14.5	12.3
City Size		
<20,000	46.8	44.7
20,000–40,000	13.1	12.4
40,000–1 million	28.8	29.6
>1 million	11.2	13.3
Region		
North	44.3	46.5
Center	19.1	18.9
South	36.6	34.7

Source: "I bilanci delle famiglie italiane nell'anno 1989," *Supplemento al Bollettino Statistico,* no. 26 (Rome: Bank of Italy, 1991), table 1.

population averages in 1989. The comparison for 1987 yields a very similar picture and for brevity has not been reported here.

In table 6.2 we report the sample means of the demographic and occupational characteristics of household heads in 1987 and 1989. The structure of the two samples is similar. There is a relatively small number of young household heads, reflecting the large proportion of young working adults living with their parents. In fact, in 1989 the fraction of income recipients under age 30 (not reported in the table) was 19.8 percent, compared with only 7.6 percent of household heads that young. The occupational breakdown reveals that over one-third of household heads were not in the labor force in 1989. Of the remaining two-thirds, 27 percent were self-employed.

Table 6.3 displays population averages and sample means of disposable income, durable and nondurable consumption, and net worth broken down into

Table 6.2   **Sample Means of Selected Demographic and Occupational Characteristics of Household Heads in the 1987 and 1989 SHIW**

Variable	1987 SHIW	1989 SHIW
Gender		
Male	82.6	81.5
Female	17.4	18.5
Age		
<30	6.9	7.6
31–40	18.4	17.5
41–50	21.3	23.1
51–65	30.2	30.4
>65	23.2	21.4
Region		
North	48.7	50.1
Center	18.8	19.0
South	32.5	30.8
Occupation		
Operative	24.0	21.0
Clerical	16.8	17.5
Manager	5.8	7.6
Entrepreneur, professional	4.0	4.5
Other self-employed	14.0	12.7
Not in the labor force	35.3	36.7
Sector		
Agriculture	5.2	4.3
Industry	21.9	20.0
Public administration	17.9	19.3
Other	19.8	19.7
Not in the labor force	35.3	36.7

Sources: For 1987, "I bilanci delle famiglie italiane nell'anno 1987," *Supplemento al Bollettino Statistico,* no. 5 (Rome: Bank of Italy, 1989), table A1. For 1989, "I bilanci delle famiglie italiane nell'anno 1989," *Supplemento al Bollettino Statistico,* no. 26 (Rome: Bank of Italy, 1991), table A1.

Table 6.3   **Comparison between National and Financial Account Data and the 1987 SHIW**

	Aggregate Data (total)[a] (1)	Average Figures (per household) Based on Aggregate Data[b] (2)	Average Figures (per household) Based on 1987 SHIW[c] (3)	Ratio of (3) to(2) (4)
Disposable income	720	37,696	30,400	80.6
Total consumption	614	32,147	21,900	68.2
Nondurables	545	28,534	19,500	68.4
Durables	69	3,613	2,400	66.7
Net worth	3,743	195,969	130,578	66.6
Real assets	2,150	112,565	98,204	87.2
Durables	414	21,675	n.a.	n.a.
Net financial assets	1,179	61,728	32,374	52.5
Financial assets	1,260	65,969	35,486	53.8
Cash and deposits[d]	515	26,963	17,887	66.3
Public debt[e]	349	18,272	13,209	72.1
Other financial assets[f]	396	20,733	4,390	21.3
Liabilities	81	4,241	3,112	73.8
Ratio of averages				
Total consumption / disposable income		0.85	0.72	
Net worth / disposable income		5.20	4.30	
Financial assets / disposable income		1.75	1.17	
Financial assets / net worth		0.34	0.27	
Deposits / financial assets		0.41	0.50	
Public debt / financial assets		0.28	0.37	
Other financial assets / financial assets		0.31	0.12	
Liabilities / financial assets		0.06	0.09	

Sources: Col. (1)—Pagliano and Rossi (1992, table 21); *Annual Report,* Statistical Appendix (Rome: Bank of Italy, 1990), table aD29. Col. (3)—SHIW for 1987. Data on financial assets are adjusted on the basis of the 1987 BNL survey, as explained in text.

[a]Trillion lire.

[b]Thousand lire. At the end of 1987 there were 19.1 million households.

[c]Thousand lire.

[d]Deposits include checking accounts, savings accounts, and postal deposits.

[e]Public debt includes BOT (Treasury bills up to one-year maturity), CCT (floating-rate Treasury credit certificates, two to four years in maturity indexed to BOT), BTP (long-term government bonds), bonds issued by the Postal Deposits and Loans Fund, and bonds issued by local governments and public sector enterprises.

[f]Other financial assets include bonds issued by private enterprises and special credit institutions, investment funds, and equities. Insurance and severance pay are included in the aggregate but not in the SHIW figure.

its main components. Like all the summary statistics in the rest of the paper, means are computed using sample weights. In column (2) we divide the national aggregates by the number of households at the end of 1987. In column (3) we report sample means for the corresponding variables in the 1987 SHIW.

The figures in column (3) are consistently lower than those in column (2), indicating that the averages based on microeconomic data are likely to be underestimates of the true population values. Disposable income appears to be underestimated by about 20 percent and consumption by about 30 percent. As a result, the average propensity to consume resulting from the 1987 SHIW is 13 percentage points lower than that based on the national accounts (72 percent vs. 85 percent). Brandolini and Cannari (1994) explain that the discrepancy between the two measures of disposable income arises mainly from self-employment income (underestimated by half), pension benefits (underestimated by a third), and interest income. On the other hand, the SHIW slightly overestimates wages and salaries relative to the national accounts data. The figures on rents and transfers are consistent.

The SHIW underestimates net worth by 33 percent, most of the discrepancy arising from financial assets. Its estimate for real assets is fairly good (an underestimate of 13 percent); the estimate of owner-occupied houses is quite close to that based on ISTAT data, but "the estimated number of houses owned by households for purposes other than owner occupation is appreciably lower than that recorded in the 1981 Census" (Cannari and D'Alessio 1990, 327).

Net financial assets come to only 52.5 percent of the corresponding financial accounts aggregate. Note that the figure for net financial assets reported in table 6.3 and used in this paper is not based on the raw SHIW variable, but is adjusted on the basis of more reliable information drawn from the 1987 BNL survey.[1]

Table 6.3 shows that the item that is most seriously underestimated is "other financial assets," the sum of corporate bonds, shares, investment funds, insurance, private pensions, and foreign assets. This is partly due to underreporting by the wealthy, who own a disproportionate share of the more sophisticated financial instruments; it also depends on important definitional differences. Insurance policies and accrued severance pay entitlements, which accounted for roughly 10 percent of financial assets in the second half of the 1980s (Jappelli and Pagano 1994a), are not included in the SHIW data. If we exclude these two items from the figure reported in column (2), the underestimate of "other financial assets" is reduced by 10 percentage points.

Table 6.4 gives more detailed figures on sample means and medians of the components of income, consumption, and wealth in the 1987 SHIW. The income and consumption variables used in this table and in the rest of the paper exclude imputed rental income from owner-occupied housing and are thus not directly comparable with those reported in table 6.3.

Table 6.4 confirms Italians' demonstrated inclination to save (the median saving rate is 0.28) and to hold a large amount of assets (the median wealth-

---

1. The raw data underestimate aggregate financial wealth by 69 percent. As described by Cannari et al. (1990), the adjustment procedure takes into account the probability of owning a particular asset and the amount of assets held. The adjustment lowers the weight given to households which report zero financial assets in the SHIW sample; the assets figure reported in the BNL survey is then used to revise upward the amount of assets of households that report positive assets in the SHIW. In this paper, we always report weighted sample statistics.

Table 6.4   **Average and Median Values of Main Variables in the 1987 SHIW (thousand lire)**

Variable	Average	Median
Income		
Disposable income	26,832	21,696
Labor income	18,877	16,000
Transfer income	155	0
Pension income	4,912	0
Property income	2,953	771
Rents	505	0
Income from financial assets	2,448	701
Consumption and saving		
Total consumption	18,364	16,000
Durable consumption	2,433	0
Saving (disposable income *minus* consumption)	8,468	5,587
Wealth		
Net worth	130,578	75,877
Real assets	98,204	58,000
Real estate	81,270	51,600
Business capital	13,410	0
Other real assets	3,524	1,000
Total net financial assets	32,374	10,573
Deposits	17,877	7,190
Public debt	13,209	0
Other financial assets	4,390	0
Liabilities	3,112	0
Ratios		
Consumption / disposable income		0.72
Saving / disposable income		0.28
Net financial assets / disposable income		0.48
Net worth / disposable income		3.48

income ratio is 3.48). Households hold substantial amounts of assets in liquid form: median financial assets are over 10 million lire, and the median ratio of financial assets to disposable income is 48 percent (about 6 months' income). Most of these assets are held in the form of bank deposits and public debt. The majority of households do not hold shares or investment funds, included in the "other financial assets" category. Liabilities are a tiny fraction of net worth and of total financial assets. This fact, which dovetails with the aggregate data in table 6.3, has been interpreted as evidence of borrowing constraints in the mortgage and consumer credit market, rather than as evidence of a low propensity to borrow (Jappelli and Pagano 1989, 1994b; Guiso, Jappelli, and Terlizzese 1992b).

6.3   Cross-Sectional Age Profiles

Table 6.5 displays the median values of disposable income, consumption, saving, and wealth by five-year age groups. The data refer to the 1987 SHIW, the only year the survey contained publicly available data for financial assets.

Median household disposable income (col. [1]) peaks in the age bracket 55–59, when it is 1.9 times the income of the youngest bracket and 2.1 times the income of the oldest bracket. As we shall see, the cross-sectional profile heavily overestimates the actual income decline in old age: in large part, the comparatively low income of the older cohorts reflects the sustained, rapid growth of income in the postwar period.

The profile of disposable income results from the different patterns of earnings, pensions, and capital income. The earnings profile is rather flat over the working life and declines around the statutory retirement age (55 for women and 60 for men); this decline is much sharper for the self-employed than for wage earners. Pensions, rents, and income from financial assets partly offset the fall in labor income.

The cross-sectional profile of consumption (col. [2]) peaks 10 years earlier and is flatter than that of disposable income, leading to a hump-shaped saving profile (col. [3]). The fact that consumption is smoother than income is consistent with the life-cycle hypothesis. However, the saving profile also shows that all households save, even those headed by the very old and the very young, which is inconsistent with the standard version of the life-cycle model: given the concave shape of the earnings profile, the young should borrow and the old should dissave. Nevertheless, the literature on earnings uncertainty and liquidity constraints can explain why optimizing households might save even during their younger years; lifetime uncertainty, health risk, and operative bequest motives can account for continued asset accumulation in old age.

One reason why the elderly appear to save so much has to do with the measurement of income: the inflation premium on nominal assets and the depreciation of housing are not subtracted from income, leading to an overestimate of nominal interest and rental income, which constitute a large part of the income of old households. This measurement error may therefore account for the high saving rate of old cohorts and also reconcile their positive gross saving with their declining net worth (col. [8]).

Columns (6)–(9) report net worth and financial assets net of liabilities by age cohort. In the cross section, net worth increases rapidly up to ages 50–54 and then declines steadily, displaying the typical hump-shaped profile predicted by the life-cycle model. The wealth-income ratio increases up to ages 60–64 and declines slightly afterward. However, cross-sectional wealth profiles are potentially misleading: to test the life-cycle theory's prediction of dissaving after retirement, one must control for differences in permanent income between age cohorts, as was done by King and Dicks-Mireau (1982) in their study of wealth decumulation after retirement. Applying this methodology to

Table 6.5   Cross-Sectional Age Profiles for Selected Variables (thousand lire)

Age Cohort	Disposable Income (1)	Consumption (2)	Saving (3)	Saving-Income Ratio (4)	Saving-Consumption Ratio (5)	Net Financial Wealth (6)	Ratio of Net Financial Wealth to Income (7)	Net Worth (8)	Ratio of Net Worth to Income (9)
<25	14,189	12,600	689	0.06	0.07	3,008	0.11	7,007	0.34
25–29	20,066	17,160	2,553	0.16	0.19	4,589	0.22	21,175	1.04
30–34	21,105	16,440	3,982	0.20	0.25	4,851	0.24	30,264	1.27
35–39	27,250	19,561	7,260	0.26	0.35	11,396	0.42	76,003	2.81
40–44	25,788	18,900	5,426	0.22	0.28	10,509	0.42	95,772	3.50
45–49	26,370	20,000	6,013	0.23	0.30	11,517	0.45	94,803	3.50
50–54	27,471	19,800	7,829	0.31	0.45	17,833	0.62	111,289	3.79
55–59	27,517	18,000	7,762	0.32	0.48	15,346	0.58	104,877	3.93
60–64	20,284	13,000	6,300	0.34	0.51	9,982	0.57	90,025	4.74
65–69	16,825	11,400	5,604	0.36	0.55	11,260	0.67	68,457	4.16
70–74	13,243	8,700	3,900	0.31	0.46	8,321	0.61	50,000	4.29
Total	29,614	20,200	5,587	0.28	0.39	10,573	0.48	75,877	3.48

Source: SHIW for 1987 (median values).

the 1984 SHIW, Brugiavini (1987) found that in Italy the elderly run down accumulated assets at a rate ranging from 1.5 to 8 percent per year, depending on model specification. This is lower than the estimate implied by a standard life-cycle model without a bequest motive and lifetime uncertainty, but higher than that found by King and Dycks-Mireaux (1982) for Canada (from 0.7 to 1.5 percent per year between ages 65 and 85) or Hubbard (1986) and Hurd (1987) for the United States (1.5 percent or less).

To assess the effect of income distribution on saving, we report a cross-tabulation of saving by age and income classes. The households in each age cohort are divided into four groups, depending on whether their disposable income is (1) below the first income quartile, (2) between the first and the second quartiles, (3) between the second and the third quartiles, and (4) above the third quartile. For each cell we then compute the median value of saving (table 6.6) and of the saving rate (table 6.7).

The two tables show that, within each age cohort, rich households save considerably more than poor ones, confirming a common finding of cross-sectional data, i.e., that the propensity to save is an increasing function of income. In the bottom two income quartiles, the median saving rate increases up to ages 65–69 and declines afterward, whereas in the top two quartiles, the rate shows no tendency to decline, possibly reflecting the stronger bequest motive of affluent households.

Taken literally, table 6.7 implies that a reduction in income inequality would be associated with a lower aggregate household saving rate. Indeed, since the late seventies, household income inequality in Italy has declined considerably, as witnessed by Brandolini (1992): the share of income going to the top 10 percent of the population declined from 30 percent in 1975 to 25 percent in 1989, while that of the bottom 50 percent rose from 24 to 27 percent.[2] The more equal income distribution may account for part of the reduction in the Italian household saving rate observed in the eighties.

However, the table could also reflect differences in transitory income shocks rather than behavioral differences between poor and rich households. The low-income cells include households that experience temporary income drops and, on the permanent-income hypothesis, reduce their saving in order to smooth consumption. Symmetrically, the high-income cells include those enjoying a positive income shock, who may increase saving to absorb the windfall. Thus the positive correlation between saving rates and income levels in table 6.7 may simply reflect the use of current rather than permanent income to define the quartiles.

Attanasio (chap. 2 in this volume) suggests that this problem might be reduced by classing households by educational attainment, which correlates with permanent income more closely than does current disposable income and is less likely to be affected by transitory shocks and measurement error. In table

2. The overall Gini coefficient declined from a value of 0.41 in 1975 to 0.33 in 1989.

Table 6.6   **Saving by Income Quartile and Age (thousand lire)**

Age	Below First Quartile	Between First and Second Quartiles	Between Second and Third Quartiles	Above Third Quartile	Whole Sample
25–29	600	2,285	4,389	12,528	2,553
30–34	709	2,872	7,828	14,522	3,982
35–39	1,166	5,960	9,996	17,653	7,260
40–44	749	4,254	9,598	20,904	5,426
45–49	1,963	5,807	7,504	20,801	6,013
50–54	2,056	5,764	11,573	26,533	7,829
55–59	1,171	5,600	14,920	25,697	7,762
60–64	1,400	5,901	12,071	24,657	6,300
65–69	1,872	4,506	7,129	19,005	5,604
70–74	943	2,204	6,419	16,971	3,900

Source: SHIW for 1987 (median values).

Table 6.7   **Ratio of Saving to Disposable Income by Income Quartile and Age**

Age	Below First Quartile	Between First and Second Quartiles	Between Second and Third Quartiles	Above Third Quartile	Whole Sample
25–29	0.05	0.14	0.17	0.33	0.16
30–34	0.06	0.16	0.29	0.37	0.20
35–39	0.09	0.25	0.30	0.37	0.26
40–44	0.05	0.21	0.29	0.41	0.22
45–49	0.14	0.23	0.23	0.34	0.23
50–54	0.17	0.24	0.33	0.43	0.31
55–59	0.12	0.23	0.41	0.45	0.32
60–64	0.17	0.34	0.42	0.46	0.34
65–69	0.23	0.33	0.36	0.46	0.36
70–74	0.13	0.24	0.40	0.48	0.31

Source: SHIW for 1987 (median values).

6.8 we divide each age cohort into four groups according to the educational attainment of the household head: elementary education (5 years of schooling or fewer), junior high school education (6 to 8 years), high school education (9 to 13 years), and college education (14 years or more). For most age cohorts, saving does increase with education, but the differences in saving rates between the cells in table 6.8 are much smaller than in table 6.7. This suggests that the positive correlation between saving and income in the latter is largely spurious.

Finally, we cross-tabulate net financial assets and net worth by age and income groups, following the same cell definition used for saving. The amount of financial assets and its ratio to income, reported in tables 6.9 and 6.10, both rise monotonically across income quartiles. The distribution of financial assets

Table 6.8   Ratio of Saving to Disposable Income by Educational
                 Attainment and Age

Age	Years of Education				Whole Sample
	≤5	6–8	9–13	≥14	
25–29	0.16	0.16	0.14	0.16	0.16
30–34	0.18	0.19	0.20	0.26	0.20
35–39	0.15	0.26	0.22	0.33	0.26
40–44	0.17	0.20	0.23	0.24	0.22
45–49	0.19	0.23	0.29	0.30	0.23
50–54	0.31	0.29	0.31	0.38	0.31
55–59	0.29	0.37	0.35	0.34	0.32
60–64	0.30	0.30	0.45	0.45	0.34
65–69	0.34	0.36	0.37	0.30	0.36
70–74	0.29	0.40	0.38	0.44	0.31

Source: SHIW for 1987 (median values).

Table 6.9   Net Financial Assets by Income Quartile and Age

Age	Below First Quartile	Between First and Second Quartiles	Between Second and Third Quartiles	Above Third Quartile	Whole Sample
25–29	775	2,236	8,221	34,308	4,589
30–34	2,538	2,604	9,292	22,782	4,851
35–39	2,117	8,771	1,553	46,337	11,396
40–44	1,899	9,918	17,358	43,776	10,509
45–49	2,503	10,980	16,580	57,573	11,517
50–54	2,582	14,211	31,255	55,950	17,833
55–59	1,553	10,569	34,687	56,568	15,346
60–64	1,365	7,326	34,405	65,549	9,982
65–69	1,955	7,827	21,868	45,071	11,260
70–74	969	4,271	16,876	81,342	8,321

Source: SHIW for 1987 (median values).

is heavily skewed toward the rich: the median ratio of financial wealth to income is 0.48 for all age groups, but it is about 1 for most cells in the highest income quartile, compared with about 0.15 for the bottom quartile. The low level of financial assets of these households conforms to Deaton's (1991) model of impatient consumers subject to liquidity constraints and earnings uncertainty. However, the correlation between financial assets and income could also be explained in the same way as for the saving rate, i.e., as the result of transitory income shocks that households buffer by adjusting their liquid assets. This is confirmed by table 6.11, where we tabulate the ratio of net financial assets to income by educational attainment. Again, the ratio increases with education, but again the differences are considerably smaller than those shown in table 6.10.

Table 6.10   **Ratio of Net Financial Assets to Income by Income Quartile and Age**

Age	Below First Quartile	Between First and Second Quartiles	Between Second and Third Quartiles	Above Third Quartile	Whole Sample
25–29	0.07	0.13	0.35	0.82	0.22
30–34	0.18	0.14	0.32	0.57	0.24
35–39	0.15	0.39	0.47	0.81	0.42
40–44	0.13	0.43	0.57	0.86	0.42
45–49	0.16	0.46	0.46	0.89	0.45
50–54	0.19	0.66	0.85	0.99	0.62
55–59	0.20	0.44	0.95	0.94	0.58
60–64	0.19	0.43	1.12	1.14	0.57
65–69	0.25	0.59	1.09	1.19	0.67
70–74	0.13	0.39	0.99	1.94	0.61

Source: SHIW for 1987 (median values).

Table 6.11   **Ratio of Net Financial Assets to Income by Educational Attainment and Age**

	Years of Education				Whole Sample
Age	≤5	6–8	9–13	≥14	
25–29	0.19	0.19	0.27	0.42	0.22
30–34	0.12	0.20	0.33	0.40	0.24
35–39	0.14	0.40	0.42	0.56	0.42
40–44	0.26	0.35	0.64	0.48	0.42
45–49	0.42	0.50	0.55	0.44	0.45
50–54	0.54	0.69	0.53	0.99	0.62
55–59	0.40	0.80	0.72	1.18	0.58
60–64	0.37	0.80	1.06	1.56	0.57
65–69	0.46	1.09	1.49	0.82	0.67
70–74	0.43	1.65	1.49	1.81	0.61

Source: SHIW for 1987 (median values).

Net worth is more evenly distributed across income quartiles than saving and net financial assets (tables 6.12 and 6.13), especially for age cohorts over 40. Presumably, the effect of transitory income shocks on net worth is smaller than on saving and financial assets: when faced with a shortfall in income, households are more likely to use savings or to spend down financial assets than to use real assets. And unlike the pattern for saving and financial assets, it turns out that the cross-tabulation of the wealth-income ratio by education (table 6.14) is similar to that by income quartile (table 6.13).

6.4 Cohort-adjusted Age Profiles

Cross-sectional age profiles of income, consumption, saving, and wealth such as those presented above can hardly be interpreted as describing the time

Table 6.12   **Net Worth by Income Quartile and Age**

Age	Below First Quartile	Between First and Second Quartiles	Between Second and Third Quartiles	Above Third Quartile	Whole Sample
25–29	4,044	10,909	27,221	114,063	21,175
30–34	8,000	18,921	57,291	78,363	30,264
35–39	16,012	66,024	86,558	198,902	76,003
40–44	18,192	72,983	127,211	228,301	95,772
45–49	44,069	94,803	92,531	186,168	94,803
50–54	49,077	86,200	141,679	245,536	111,289
55–59	46,411	82,021	139,508	283,236	104,877
60–64	45,089	76,294	128,337	270,004	90,025
65–69	30,959	53,755	90,149	170,240	68,457
70–74	21,455	47,940	69,826	225,408	50,000

Source: SHIW for 1987 (median values).

Table 6.13   **Ratio of Net Worth to Disposable Income by Income Quartile and Age**

Age	Below First Quartile	Between First and Second Quartiles	Between Second and Third Quartiles	Above Third Quartile	Whole Sample
25–29	0.33	0.66	1.16	2.90	1.09
30–34	0.68	1.05	2.09	1.94	1.27
35–39	0.98	2.91	2.80	4.11	2.81
40–44	1.49	3.55	4.24	4.02	3.50
45–49	4.31	3.88	2.84	3.31	3.50
50–54	3.69	3.90	3.80	3.76	3.79
55–59	3.99	3.36	3.71	4.58	3.93
60–64	5.52	4.33	4.71	5.05	4.74
65–69	3.94	4.02	4.72	4.16	4.16
70–74	4.62	4.44	4.29	6.52	4.29

Source: SHIW for 1987 (median values).

path of these variables over the lifetime of a representative household. In fact, each cohort in the cross section is affected by differences in mortality rates, productivity, preferences, and institutional arrangements (such as taxes and social security). Only studies that employ relatively long panel data on households can fully disentangle individual behavior from cohort effects. Since no such data are available for Italian households, one must rely on repeated cross-sectional data, i.e., exploit the variation in the behavior of each cohort over time to estimate cohort-specific profiles from several waves of cross-sectional data.

We use the method proposed by Deaton (1985) and the data set constructed by Attanasio, Guiso, and Jappelli (1993). We stack four waves of SHIW data (1984, 1986, 1987, and 1989) and regress each variable (e.g., consumption)

Table 6.14   **Ratio of Net Worth to Disposable Income by Educational Attainment and Age**

Age	Years of Education ≤5	6–8	9–13	≥14	Whole Sample
25–29	0.31	0.58	1.36	1.39	1.09
30–34	0.56	0.75	2.09	1.75	1.27
35–39	2.26	1.41	2.52	3.83	2.81
40–44	2.99	3.06	4.31	3.97	3.50
45–49	3.33	3.24	4.07	3.60	3.50
50–54	3.66	3.20	4.16	6.49	3.79
55–59	3.71	3.15	3.98	8.31	3.93
60–64	4.42	4.10	4.74	7.85	4.74
65–69	3.94	4.55	4.78	6.34	4.16
70–74	3.81	4.89	4.75	7.17	4.29

Source: SHIW for 1987 (median values).

against a set of cohort-specific dummies and a fifth-order polynomial in age. The hypothesis implicit in this method is that the relevant profile (e.g., the consumption profile) of the typical household differs across cohorts only by a constant and that its shape depends only on time. An estimate of the cross-sectional profile unadjusted for cohort effects is obtained by running the same regression but dropping the cohort dummies. The difference between the fitted values of the age polynomial in the two regressions is an estimate of the cohort effect.

Consumption and income are defined differently here from the previous section. To guarantee comparability between the different waves of the SHIW used in the estimation, consumption and disposable income include imputed rents from owner-occupied housing, while disposable income excludes interest and dividends, which are available only for the 1987 and 1989 cross sections. Lack of data on wealth for all SHIW surveys except 1987 and 1989 prevents us from gauging the distortion induced by cohort effects on the age profiles of financial assets and net worth. All figures have been converted into 1989 lire using the consumer price index as deflator.

Cohorts are defined over five-year intervals. The first of 10 cohorts consists of households with heads born between 1955 and 1959 (aged 25–29 in 1984), the last cohort, of those born between 1910 and 1914 (aged 70–74 in 1984). Regressions are carried out by least absolute deviations (LAD), to obtain consistent estimates of the median values of each profile. This estimator is preferred to OLS because it is robust with respect to the presence of influential values and because the estimated profiles are more closely comparable with those of the previous section.[3] Rather than reporting the estimated coefficients

3. Still, they are not fully comparable, for two reasons: first, as noted, the definitions of income and consumption differ in the two sections; second, the cross-sectional profiles in section 6.3 refer

of each regression, we plot the fitted values of the age polynomials of the regression that includes cohort dummies and of the one that excludes them.

Figures 6.1 and 6.2 display the fitted values of the regressions for disposable income and earnings. The profiles adjusted for cohort effects are shaped quite differently from the cross-sectional profiles: (1) they rise more steeply at younger ages, (2) they peak about 10 years later (at ages 55–59 rather than 45–49), and (3) they stay at a higher level beyond retirement (at age 75 the estimate of disposable income adjusted for cohort effects is more than twice as great as the unadjusted estimate).

The conclusion drawn from figure 6.3, which reports the estimated profiles of total consumption, is similar. Here, however, the cohort adjustment raises the consumption of the elderly more than their income. As a result, while unadjusted saving increases steadily with age, adjusted saving declines from age 34 onward. This is shown by figure 6.4 (saving rate) and figure 6.5 (saving-consumption ratio) which provide a striking reminder of the fallacies concerning individual behavior that can result from reliance on cross-sectional data. The unadjusted profile indicates that in Italy the old are the big savers, whereas the adjusted profile shows that it is the young that do most of the asset accumulation, possibly anticipating future family needs and the purchase of housing and durable goods.

The regression technique used so far to control for cohort effects can also be used to describe other features of household saving behavior. In table 6.15 we expand the list of regressors by adding demographic variables and schooling, residential, and occupational dummies to the cohort dummies and the age polynomial. In columns (1) and (2) the dependent variable is the saving rate; in columns (3) and (4) the dependent variable is the ratio of saving to consumption, which is less subject than income to extreme value problems and is a better measure of permanent income.[4]

The saving rate proves to increase with the number of adults in the household and to decline with the number of children; the former effect dominates the latter, so that larger households save proportionately more than smaller ones. Married couples save less, and households with male heads save more.

Column (1) shows that households in the South save 5 percentage points less than those in the Center and 3.3 points less than those living in the North. This may be due to an absolute income effect (per capita income is substantially lower in the South): if preferences are not homothetic (e.g., they are represented by a Stone-Geary utility function), the saving rate can be a positive

---

to the 8,027 households of the 1987 SHIW, whereas those estimated in this section are based on the larger cross section of 28,324 observations obtained by pooling the 1984, 1986, 1987, and 1989 surveys.

4. In the first regression we exclude observations referring to households whose disposable income is below 1 million lire (311 observations); in the second we also exclude those whose consumption is below that level (14 observations).

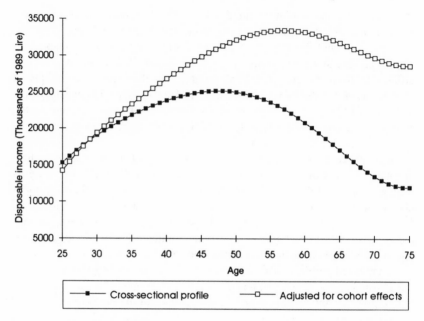

Fig. 6.1   Age-income profile

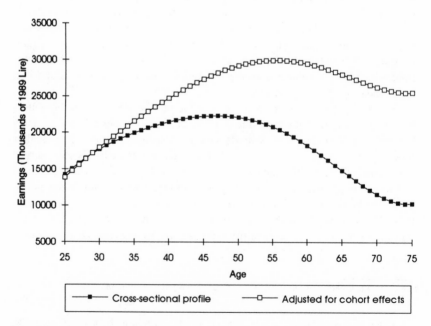

Fig. 6.2.   Age-earnings profile

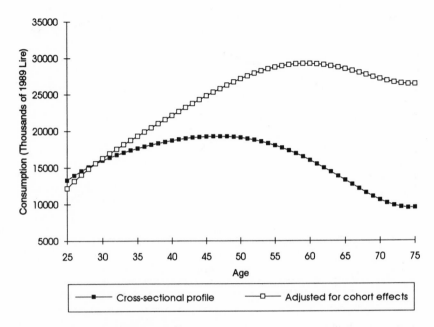

Fig. 6.3   Age-consumption profile

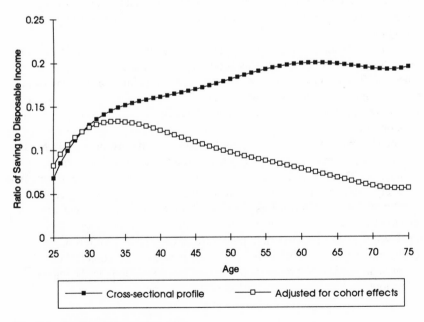

Fig. 6.4   Profile of the saving rate

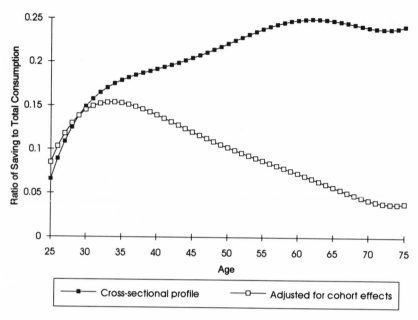

Fig. 6.5   Profile of the saving-consumption ratio

function of permanent income. Another explanation could be greater underreporting of income in the South, which would produce an underestimate of the saving ratio.[5]

As is already apparent from the descriptive evidence given in table 6.5, the saving rate is associated with education: column (1) shows that 10 years of schooling increase the saving rate by 3 percentage points. On the one hand, education may proxy for permanent income; on the other, it may be associated with a lower rate of time preference and give access to more attractive investment opportunities.

If employment status is a proxy for earnings uncertainty, household heads with riskier jobs may be expected to save more to buffer uninsurable income fluctuations. Thus the saving rate of wage and salary earners, whose income is relatively stable, can be expected to be lower than that of self-employed workers. But no such pattern emerges from table 6.15: for instance, clerical workers tend to save less than entrepreneurs, but more than professionals and other self-employed workers. The pattern of the coefficient estimates parallels the results in Skinner (1988): controlling for other variables, he finds no correlation between saving and employment status. A possible explanation may be that those who choose riskier jobs are less risk averse in general.

---

5. Cannari et al. (1990) find that financial assets are more under reported in the South than in the Center and North.

Table 6.15   **Saving Rate Regressions**

Variable[a]	Coefficient (1)	t-statistic (2)	Coefficient (3)	t-statistic (4)
Number of adults	0.047	13.09	0.081	15.12
Number of children	−0.003	−1.90	−0.004	−1.44
Married	−0.035	−4.88	−0.064	−6.01
Male	0.034	4.58	0.051	4.63
Living in the Center	0.050	10.77	0.073	10.58
Living in the North	0.033	8.30	0.047	7.85
Living in a city[b]	−0.035	−8.51	−0.050	−8.24
Years of education	0.003	6.74	0.005	6.65
Clerical worker	0.034	6.53	0.048	6.19
Manager	0.057	4.62	0.089	4.87
Entrepreneur	0.040	3.13	0.061	3.19
Professional	0.014	2.75	0.021	2.75
Other self-employed	0.020	2.12	0.028	2.07
Born in 1955–59	−0.101	−2.83	−0.162	−3.05
Born in 1950–54	−0.099	−2.97	−0.159	−3.22
Born in 1945–49	−0.076	−2.44	−0.128	−2.78
Born in 1940–44	−0.064	−2.21	−0.113	−2.62
Born in 1935–39	−0.047	−1.72	−0.090	−2.24
Born in 1930–34	−0.018	−0.74	−0.048	−1.29
Born in 1925–29	−0.008	−0.35	−0.032	−0.98
Born in 1920–24	−0.006	−0.34	−0.025	−0.94
Born in 1915–19	0.015	1.13	0.009	0.45
Constant	0.074	2.66	0.075	1.80
Number of observations	25,829		25,815	

Note: Dependent variable is saving-income ratio in cols. (1) and (2) and saving-consumption ratio in cols. (3) and (4). Estimation method is least absolute deviations.

[a]The regression also includes a fifth-order age polynomial. Excluded attributes are: head of household not married, households headed by a female, households living in the South, households living in towns with less than 500,000 inhabitants, operative and laborer, households with heads born in 1910–14.

[b]A city is defined as a town with over 500,000 inhabitants.

Finally, the cohort dummies indicate that younger generations save a smaller fraction of their income. This may be attributed to a preference shift, as well as to a diminished need for precautionary saving: postwar generations have grown up in a more stable environment, with public insurance schemes unavailable to their parents.

6.5   Institutional Factors

The availability of housing finance, the public provision of health care, and the rules of the social security system are likely to affect the saving decisions of Italian households in a powerful fashion. In this section we evaluate the potential impact of these institutional arrangements. Data on the timing and financing of home acquisition illustrate the role of housing purchases in asset accumulation. Figures on the incidence of private health expenditure are used to evaluate the importance of uninsured health risk as a motive for saving. Finally, the role of social security wealth in saving decisions is assessed by focusing on ex post and ex ante replacement rates.

6.5.1   Credit Markets and the Acquisition of Housing

Housing is the only durable item for which the SHIW reports detailed information. Italian households acquire homes comparatively late in life: most buy their homes in their forties or fifties, whereas most Americans and Britons purchase their first house in their twenties or early thirties (Jappelli and Pagano 1989). Table 6.16 shows that the fraction of home owners starts at 25 percent, increases gradually to 34 percent at ages 30–34, and reaches a plateau of around 70 percent in the age brackets between 55 and 69.

Previous work suggests that this pattern derives from mortgage market imperfections that keep young households from borrowing to buy their home (Guiso, Jappelli, and Terlizzese 1994). Indirect evidence in this sense is provided by table 6.17, which shows that in 1987 the average liabilities of Italian households—consisting mainly of housing loans—were just over 3 million lire (11.6 percent of average disposable income and 2.4 percent of average net worth) and that only 21 percent of households were indebted. Average household debt peaks between ages 40 and 44, when most Italians purchase their first house. But since these liabilities are fairly small, home buyers must rely mainly on accumulated savings, inter vivos transfers, and bequests.

The relative importance of saving, transfers, and bequests in the acquisition of housing is detailed in table 6.16, which distinguishes between households

Table 6.16   **Profile of Home Ownership by Age (% of households in the age group)**

Age	Home Ownership	Purchased	Received as Bequest	Received as Gift
<25	0.25	0.13	0.11	0.02
25–29	0.34	0.21	0.06	0.06
30–34	0.34	0.27	0.04	0.04
35–39	0.52	0.38	0.12	0.02
40–44	0.59	0.42	0.13	0.04
45–49	0.63	0.49	0.13	0.02
50–54	0.68	0.52	0.16	0.02
55–59	0.69	0.54	0.16	0.01
60–64	0.72	0.53	0.19	0.00
65–69	0.72	0.51	0.20	0.01
70–74	0.61	0.44	0.17	0.00
Total	0.60	0.45	0.14	0.02

Source: SHIW for 1987.

Table 6.17   **Household Liabilities by Age**

Age	Number of Households with Liabilities	Fraction of Households with Liabilities in Cell	Mean Value of Total Liabilities (thousand lire)
<25	9	0.18	2,100
25–29	103	0.27	2,691
30–34	190	0.31	4,860
35–39	274	0.31	4,947
40–44	255	0.28	5,904
45–49	248	0.26	3,640
50–54	232	0.25	3,242
55–59	155	0.19	3,192
60–64	125	0.17	2,809
65–69	67	0.10	1,048
70–74	54	0.05	356
Total	1,712	0.21	3,112

Source: SHIW for 1987.

who purchased or built their house themselves, those who inherited it, and those who received it as a gift. The profile of buyers dominates the pattern of owner-occupation over the life cycle: only 16 percent of households report that their house came as a bequest or as a gift, regardless of age. Thus most young households do not rent in anticipation of a bequest, but of a future house purchase.[6]

6.5.2 Health Risks and the Public Provision of Health Care

One reason for saving is to cover uninsured health expenditures. Measuring the subjective assessment of health hazards is virtually impossible in the absence of specifically designed surveys, so that one must rely on indirect indicators of the effects of health risk. In a 1990 survey conducted by the BNL and the Centro Einaudi,[7] only 7 percent of the respondents reported that medical assistance was their primary reason for saving (3.2 percent of those younger than age 30 and 14 percent of those older than age 60). The apparently low weight attached to health risk in saving decisions can be explained by the universal coverage of the Italian National Health Service. Although the quality of

6. Some direct purchases of housing are inter vivos transfers in disguise, being financed by monetary transfers from parents, friends, or other relatives. To the extent that this is a valid concern, the gift component reported in table 6.16 is an underestimate of its true value.

7. The results of this survey are published in the *Rapporto BNL-Centro Einaudi sul risparmio e sui risparmiatori in Italia* (Rome: Editoriale Lavoro, 1990); the data in the text are drawn from table 2.2 of this publication. The survey has been conducted annually since 1984 and oversamples medium- and high-income households, because it selects about 1,000 households holding a bank account, T-bills, or bonds. The breakdown between the various motives for saving reported in the text is quite stable over time.

its medical services is quite uneven and generally poorer than in most EC countries, this system does insure all health risks for any amount.

As a result, Italian households spend little out of pocket on health. According to the 1989 SHIW, health expenditure (whether privately insured or not) accounts for just 1.8 percent of disposable income and 2.3 percent of consumption. Average health expenditure, however, does not convey the full picture. Precautionary saving depends on the variance, not the level, of health hazards. In fact, the coefficient of variation of health expenditure is 2.1, to be contrasted with 0.6 for total consumption. This results from a small fraction of households incurring substantial health costs: 1 percent of the sample allocate more than 20 percent of their consumption expenditure to health, and 3.7 percent spend between 10 and 20 percent. But, for the vast majority, the incidence of health expenditure is low: less than 5 percent of consumption for 86.9 percent of the sample, and between 5 and 10 percent for 8.5 percent of the sample.

The ratio of health expenditure to total consumption does not rise much in old age (table 6.18), showing that the National Health Service provides effective insurance against health risks. The table's data on out-of-pocket health expenditure tally with those reported by the 1987 ISTAT survey, which contains very accurate data on the composition of household consumption. They also square with the low incidence of health insurance in the population: only 4 percent of households hold a private health insurance policy, and only 1.5 percent spend more than half a million lire a year on such coverage. The sample average of health insurance premiums is a tiny 0.1 percent of total consumption.

Table 6.18   Ratio of Private Health Expenditure to Disposable Income and Total Consumption Expenditure by Age

Age	Ratio of Health Expenditure to Disposable Income	Ratio of Health Expenditure to Consumption Expenditure
<25	0.012	0.014
25–29	0.014	0.017
30–34	0.018	0.022
35–39	0.019	0.023
40–44	0.020	0.025
45–49	0.019	0.023
50–54	0.020	0.024
55–59	0.018	0.022
60–64	0.018	0.023
65–69	0.020	0.025
70–74	0.017	0.022
Total	0.018	0.023

Source: SHIW for 1989 (mean values).

Table 6.19   **Replacement Rate by Income Class**

Income Class (million lire)	*Ex Post* Replacement Rate (1)	*Ex Ante* Replacement Rate (2)
<10	0.65	0.68
10–15	0.67	0.76
15–20	0.67	0.79
20–25	0.74	0.78
25–30	0.76	0.79
30–35	0.73	0.79
35–40	0.75	0.80
45–50	0.76	0.79
50–60	0.76	0.80
60–70	0.77	0.80
70–80	0.78	0.80
80–90	0.80	0.79
90–100	0.72	0.81
>100	0.69	0.80
Total	0.73	0.79

Source: SHIW for 1989 (mean values).

Note: The *ex post* replacement rate is based on 877 responses by retired workers concerning the ratio of their first monthly pension check to their last monthly salary. The *ex ante* replacement rate is based on 2,831 responses by people still in the labor force in 1989 about their expectation of the ratio of their first monthly pension to their last monthly income.

6.5.3   Pension Arrangements and Life Insurance

The income replacement rate, defined as the ratio between pension benefits and preretirement earnings, is a key determinant of how much households choose to save for retirement. In 1989 the SHIW for the first time included a special section on pensions, providing data on both actual replacement rates and the subjective assessment of expected retirement income by people still in the labor force.

We have tabulated the average ex post replacement rate by classes of disposable income (table 6.19), based on responses to this question: "Consider the moment when you received your first monthly pension. Setting your last monthly salary equal to 100, what was your first monthly pension?"[8] We concentrate on retirement pensions only, thus excluding disability pensions and veterans' pay. Out of 2,385 pension recipients, 877 replied to the question; of these, 826 receive retirement benefits. The overwhelming majority of respondents (99.4 percent) are public pension recipients.

The average ex post replacement rate is 73 percent. The rate is some 10 percentage points lower for pension recipients whose current disposable in-

8. This question is asked separately for up to three pensions. The figures in table 6.19 are based on the response for the first pension only, because the number of respondents who received second and third retirement pensions is negligible (13 and 0, respectively).

come was below 20 million lire, possibly because these workers retired with relatively low seniority. It is also lower than average for pensioners with current incomes above 90 million lire in 1989: this reflects the ceiling on pension benefits, which is independent of social security contributions (33.5 million lire after 40 years of contributions in 1988). Overall, these figures reflect the high benefits and broad eligibility criteria of the Italian social security system (Jappelli and Pagano 1994a).

To understand the determinants of saving, however, what matters is not the effective (ex post) rate, which reflects the retirement rules that applied to the cohorts of retirees alive at the time of the interview, but the expected replacement rate. An estimate of this ex ante rate can be inferred from the following question posed to all income recipients in the labor force (both employees and the self-employed) in 1989: "Consider the moment when you will retire. Setting your final monthly income before retirement equal to 100, what do you expect your first monthly pension to be?"

A total of 2,831 household heads answered this question; the responses are tabulated by income classes in column (2) of table 6.19. The average expected replacement rate is 79 percent, and it ranges between 76 and 81 percent for all income classes except the lowest. Even high-income households expect their pension to make up almost fully for the fall in earnings at retirement. This is striking, considering that in 1989 the Italian social security system was already financially unsustainable, due to the increase in benefits in the 1970s and 1980s and the rapid growth in the number of recipients. Clearly the apparent long-run unsustainability of the system, well known to policymakers and experts, was not evident to the vast majority of households in 1989.

The pattern of expected replacement rate by age of the worker (table 6.20) is perhaps even more surprising. If the system were perceived to be unsustainable, one would expect young workers to be less optimistic than older ones

Table 6.20   **Replacement Rate by Age**

Age	Ex Ante Replacement Rate
< 25	0.82
25–29	0.79
30–34	0.78
35–39	0.79
40–44	0.81
45–49	0.80
50–54	0.79
55–59	0.79
60–64	0.76
65–69	0.74
Total	0.79

Source: SHIW for 1989 (mean values).

about their future benefits, but the actual pattern is just the opposite: the young and the middle aged expect a higher replacement rate than older respondents.

An increase in the replacement rate for social security may reduce saving if households regard social security wealth as a substitute for private asset accumulation. A potential countereffect, however, is the possibility of earlier retirement, which would increase the need for retirement saving. The simple correlation between the expected replacement rate and the saving rate is very small and positive (0.0024). Regression analysis indicates that the conditional correlation (controlling for demographics and other economic variables) between the propensity to save and the expected replacement rate is small and not significantly different from zero, suggesting that the two effects largely offset one other.

A confirmation that in 1989 Italian households anticipated a high replacement rate is that they planned to rely mostly on social security income after retirement: in fact their recourse to private pension schemes was very limited. The SHIW does not tally private pension benefits and income from life insurance policies, but their quantitative importance can be judged indirectly by looking at private pension contributions and life insurance premiums, which averaged 84,000 lire (0.2 percent of disposable income) and 147,000 lire (0.4 percent of disposable income), respectively, in 1989. Households reporting significant private pension plan contributions (more than 500,000 lire) are 4.4 percent of the sample; those contributing more than 500,000 lire to a life insurance fund are 8.6 percent.

6.6   Conclusions

The stylized facts about household saving in Italy presented here are based on the Survey of Household Income and Wealth. Without estimating structural models and explicitly testing competing hypotheses, one cannot discriminate between different motives for saving or assess their relative importance. However, this kind of description of the microeconomic data can disclose broad patterns of saving behavior.

First of all, the data confirm the well-known fact that Italian households on average are high savers. More interesting, perhaps, is the very widespread nature of the saving impulse. The median saving rate is 0.28, the median wealth-income ratio is 3.48, and even the lowest-income quartile features high saving rates and wealth-income ratios. To be sure, there are important differences in saving behavior between population groups: the saving rate is higher for the richer and better educated households, and lower in the South and for postwar generations.

Our analysis also underscores the importance of cohort effects. Unless these are controlled for, cross-sectional data can be misleading in studying the life-cycle behavior of households. While the cross-sectional data indicate that the saving rate increases with age up to retirement, our cohort analysis shows that it is the young who exhibit the highest saving rates, possibly anticipating future family needs and the purchase of their first house. In fact, in direct interviews conducted in 1990 by the BNL and the Centro Einaudi, the majority of Italian households (52 percent) mention the purchase of a house as their main motive for saving. The data on home acquisition presented here show that Italians buy their first house drawing mainly on self-financing rather than borrowing; only a minority rely on private transfers and bequests.

The next most common reason for saving mentioned by households (19.5 percent) is to supplement pension income after retirement. The relatively low weight assigned to retirement saving is probably explained by the generosity of the Italian social security system, which survey respondents, at the time, expected to continue. In fact, in the 1989 SHIW most working-age household heads expected that pension benefits would nearly equal their preretirement earnings.

Saving for one's descendants is probably even less important for the average household: only 9 percent of the respondents to the BNL–Centro Einaudi survey report this as their main reason for saving. Finally, although recent research stresses the importance of precautionary saving, only 7 percent of Italian households cite uninsured health and disability risks in old age as their main saving motive,[9] evidently reflecting the full insurance and universal coverage provided by the National Health Service. It is also consistent with the evidence from cross-sectional data, which register private health-related expenditure as only a minor item in the consumption basket of most households.

Appendix A
Microeconomic Data in Italy

In this appendix we briefly describe the characteristics of the three main surveys that provide microeconomic data on Italian households: the Bank of Italy Survey of Household Income and Wealth (SHIW; Indagine sui bilanci delle famiglie italiane), conducted by the Bank of Italy, the survey conducted by the Banca Nazionale del Lavoro (BNL), and the Survey of Family Budgets (Indagine sui bilanci di famiglia) conducted by the National Institute of Statistics (ISTAT).[10] Each has its own distinct purpose and characteristics.

The SHIW

Since 1965 the Bank of Italy has sponsored a survey of consumer finances and characteristics. The survey was conducted yearly until 1987 (except for

9. A residual fraction of responses is allocated to "saving for other purposes" (12.5 percent).
10. In addition, the Centro Einaudi and BNL publish (yearly since 1984) the results of a survey with few demographic characteristics but many "qualitative" variables related to households' motivations for saving and their behavior in financial markets.

1985); since then it has been conducted every two years. Until 1984 each survey covered about 4,000 households; starting in 1986 the sample size was doubled. In this paper we use data for 1984 (4,001 households), 1986 (8,022 households), 1987 (8,027 households), and 1989 (8,274 households). A major innovation of the 1989 SHIW was the inclusion of a small panel component. In fact, the 1989 SHIW included 1,208 households that were also interviewed in 1987, plus a random sample of 7,066 households interviewed for the first time. The 1991 SHIW has a similar structure.[11]

The SHIW is representative of the Italian resident population. Selection is by a two-stage stratified sampling procedure (towns, then households). In the first stage, all Italian metropolitan areas and towns are divided into strata. Towns with more than 40,000 inhabitants and a random sample of all towns with fewer than 40,000 inhabitants (of which there are more than 9,000) are selected. In the second stage, households are drawn by a random sampling procedure from the list of all resident households in a given city. Probability selection is enforced at all stages of sampling.

Interviews are conducted by a specialized agency with professional interviewers. The interviews are preceded by extensive training and several meetings with Bank of Italy representatives who instruct the interviewers. The latter are given no discretion in the choice of households and families to be interviewed. Interviews take place in person, by visiting the residence of the household. Nonrespondents are replaced by households with similar characteristics.

Brandolini and Cannari (1994) report that "the response rate was slightly above 50 percent in the mid-seventies and oscillated around 60 percent until 1987, but it dropped to only 37 percent in . . . 1989." Cannari and D'Alessio (1992), focusing on the small panel section of the 1987 survey, find that the response rate is inversely correlated with family income and wealth, leading to an underestimate of respondents' income of about 5 percent.

The interviews usually take place in January and February. Balance sheet items are reported as of December 31 of the preceding year, while income is reported for the previous calendar year. Thus, the 1989 SHIW was conducted at the beginning of 1990. The survey data are available to the public.[12]

The SHIW contains detailed demographic, income, and wealth data and some information on household expenditures. The major weakness of the SHIW is that, by comparison with the national financial accounts, it seriously underestimates the financial wealth of households. For this reason, the SHIW data on financial wealth are not released to outside users. However, Bank of

11. The main source of information about the SHIW is a series of Bank of Italy publications in Italian. For the 1987 SHIW, see "I bilanci delle famiglie italiane nell'anno 1987," *Supplemento al Bollettino Statistico,* no. 5 (Rome: Bank of Italy, January 1989). For the 1989 SHIW, see "I bilanci delle famiglie italiane nell'anno 1989," *Supplemento al Bollettino Statistico,* no. 26 (Rome: Bank of Italy, October 1991). The main reference in English is Brandolini and Cannari (1994).

12. The tape, questionnaire, reference material, and description of the SHIW can be requested by writing to: Statistical Office, Research Department, Bank of Italy, Via Nazionale 91, 00186 Rome, Italy.

Italy and BNL statisticians have recently adjusted the financial wealth figures of the 1987 survey using the 1987 BNL survey (see below) as the benchmark. These adjusted 1987 data have been made available to us on special request to the Research Department of the Bank of Italy, and are used in this paper. The 1989 survey contains unique information on health expenditures, social security benefits, insurance premiums, and private pension contributions.

Empirical studies have used the SHIW (especially the 1987 and 1989) for econometric tests of various hypotheses about consumer behavior. Many of the most recent studies are part of a research project on household behavior sponsored by the Bank of Italy. Brugiavini (1987) and Ando, Guiso, and Terlizzese (1994) test whether the decumulation of wealth after retirement conforms to the predictions of the life-cycle model. Barca, Cannari, and Guiso (1994) estimate the fraction of housing wealth received as a bequest. Guiso, Jappelli, and Terlizzese (1992a) test whether a self-reported measure of earnings uncertainty affects saving and wealth accumulation. Cannari and Franco (1990) focus on pension benefits and household retirement income, while Ando et al. (1992) analyze young households' behavior. Attanasio, Guiso, and Jappelli (1993) merge five successive surveys and study the microeconomic causes of the decline in saving experienced by the Italian economy in the eighties. Jappelli and Pagano (1988) find that desired consumption exceeds actual consumption for liquidity-constrained households. According to Guiso, Jappelli, and Terlizzese (1994) imperfections in the mortgage market increase the saving rate of households with plans to purchase a house. Brugiavini and Weber (1994) examine the connection between liquidity constraints and durable goods purchases. Guiso and Jappelli (1991) test whether inter vivos transfers help to relax credit constraints.

The BNL Survey

The BNL survey has been conducted each year since 1984. The sample is a rotating panel of about 1,000 households drawn from among BNL customers. The sample is not representative of the population, overrepresenting high-income households. The BNL sample is stratified according to two criteria: occupation (entrepreneur, self-employed, manager, employed worker, and a residual class including retired and nonemployed customers) and the BNL branch. This survey contains information on demographic characteristics (household head's occupation, sector, age, sex and education, residence, and family size and number of income recipients), income (earnings, real and financial income, and transfers), and main categories of expenditure. The strength of the survey is its detailed and highly disaggregated information on assets and liabilities. The customer relationship between the BNL and survey respondents makes this source of information the least subject to underreporting: it is the best source for data on financial wealth at the household level in Italy. Unfortunately, it is not publicly available, apart from summary statistics published by the Research Department of the BNL itself. However, a recent study by Cannari et al. (1990) has used the BNL data to revise the data on financial wealth of the 1987 SHIW.

The ISTAT Survey

The ISTAT survey contains detailed data on consumption, some information on income, and none on wealth (with the exception of ownership of the house of residence).[13] The survey has been conducted yearly since 1980. The sample is a random stratified sample and is fairly large (over 30,000 households); one-twelfth of the sample is interviewed each month. Demographic characteristics are available with some detail: households are asked to report age, schooling, region of residence, sector, occupation, family size, gender, and number of income recipients. Consumption data are collected accurately and at a highly disaggregated level, the main purpose of the survey being the collection of data on the composition of consumer durables and nondurable expenditure. Households are also asked to report monthly income and annual saving, choosing between 16 predetermined income and saving classes. The income question is meant to capture "normal" monthly after-tax disposable income, including imputed rents from owner-occupied dwellings (asked about separately). No distinction is available as to the source of income (labor income, transfers, capital income, etc.). Since many income components do not accrue on a monthly basis, the income measure is likely to be seriously underestimated.

Appendix B
Definition of Variables

Head of household: Normally the husband or the father. If the person who would usually be considered the head of the household has migrated or works abroad, the household head is the person responsible for the economic activity of the family.

Household size: Total number of persons in the family. Persons include head, spouse (whether married or not married), children, and other relatives and nonrelatives living in the household.

Education of head of household: Years of education. Coded as: 0 (no education), 5 (completed elementary school), 8 (completed junior high school), 13 (completed high school), 18 (completed university degree), and 20 (postgraduate education).

Occupation of head of household: Main occupation of household head.

---

13. Descriptive statistics have appeared regularly in ISTAT publications. For the 1989 survey, see *Collana d'Informazione,* no. 21 (Rome: ISTAT, 1989).

Coded as: 1 (operative or laborer), 2 (clerical), 3 (professional), 4 (manager), 5 (entrepreneur), and 6 (self-employed).

Sector of occupation of head of household: Refers to the main sector of occupation. Coded as: 1 (agriculture), 2 (industry), 3 (public administration), and 4 (service).

Region of residence: Coded as: 1 (North—Piemonte, Valle D'Aosta, Liguria, Lombardia, Trentino, Friuli, Veneto, and Emilia-Romagna), 2 (Center—Marche, Umbria, Toscana, and Lazio), and 3 (South—Abruzzi, Molise, Campania, Basilicata, Puglia, Calabria, Sicilia, and Sardegna).

Labor earnings of household: All income from labor net of taxes and contributions.

Disposable income of household: In the cross-sectional data referring to 1987, disposable income is the sum of wages and salaries, self-employment income, property income, and transfers, less income taxes and social security contributions of each member of the household. Wages and salaries include overtime bonuses, fringe benefits, and payments in kind, and exclude tax withholdings. Self-employment income is net of taxes and includes the income from unincorporated business, net of depreciation of physical assets. Property income is the sum of rental (excluding imputed rental income from owner-occupied housing) and income from financial assets (interest received, less interest paid, plus dividends). Transfers are the sum of pension benefits, pension arrears, severance pay, unemployment and illness compensation, student grants, alimony, bequests, and inter vivos transfers. For reasons of data availability, in the pooled data formed by the 1984, 1986, 1987, and 1989 surveys, property income is defined simply as rents (inclusive of imputed rents from owner-occupied housing).

Consumption of household: Sum of the expenditures on nondurable items (food, clothing, medical expenses, insurance, fuel, entertainment, education, house maintenance, and rents) and durable goods (vehicles, furniture and appliances, and valuables). Imputed rents on owner-occupied housing are not included. For reasons of data availability, in the pooled data formed by the 1984, 1986, 1987, and 1989 surveys, consumption includes imputed rents from owner-occupied housing.

Household net worth: Sum of household's net financial assets and real assets. Net financial assets are the sum of checking accounts, saving accounts, money market accounts, certificates of deposit, stocks, and government bonds and other bonds, less household liabilities (consumer credit and real estate mortgages). Real assets are the sum of real estate and unincorporated business holdings.

References

Ando, Albert, Luigi Guiso, and Daniele Terlizzese. 1994. Dissaving by the old, transfer motives and liquidity constraints. In *Saving and the accumulation of wealth: Essays on Italian household and government saving behaviour,* ed. Albert Ando, Luigi Guiso, and Ignazio Visco. New York: Cambridge University Press.

Ando, Albert, Luigi Guiso, Daniele Terlizzese, and Daniel Dorsainvil. 1992. Saving among young households: Evidence from Japan and Italy. *Scandinavian Journal of Economics* 94: 233–50.

Attanasio, Orazio, Luigi Guiso, and Tullio Jappelli. 1993. The consumption boom in Italy: Microeconomic implications of macroeconomic evidence. Mimeograph.

Barca, Fabrizio, Luigi Cannari, and Luigi Guiso. 1994. Bequests and saving for retirement: What impels the accumulation of wealth? In *Saving and the accumulation of wealth: Essays on Italian household and government saving behaviour,* ed. Albert Ando, Luigi Guiso, and Ignazio Visco. New York: Cambridge University Press.

Brandolini, Andrea. 1992. A description and an assessment of the sample surveys on the personal distribution of incomes in Italy. Rome: Bank of Italy. Mimeograph.

Brandolini, Andrea, and Luigi Cannari. 1994. Methodological appendix: The Bank of Italy's Survey of Household Income and Wealth. In *Saving and the accumulation of wealth: Essays on Italian household and government saving behaviour,* ed. Albert Ando, Luigi Guiso, and Ignazio Visco. New York: Cambridge University Press.

Brugiavini, Agar. 1987. Empirical evidence on wealth accumulation and the effects of pension wealth: An application to Italian cross-section data. Financial Markets Group, Discussion Paper no. 20. London School of Economics.

Brugiavini, Agar, and Guglielmo Weber. 1994. Durable and nondurable consumption: Evidence from Italian household data. In *Saving and the accumulation of wealth: Essays on Italian household and government saving behaviour,* ed. Albert Ando, Luigi Guiso, and Ignazio Visco. New York: Cambridge University Press.

Cannari, Luigi, and Giovanni D'Alessio. 1990. Housing assets in the Bank of Italy's Survey of Household Income and Wealth. In *Income and wealth distribution, inequality and poverty,* ed. C. Dagum and M. Zenga. Berlin: Springer.

———. 1992. Mancate interviste e distorsione degli stimatori. Temi di Discussione, no. 172. Rome: Bank of Italy.

Cannari, Luigi, Giovanni D'Alessio, Giovanni Raimondi, and Ambrogio Rinaldi. 1990. Le attività finanziarie delle famiglie italiane. Temi di Discussione, no. 136. Rome: Bank of Italy.

Cannari, Luigi, and Daniele Franco. 1990. Sistema pensionistico e distribuzione dei redditi. Temi di Discussione, no. 137. Rome: Bank of Italy.

Deaton, Angus. 1985. Panel data from time series of cross sections. *Journal of Econometrics* 30: 109–26.

———. 1991. Saving and liquidity constraints. *Econometrica* 59: 1221–48.

Guiso, Luigi, and Tullio Jappelli. 1991. Do intergenerational transfers offset capital market imperfections? Evidence from a cross-section of Italian households. *European Economic Review* 35: 103–20.

Guiso, Luigi, Tullio Jappelli, and Daniele Terlizzese. 1992a. Earnings uncertainty and precautionary saving. *Journal of Monetary Economics* 30: 307–37.

———. 1992b. Saving and capital market imperfections: The Italian experience. *Scandinavian Journal of Economics* 94: 197–213.

———. 1994. Housing finance arrangements, intergenerational transfers and consumption: The Italian experience. *Economic Modeling* 11 (April).

Hubbard, R. Glenn. 1986. Pension wealth and individual saving: Some new evidence. *Journal of Money, Credit and Banking* 22: 167–78.

Hurd, Michael D. 1987. Savings of the elderly and desired bequests. *American Economic Review* 79: 298–313.

Jappelli, Tullio, and Marco Pagano. 1988. Liquidity constrained households in an Italian cross-section. CEPR Discussion Paper no. 257. London: Centre for Economic Policy Research.

———. 1989. Consumption and capital market imperfections: An international comparison. *American Economic Review* 79: 1088–1105.

———. 1994a. Government incentives and household saving in Italy. In *Public policies and household saving,* ed. J. M. Poterba, 105–32. Chicago: University of Chicago Press.

———. 1994b. Saving, growth and liquidity constraints. *Quarterly Journal of Economics* 109: 83–109.

King, Mervyn, and Louis Dicks-Mireau. 1982. Asset holdings and the life-cycle. *Economic Journal* 92: 247–67.

Pagliano, Patrizia, and Nicola Rossi. 1992. Il risparmio nazionale, privato e pubblico: una ricostruzione dal 1951 al 1990. Temi di Discussione, no. 169. Rome: Bank of Italy.

Rossi, Nicola, and Ignazio Visco. 1994. Private saving and government deficit. In *Saving and the accumulation of wealth: Essays on Italian household and government saving behaviour,* ed. Albert Ando, Luigi Guiso, and Ignazio Visco. New York: Cambridge University Press.

Skinner, Jonathan. 1988. Risky income, life-cycle consumption and precautionary saving. *Journal of Monetary Economics* 22: 237–55.

Contributors

Orazio P. Attanasio
Universita di Bologna
Dipartimento di Scienze Economici
Strada Magglore 45
40125 Bologna
Italy

James Banks
Institute for Fiscal Studies
7 Ridgemount Street
London WC1E 7AE
England

Richard Blundell
Institute for Fiscal Studies
7 Ridgemount Street
London WC1E 7AE
England

Axel Börsch-Supan
Department of Economics
University of Mannheim
D-68131 Mannheim
Germany

John B. Burbidge
Department of Economics
McMaster University
Hamilton, Ontario
L8S 4M4
Canada

James B. Davies
Department of Economics
Social Science Centre
University of Western Ontario
London N6A 5C2
Canada

Tullio Jappelli
Istituto di Studi Economici
Istituto Universitario Navale
Via Acton 38
80133 Napoli
Italy

Yukinobu Kitamura
Institute for Monetary and Economic
    Studies
2-1-1 Hongoku-cho
Nihonbashi, Chou-ku
Tokyo
Japan

Marco Pagano
Universitá Commerciale
Luigi Bocconi
Via Sarfatti 25
20136 Milano
Italy

James Poterba
Department of Economics
Massachusetts Institute of Technology
50 Memorial Drive
Room E52-350
Cambridge, MA 02139

Noriyuki Takayama
Hitotsubashi University
Institute of Economic Research
2-1, Naka
Kunitachi, Tokyo 186
Japan

Author Index

Subject Index

273